# The Grea n

## Anglo-American Power and World Order

**Mark Curtis**

LONDON • STERLING, VIRGINIA

First published 1998 by Pluto Press
345 Archway Road, London N6 5AA
and 22883 Quicksilver Drive,
Sterling, VA 21066–2012, USA



British Library Cataloguing in Publication Data
A catalogue record for this book is available from the British Library

ISBN 0 7453 1239 X hbk

Library of Congress Cataloging in Publication Data
A catalog record for this book is available.

Designed and produced for Pluto Press by
Chase Production Services, Chadlington, OX7 3LN
Typeset from disk by Stanford DTP Services, Northampton
Printed in the EC by T J International, Padstow

# Contents

## Part III
## The Middle East



## Part IV
## The United Nations

# List of Abbreviations and Acronyms

| | |
|---|---|
| ADB | Asian Development Bank |
| ATP | Aid and Trade Provision |
| AWACS | Airborne Warning and Control System |
| BHRO | Bahrain Human Rights Organisation |
| BP | British Petroleum |
| CBI | Confederation of British Industry |
| CDC | Colonial Development Corporation |
| CENTCOM | Central Command |
| CIA | Central Intelligence Agency |
| DTI | Department of Trade and Industry |
| EC | European Community |
| ESAF | Enhanced Structural Adjustment Facility |
| EU | European Union |
| FCO | Foreign and Commonwealth Office |
| GATT | General Agreement on Tariffs and Trade |
| GCC | Gulf Cooperation Council |
| GCHQ | Government Communications Headquarters |
| GDP | gross domestic product |
| GNP | gross national product |
| ICJ | International Court of Justice |
| IDA | International Development Agency |
| IFC | International Finance Corporation |
| IFI | international financial institution |
| IISS | International Institute for Strategic Studies |
| IMF | International Monetary Fund |
| ITO | International Trade Organisation |
| JRDF | Joint Rapid Deployment Force |
| LDC | less developed country |
| MEW | Middle East Watch |
| MI5 | Military Intelligence – domestic security division |
| MI6 | Military Intelligence – secret intelligence division |
| MoD | Ministry of Defence |
| MSF | Médecins Sans Frontières |
| NAFTA | North American Free Trade Agreement |

| | |
|---|---|
| NATO | North Atlantic Treaty Organisation |
| NGO | non-governmental organisation |
| NIC | newly industrialising country |
| NSA | National Security Agency |
| NSC | National Security Council |
| ODA | Overseas Development Administration |
| OECD | Organisation for Economic Co-operation and Development |
| OEEC | Organisation for European Economic Co-operation |
| OPEC | Organisation of Petroleum Exporting Countries |
| PKI | Indonesian Communist Party |
| PLO | Palestine Liberation Organisation |
| R&D | research and development |
| RAF | Royal Air Force |
| RDF | Rapid Deployment Force |
| SANG | Saudi Arabian National Guard |
| SAP | structural adjustment programme |
| SAS | Special Air Service |
| SAVAK | Iranian secret police |
| SIGINT | signals intelligence |
| SIS | Secret Intelligence Service |
| SUNFED | Special United Nations Fund for Economic Development |
| TAPOL | Indonesian Human Rights Campaign |
| TASM | Tactical Air to Surface Missile |
| TNC | transnational corporation |
| TRIPS | Trade-related intellectual property rights |
| UAE | United Arab Emirates |
| UAR | United Arab Republic |
| UN | United Nations |
| UNAMIR | United Nations Assistance Mission in Rwanda |
| UNCTAD | United Nations Conference on Trade and Development |
| UNDA | United Nations Development Authority |
| UNDP | United Nations Development Programme |
| UNESCO | United Nations Educational, Scientific and Cultural Organisation |
| USAF | United States Air Force |
| WTO | World Trade Organisation |

# Introduction

This study attempts to analyse past and present US and British foreign policy, the 'special relationship' between them and their policies towards 'development', the Middle East and the United Nations. Their policies in these three areas are especially important to consider since they are central to sustaining current world order: US and British priorities determine much of the development agenda, especially in the area of the international economy; the US remains the de facto controlling power in the Middle East, with Britain playing a key role in the Gulf; and the two states' agendas largely determine the functioning or otherwise of the UN Security Council. By consulting the formerly declassified planning record, as well as a variety of contemporary sources, it is possible to show the reality of policy in these areas, and the radical difference between this reality and that presented by mainstream media and academic commentators.

Citizens of the United States and Britain bear a heavy burden. These two countries have largely shaped the post-Second World War world and the current international order, usually in close alliance with each other. The human consequences of their policies are immense. 'World order' currently means three-quarters of the world's population living in poverty (an average income of $2 a day) and works only to the benefit of a minority elite. It also signifies economic and political power increasingly concentrated in unaccountable private organisations in whose interests international relations increasingly function. Any honest inquiry shows that the policies carried out in the names of the people of these two great democracies are in fact responsible for much of humanity's suffering at the end of the twentieth century. The magnitude of this culpability is matched by the degree to which it is overlooked or suppressed by the so-called free press and independent academia in these two countries.

The United States is the most powerful nation in the world and, with the disappearance of the Soviet Union, the sole global superpower. More than any other single state, it is responsible for the contours of world order. Former US Secretary of State Warren Christopher once correctly noted that this 'is a world that has been shaped by the successful use of American power'.[1] US interest in maintaining international order is so great that, as one prominent US academic notes in a 1995 study: 'the United States by some estimates will be spending more for defence [sic] in the coming four years than the rest of the world combined'.[2]

Britain is not in the same league but its current power and influence in the world are generally greatly underestimated. The two dominant views about British foreign policy are, first, the conservative one, which asserts that Britain remains a global power, and exercises that power in an essentially benign way; and, second, the liberal one, which asserts that Britain is really a marginal power (with only pretensions to great power status), and acts generally in a benign way but sometimes errs. Neither is quite correct: the basic fact is that Britain is a global power, whose influence remains great, and pursues policies that are in effect quite consistently abhorrent. The facts of history and the contemporary record clearly bear this out, and I attempt to outline some aspects of this below.

The idea that Britain is a bit player on the world stage, a mere European power, and is not greatly responsible for what happens in the world, does not accord with the evidence. Britain is one of a handful of nuclear powers, one of five permanent members on the UN Security Council, one of the world's largest exporters of arms and military training, is a major financial centre, home to many of the world's most significant transnational corporations and a major source of foreign investment (and thus one of the world's greatest champions of a horribly unjust international economic order).

British planners have stated that national interests entail 'the promotion of an international framework that will favour our democratic, economic, trading and social values'.[3] The problem is precisely that the current international order largely achieves these goals viewed from the perspective of the British establishment; at the same time it consigns the overwhelming majority of people on the planet to a life of poverty. This simple statement shows the degree to which the British (and US) policy of promoting the international status quo is, at its most basic level, responsible for terrible human conditions.

George Bush noted before the war against Iraq that the US would inflict a crushing defeat on Saddam Hussein because 'what we say goes'.[4] Similar reasoning applies when a US analyst notes that:

> For those of us who believe that the extension of US influence – with all its faults – benefits the United States and the world

> community, preserving the position of the United States as the dominant global power is a pragmatic and moral necessity.[5]

Similarly, Margaret Thatcher once said:

> We need to ensure that military superiority – particularly technological superiority – remains with nations, above all the United States, that can be trusted with it. We must never leave the sanction of force to those who have no scruples about its use.[6]

Establishment academics encourage the same tendencies towards upholding international order on the part of Anglo-American power. Oxford Professor Robert O'Neill, for example, notes that 'Britain has a very demanding and influential security role to play in the decades ahead. The US needs more support and company.' Therefore, 'Britain's global experience, capability and good standing places her next in importance to the US as an upholder of international security'.[7] Prince Charles has also praised the 'immense skills displayed by our armed forces' and stated that 'I happen to think that Britain has a special contribution to make to the challenges of the new disorder of the post-Cold War world, and to help in the creation of a better and more orderly world.' This is an area in which 'our armed forces have particular expertise' as well as 'a long and proven tradition of excellence and professionalism which is recognised and admired the world over'.[8]

Many key features of the current era closely resemble those of the imperial era. Independent academic Frank Furedi correctly points out that 'the aftermath of the 1991 Gulf War against Iraq was marked by a tendency expressly to celebrate imperial conquest in Britain and the United States'. 'By the time of the war against Iraq', he notes, 'there was virtually no intellectual critique of the West's right to intervene militarily in the Third World.'[9] What was being intellectually defended and celebrated was 'the most sophisticated and violent air assault in history against a virtually defenceless people', a report by the Clark Commission, under former US Attorney General Ramsey Clark, concluded.[10] Fittingly, the British forces in this war were commanded by a former Commander of the Special Air Service (SAS), Peter de la Billiere, who in the 1960s in Aden led terrorist-style hit squads by 'select[ing] a group of men who, disguised as Arabs, were to sally out in small groups into the town, looking for targets. If prisoners were to be taken and interrogated that was a bonus, but essentially the purpose was to meet terrorism with terrorism.'[11]

In this quest for basic control over world order US and British foreign policy has been remarkably consistent following the end of the Cold War. This consistency is now often stated in mainstream analyses, even though it contradicts everything that these commentators said the US stood for in the Cold War period (that is, that its foreign policy was based on containing the Soviet Union). Michael Cox, for example, in a major analysis of US foreign policy for Chatham House notes:

> Many of the broader objectives sought by the United States since 1989 actually bear a strong resemblance to those it pursued before the end of the Cold War and the fall of the USSR. Admittedly the geopolitical context has altered. But the underlying aim of the US – to create an environment in which democratic capitalism can flourish in a world in which the US remains the dominant actor – has not significantly altered.[12]

The primacy of retaining control is a logical continuation of the main features of past decades. The 1970s saw setbacks for the West through a series of anti-Western revolutions in the Third World; the 1980s was a decade of rollback with the debt crisis disciplining the Third World and aggressive Western foreign policies under Reagan and Thatcher; the 1990s seals the success of rollback with the unhindered promotion of economic 'liberalisation' in the South, especially through the creation under Northern auspices of the World Trade Organisation (WTO), and with the US as the sole superpower – there are now few barriers to the promotion of Western (more properly, Northern) policies in the South. This was well put by the South Commission at the beginning of the 1990s, and is even more true today:

> The widening disparities between South and North are attributable not merely to differences in economic progress, but also to an enlargement of the North's power vis-a-vis the rest of the world. The leading countries of the North now more readily use their power in pursuit of their objectives. The 'gunboat' diplomacy of the nineteenth century still has its economic and political counterpart in the closing years of the twentieth. The fate of the South is increasingly dictated by the perceptions and policies of governments in the North, of the multilateral institutions which a few of those governments control, and of the network of private institutions that are increasingly prominent.[13]

International relations at the turn of the century in many ways reveal the success of the post-Second World War project of the US to exert unadulterated control over the international economy and international relations more generally. John Ikenberry, writing in the US journal *Foreign Affairs* notes that 'the world order created in the 1940s is still with us, and in many ways stronger than ever'. With the end of the Cold War came the end of bipolarity, the nuclear stalemate and containment of the Soviet Union, Ikenberry notes, but other aspects of world order created in the 1940s endure: 'the commitment to an open world economy and its multilateral management, and the stabilization of socioeconomic welfare'. The post-Second World War system created by the US 'remains the core of world order', based on 'economic openness', 'joint management of the Western political-economic order' and rules and organisations that 'support domestic economic stability and social security'. To Ikenberry, 'the post-Cold War order is really a continuation and extension of the Western order forged during and after World War II'.[14] It has not quite worked out for the US, however, since although the Soviet Union has disappeared, it is forced to confront other major competitors, both within the capitalist West and in a rising Asia.

If we were to look at the world with honesty, we would clearly see that the United States and Britain are responsible for the most basic and routine flouting of international law. They are certainly not alone in this but they play a significant leading role. The Universal Declaration of Human Rights, for example, calls on all states to uphold the most basic human rights provisions. The final article reads: 'Nothing in this declaration may be interpreted as implying for any state, group or person any right to engage in any activity or to perform any act aimed at the destruction of the rights and freedoms set forth herein.'[15] Similarly, one might cite the Declaration on the Right to Development, which was adopted by the UN General Assembly in 1986, and which affirms the right to development of every person on the planet. Here, states are required to pursue policies that promote the improvement of the welfare of the entire population of states. These universal values are flouted as a matter of daily routine, by, for example, pursuing arms exports, continuing diplomatic support for repressive governments or promoting certain international economic instruments, some of which are considered in this study.

The independent US analyst Edward Herman has noted that 'the question of "who will contain us" is an oxymoron in the United States'.[16] The same applies in Britain. It would simply be inviting ridicule in mainstream circles to suggest that the United States and Britains of the world, and not the Iraqs, the Irans and the Libyas, are the major causes of suffering and abuses of civilised norms. Indeed, the comparison is unfair. Although the official 'rogue states' often pursue policies of unmitigated evil, the basic fact is that our governments are incomparably more powerful, and therefore bear more responsibility overall for the horrors in the world, than any of the threats designated by the establishment. The question of who will contain the powerful in our societies is a relevant one. This study attempts to elucidate on some of their most important policies.

# Part I

# Foreign Policy

# 1

# Postwar Foreign Policy and the Special Relationship

If we extricate ourselves from the view of foreign policy promoted in the mainstream and instead consider actual reality from the declassified documents and historical record, a fairly clear picture emerges as to the roots and effects of US and British foreign policy. In the US, there are a number of independent scholars – perhaps most prominently, Gabriel Kolko and Noam Chomsky – who have extensively analysed the historical and documentary record of US foreign policy. With British foreign policy, there is a paucity of independent sources and much of the secret record awaits documentation, which I tried to do in my previous book, *The Ambiguities of Power*. Below I try to outline, albeit very briefly, some main themes of postwar US and British foreign policy and the special relationship.

## Key themes in postwar US foreign policy

Postwar US foreign policy has been based on securing control over what was called the 'Grand Area', which encompassed virtually the entire non-Soviet world. US leaders incessantly outlined their primary goal within this area of an 'open door' in international trade and investment whereby 'American enterprises in other countries should be assured the right of access to raw materials and markets and to labour supply of the host country on the same terms as business enterprises operated therein by its citizens or by citizens of third countries'.[1] Given the predominant role of US business in the international economy after the Second World War, the overall US goal was nothing less than control of the international economy.[2] Cordell Hull, the US Secretary of State and architect of US postwar planning, had noted during the war that:

> Leadership towards a new system of international relationships in trade and other economic affairs will devolve very largely upon

> the United States because of our great economic strength. We should assume this leadership, and the responsibility that goes with it, primarily for reasons of pure national self-interest.[3]

It also involved control over world order more generally. As a State Department memorandum of 1948 put it: the establishment of a 'truly stable world order can proceed ... only from the older, mellower and more advanced nations of the world'.[4] This view echoed Winston Churchill, who had noted in 1940:

> Power in the hands of these two great liberal nations, with the free nations of the British Commonwealth and the American Republics associated in some way with them so as to ensure that power is not abused, offers the only stable prospect of peace.[5]

Noam Chomsky states that:

> In the international system envisioned by US planners, the industrial powers were to reconstruct, essentially restoring the traditional order and barring any challenge to business dominance, but now taking their places within a world system regulated by the United States. This world system was to take the form of state-guided liberal internationalism, secured by US power to bar interfering forces and managed through military expenditures, which proved to be a critical factor stimulating industrial recovery. The global system was designed to guarantee the needs of US investors, who were expected to flourish under the prevailing circumstances.[6]

Of particular importance to US planners were the raw material supplies, markets and investment opportunities of the Middle East, Southeast Asia and Latin America. Leading historian Gabriel Kolko notes that 'by no later than 1960, America's ideals and assumptions regarding institutional issues, above all foreign investment and raw materials exports, had been repeated so often, both in its policy guidelines and its routine diplomacy, that one can fairly say that ... there remains no mystery whatsoever regarding American formal premises and aims'.[7] Indeed, reviewing US foreign policy from 1945 until 1980, Kolko asserts that despite the risk of oversimplification, 'the economic component remains the single most important factor in its postwar conduct in the Third World'.[8]

In the Middle East, US planners undertook to secure overall control of the region's oil supplies in alliance with US oil corporations and based on a close relationship principally with the Saudi royal family and regime that lasts until today. This involved US arms sales to the regime, which helped to 'keep the goodwill of the King and other important Saudi Arabs', as it was put in 1947, and which remains relevant today.[9] US petroleum policy towards Britain – the other power with a controlling interest in Middle Eastern oil – was described in 1947 as predicated upon 'a very extensive joint interest and upon a control, at least for the moment, of the great bulk of the free petroleum resources of the world'.[10]

The need to exert control over the international economy's most important commodity meant gradually displacing the British from the region, the first major act of which was the joint CIA–MI6 coup in 1953 against the Iranian government that had nationalised the British-controlled oil industry. The new regime under the Shah reduced the British concession and gave US oil corporations an increased share in the country's oil business. Throughout the postwar period overall strategic control of the region has remained an overriding priority of US foreign policy (referred to as 'defence' in the propaganda system in a region where the US has 'security interests'). The interventions in Lebanon in 1958 and in Iraq in 1991, the strategic alliance with the Shah of Iran from 1953–78, Turkey and Israel and constant support for the regimes of the oil-rich Gulf states have all been in order to secure this fundamental goal (see also Chapters 5 and 6).

Contrary to popular myth, another key US postwar policy was general support for continuing control of colonial territories by the European powers, especially in Africa. 'In general', the State Department noted in 1950, 'we believe that our economic goals in Africa should be achieved through coordination and cooperation with the colonial powers.'[11] European colonial powers' plans to 'undertake jointly the economic development and exploitation' of the colonial areas 'has much to recommend it', the State Department noted in 1948.[12] In 1950, the State Department supported the European policy of the 'development of Africa as a means of strengthening their overall economic and strategic position in the world'.[13] By 1960, a National Security Council (NSC) report on Africa confirmed that the policy continued, and US interests involved 'the development of the dependent territories, in an orderly manner and in cooperation with the European metropoles, toward ultimate self-determination'. This transition should take place 'in a way which preserves the essential ties which bind Western Europe and Africa'. It also stated:

> As areas achieve independence [US policy is to] encourage them (1) to make the maximum contribution to their own economic development, (2) to eliminate barriers to trade and investment, (3) to take measures capable of attracting maximum amounts of external private capital, and (4) to look essentially to Western Europe, to the Free World international financial institutions and to private investment to meet their needs for external capital so long as this is consistent with US security interests.[14]

The US Joint Chiefs of Staff noted in 1947 that 'the United States is, by reason of its strength and political enlightenment, the natural leader of this hemisphere', referring to Latin America.[15] Similarly, then CIA Deputy Director of Intelligence, Robert Gates, noted in 1984 that 'the fact is that the Western hemisphere is the sphere of influence of the United States'.[16] In Latin America, Kolko notes, the US confronted 'an alternative concept of national capitalist economic development that rejected fundamentally its historic objective of an integrated world economy based not simply on capitalism but also on unrestricted access to whatever wealth it desired'. 'Nowhere else', Kolko states, 'were the underlying bases and objectives of US foreign policy revealed so starkly' in which the 'open door' was a myth and 'power and gain for the United States' the real foundation of its policies.[17]

The US intervention in Guatemala in 1954 was the first major postwar example of a familiar pattern of intervention, especially in Latin America. The pattern is that an essentially nationalist government (in this case under Jacobo Arbenz, democratically elected) threatens established US business interests in the country and/or region (in this case specifically the United Fruit Company, a major landowner) and the traditional economic and political order by pursuing a reform programme of benefit to the majority impoverished population. The political programme is then publicly labelled by US leaders as 'communist', usually backed by the Soviet Union, providing a pretext for intervention. The overt or covert US intervention occurs (in the Guatemala case with the CIA organising an invasion of the country, and conducting bombing raids) in an attempt to return to the traditional order under the pretext of restoring 'democracy'. This pattern was repeated in covert or overt US operations in Cuba from 1959, the Dominican Republic in 1965, Vietnam from the 1950s and in US-aided coups such as in Brazil in 1964 and Chile in 1973.

Another element in the basic pattern was sympathetic ideological framing of the issues by the US and British media and academia. Thirty years after the intervention in Guatemala, the US-organised contra war in Nicaragua showed the pattern was alive and well. The latter has been extensively documented by independent analysts, and involved the systematic pursuit of acts of terrorism by the US-backed forces and the undermining of possible diplomatic solutions to the conflict. The overall US goal in Nicaragua – and in the wider Central America region – was most reasonably understood as the destruction of the prospects for independent development. As in many other US interventions, the official assertions about the primacy of the Soviet or communist threat as an explanation for US policy were too ludicrous to be taken seriously on the evidence. However, as I documented in a study of British press reporting of the war in Nicaragua, this was indeed the lens through which the war was consistently reported in Britain, as well as in the US.[18]

A further element in the pattern was support for US policy from Britain, which has usually been the primary (and sometimes only major) supporter of US acts of aggression throughout the postwar period. For example, the Thatcher government strongly backed the US war against Nicaragua, adopting supportive positions in international fora and publicly declaring strong diplomatic backing. 'We support the United States' aim to promote peaceful change, democracy and economic development' in Central America, Thatcher stated in January 1984, by which time the US aim of destroying the prospects for these was quite clear to any rational observer (which thus excluded 99 per cent of the British press).[19] British mercenaries took part in the war, one British private 'security' company was involved in the sabotage of installations in Nicaragua, and British aircrew made 'flights into Nicaragua so that American nationals could not be captured if anything happened', John Prados notes in a study of CIA operations.[20] Security services expert Stephen Dorril notes that 'it is almost inevitable' that these deals between the US and British mercenaries were made with the agreement of Britain's MI6 'since there is agreement between the American and British intelligence services about recruiting each other's citizens'.[21] Arms for the Contras were contracted and forwarded from British companies, and attempts were made to supply surface-to-air missiles, though British government involvement is unclear.[22]

The principal threat to US foreign policy was always upheld by US officials as being the Soviet Union. The interventions from Guatemala in 1954 to Grenada in 1983 – as well as other policies, such as human rights and arms control – were invariably described in this light. Mainstream academia and the media, including many left-leaning commentators, promoted this line, in Britain as well as in the US, with as much frequency. Although 'containment' of the Soviet Union explains much about US postwar strategy, and the Cold War was a key issue in many policies, postwar US foreign policy was never in reality based mainly on containment. As I have shown elsewhere,[23] with reference to the planning documents of the US and Britain, much of postwar foreign policy is explicable more in terms of dividing up the world by reaching a tacit understanding with the Soviet Union. A British Foreign Office memorandum of 1951 noted that the current Western policy of 'containment' must 'give way as soon as possible' to 'the positive purpose of reaching an accommodation, or rather a modus vivendi ... with the Communist half of the world'.[24] This largely occurred in Eastern Europe – to be controlled by the Soviet Union – and virtually the whole of the Third World – to be controlled by the US and its allies and in which, in reality, there was very little direct interference by the Soviet Union.

The declassified documents and historical record show that the main threat in the Third World was from internal nationalist forces, sometimes popular and democratic, that threatened US and foreign control over the country's resources. Such threats were sometimes labelled 'internal aggression' in the planning records.[25] Noam Chomsky has unearthed much evidence to this effect: the major threat to US interests is posed by 'nationalistic regimes' that are responsive to popular pressures for 'immediate improvements in the low living standard of the masses' and diversification of the economies. This tendency conflicts with the need to 'protect our resources' and to encourage 'a climate conducive to foreign investment' and 'in the case of foreign capital to repatriate a reasonable return'.[26] This threat remains essentially the same today, although the forces that oppose US policy are as likely to be independent civil society groups as political, liberation movements as such.

The overturning of nationalist regimes and the undermining of nationalist movements were therefore standard features of US (and British) postwar foreign policy. Control over key states and regions was to be effected by maintaining the established order ('internal security') in these areas, through an alliance with often repressive and military-dominated elites. Arms exports and military training played (and continue to play) an important role in cementing such alliances; military intervention is an option when things get really out of control. Former Reagan administration official Thomas Carothers has noted that in Central America (and elsewhere, one might add), the US 'inevitably sought only limited, top-down forms of democratic change that did not risk upsetting the traditional structures of power with which the United States has long been allied'. Thus US policy was to support 'the basic order of ... quite undemocratic societies' and to avoid 'populist-based change' that might upset 'established economic and political orders' and open 'a leftist direction'.[27]

A major reason why nationalist forces presented such a threat to US policy was the fear that success would be repeated elsewhere – the 'threat of a good example', to use the title of a book by Oxfam, explaining US fears that the success of the Sandinista revolution in Nicaragua might be repeated elsewhere in Central America.[28] The Castro revolution in Cuba was feared partly 'because it could encourage expropriations of American property in other Latin American countries'.[29] CIA Director John McCone said that 'Cuba is the key to all Latin America; if Cuba succeeds, we can expect all of Latin America to fall'.[30] Similarly, during the US preparations to overthrow the Guatemalan government in 1954, a State Department official noted that Guatemala:

> has become an increasing threat to the stability of Honduras and El Salvador. Its agrarian reform is a powerful propaganda weapon; its broad social programme of aiding the workers and peasants in a victorious struggle against the upper classes and large foreign enterprises has a strong appeal to the populations of Central American neighbours where similar conditions prevail.[31]

Nationalist grievances should have been well understood by US planners, since they are revealed in many of the declassified US documents. The US Department of Agriculture noted in 1950 that 'the central agricultural and, indeed, economic and social problem throughout Asia is the abject poverty of the large masses of the peasants'. One of the basic reasons for this 'has been the landlord–tenant system in many parts of Asia, under which large groups of peasants are cultivating somebody else's land and paying exorbitant rents for it'. A danger was that 'the success of the communists in China, where they largely won the support of the peasants by promising land in drastic revision of landlord–tenant relationships, may be repeated in other parts of Asia'.[32] Such inequities in land ownership were the principal cause of many revolutionary or reformist movements the US sought to crush, such as in the Philippines in the 1950s, in Vietnam from the 1950s and El Salvador and Nicaragua in the 1980s.

Outside of the Third World, the US has faced major challenges from its Western 'allies', long understood by US planners also as competitors. The rise of Japan and Germany, in particular, but also the newly industrialising countries (NICs) in Asia has posed major problems. The Soviet Union's collapse would have opened up the entire world to potential US penetration had US power in the 1990s been as great as in the 1940s. However, German capital is more likely to benefit from the 'opening' of Russia and Eastern Europe, and Japan is the major economic power in East Asia. Also, the disappearance of the Soviet 'threat' obviates the need for US security guarantees to its allies, removing a major lever to discipline them into accepting US 'leadership' on other issues. The US is still the world's major power, however, both militarily and in many ways economically, and its policies in key areas – the United Nations, the Middle East and the WTO, for example – remain the dominant ones. As discussed below, US foreign policy increasingly acts on behalf of a transnational rather than purely US elite with interests in pursuing globalisation and securing the political systems that are required to promote it. The continuation of a controlling role in the 'era of globalisation' is consistent with the goals outlined, and largely secured, following the Second World War.

There is an enormous amount of goodwill extended to US foreign policy in mainstream analysis. In Britain, serious independent criticism of US foreign policy is often ridiculed as 'anti-American' – a term of abuse that suggests some personal grudge – and my experience in the academic world is that it is simply considered as 'not the done thing' to criticise US policy in a systematic way. In the mainstream, it is often recognised that the US is the world's hegemonic power – a fact invariably to be applauded – and that it has occasionally pursued policies that deviate from the promotion of grand principles like democracy, human rights and human development. But the historical record – it has been touched on only briefly here and is considered throughout the rest of this study – shows simply that the US is a fundamentally malevolent power if judged by the extent of its promotion of those same values.

In the words of Colonel Philip Roettinger, the CIA Station Chief in Guatemala during the 1954 US-sponsored coup, 'we are plunderers ... We go into primitive countries in order to destroy for power and money.'[33] This view is consistent with the US record of millions dead in the war in Southeast Asia, thousands dead in a terrorist war in Nicaragua and hundreds of thousands killed in US-supported mass killing in Indonesia in 1965, to cite some of the worst examples. To cite just one example of US goals from the declassified record, a 1954 government report noted that 'hitherto accepted norms of conduct do not apply ... to survive, long standing American concepts of "fair play" must be reconsidered. We must ... learn to subvert, sabotage and destroy our enemies by more clever, more sophisticated and more effective methods than those used against us.'[34] US power has been, and continues to be, largely responsible for the international economic system that impoverishes billions of people at the same time as enriching a minority; a system which, not surprisingly, also has the same consequences domestically. The domestic gains that many American people can claim their system offers are certainly real, especially in comparison with other societies around the globe, but there can be no doubt that the US interaction with the world has been grave.

The reality of US policy is, however, invariably buried, to the degree that when the US President announced the intention to promote a benign 'New World Order' in 1990, virtually the whole of the press and academia greeted the proposal with solemnity (albeit sometimes critical) rather than simply ridicule. Similar reactions invariably follow US government announcements of 'humanitarian' interventions, for example in Somalia or Haiti. Kolko has correctly noted that 'the fundamental assumption that the United States retains the right and obligation to intervene in the Third World in any way it ultimately deems necessary, including militarily, remains an article of faith among the people who guide both political parties'.[35] One might add that it is also an article of faith for media and academic commentators in both the US and Britain to accept that basic right, a privilege not extended to any other country.

## Key themes in postwar British foreign policy

British foreign policy has been subject to arguably more myth than even that of the US. Scholars who have exposed US policy through the declassified planning records have been largely absent from Britain, where analysis has been dominated by former officials and absurdly sycophantic academics. The basic contours of British policy can be outlined by taking a brief look at recent history.

Policy since 1945 has been guided by two main aims. The first has been to maintain as far as possible Britain's power status: in the early postwar years as a 'great power' and latterly as a second-rank global power that should not descend into a mere European one. Referring to great power status, the British Ambassador to the US noted in 1954 that 'we take this for granted' and that it was 'a principle so much at one with our outlook and character that it determines the way we act without emerging itself into clear consciousness'.[36]

The second aim has been to ensure that the international system is organised to benefit British and Western commercial interests and that the world's economically most important states and regions remain under effective Western control. The Foreign Office noted in 1949 the 'importance of our maintaining control of the periphery [around the Soviet Union] which runs round from Oslo to Tokyo'. In this task, 'we should try to look on the periphery as a whole' and 'this policy should, if possible, be concerted with the United States'.[37] Another report, from 1947, noted that 'the area from Suez to Singapore' was also 'of decisive importance to us', since it provided significant dollar earnings and thus 'could continue to buy heavily from us'.[38] The interrelated goals of maintaining power status and ensuring economic interests in key areas were outlined by the Foreign Office in 1950:

> If the United Kingdom were voluntarily to abandon her position of political influence in selected areas, she would probably find herself not only without economic access to those areas but unable, through loss of prestige, to prevent a further involuntary decline in her influence elsewhere and consequently a general decline in the strength of the Western powers.[39]

The basic strategy, as with the US, has hardly altered throughout the postwar period – tactics for achieving these aims have changed as a result of declining power, not changing interests.

Britain's first postwar (Labour) government intensified the economic exploitation of Britain's colonies in order to help a British economy ravaged by war, a policy that was supported and encouraged by the US. Africa was described as 'an important source of raw materials in peace and war', and Southeast Asia as 'a substantial economic asset and a net earner of dollars'.[40] Use of the sterling area – the large part of the world where the pound was the trading currency – as a device for supporting the pound, and the system of bulk-buying of colonial commodities by Britain at prices below the world market price, became weapons to 'extract wealth from peasant producers', imperial historian David Fieldhouse notes.[41] The British Treasury had outlined in 1945 that 'we have to devise techniques for bringing influence to bear upon other countries' internal decisions', which involved economic measures to force countries to 'accept our advice on the general course of their development'.[42]

Labour government leaders explicitly sought to preserve Britain's Great Power status and initially explored the possibility of becoming a 'Third Force' between the US and the USSR. This was to involve an alliance of the European colonial powers together with their colonies to achieve an 'African Union under European auspices', as a British ambassador put it.[43] Foreign Secretary Ernest Bevin noted in 1948 that 'it should be possible to develop our own power and influence to equal that of the United States of America and the USSR' since 'we have the material resources in the colonial empire, if we develop them'. This policy would 'show clearly that we are not subservient' to either superpower.[44] However, by 1949 this policy was rejected as it was clear that British power was insufficient to support it. Instead, Britain opted for a special relationship with the United States that endures to this day. British leaders believed this policy would ensure that Britain would achieve its foreign policy goals, although adjustment to a junior status to the senior power would be inevitable.

'Decolonisation' is a misleading term to describe the change from colonial control to formal independence on the part of Britain's colonies. First, the term implies a voluntary process, which it was not in many cases – rather, Britain was often forced to withdraw either by nationalist political forces or domestic pressures. Planners understood in 1947 that 'the greater part of the world' was opposed to British and other colonialism. Indeed, 'the only quarter from which effective support' was available or likely 'is the United States'.[45] Imperialists like Churchill were staunchly opposed to giving up empire – the famous 'finest hour' speech in 1940 finished with a call to defend not just Britain from Hitler but also the British empire, and to keep it intact for a thousand years.[46] Hitler used similar 'thousand-year' rhetoric for his dream for the Reich.

Second, colonial control was often replaced by a form of neocolonialism intended to continue British economic and political interests after formal independence. This was the explicit intention of much British post-independence planning, for example in Kenya, where policy was largely to ensure land remained in the same (white) hands as before independence. Generally, Britain feared 'irresponsible extremist leaders' filling the vacuum after it left, with the aim being 'to leave behind us stable societies' ('stable' being a regular term used in the planning files to mean 'pro-Western').[47] It was therefore correct (then as now) of Prime Minister Clement Attlee to state in 1947, referring to the Middle East, that 'we shall constantly appear to be supporting vested interests and reaction against reform and revolution in the interests of the poor'.[48] Aid, trade and military contacts perform similar functions today of maintaining relations with favoured elites.

Britain conducted many unilateral military and other interventions in the Third World in the 25 years following the end of the Second World War. Nationalist elements who threatened Western control over countries' resources were far and away the most significant problem to British planners. The Soviet threat was virtually non-existent in most of the major policy areas in these years, despite attempts by planners and commentators, both then and now, to claim the opposite. The formerly secret documents show that the wars fought in Malaya and Kenya were much more brutal than usually presented. In Kenya in the 1950s, for example, British forces and their local allies indulged in routine torture, an apparent shoot-to-kill policy, draconian police measures and mass 'resettlement' programmes to combat the dual threat of the Mau Mau movement and indigenous nationalism. In some of the prisons set up by the British, 'short rations, overwork, brutality, humiliating and disgusting treatment and flogging' were all practised, according to a British officer who worked in them.[49] Some prisons were 'probably as bad as any similar Nazi or Japanese establishments', imperial historian Victor Kiernan comments.[50]

The pattern of postwar US military intervention in Latin America noted in the previous section was begun by Britain. A long-forgotten British intervention occurred in British Guiana (now Guyana) in 1953, when Britain overthrew the democratically elected government of Cheddi Jagan, who threatened control of the country's economic resources by British and foreign companies. Jagan's mildly socialist programme of economic reform to improve the conditions of the majority impoverished population was described by the then Colonial Secretary as 'threatening the order of the colony' and 'destroying the confidence of the business community'. After the overthrow, and with some elected leaders in jail, further elections were ruled out because 'the same party would have been elected again', the Colonial Secretary noted.[51]

Britain was, and remains, especially active in the Middle East, an area that to British planners was 'a vital prize for any power interested in world influence or domination'.[52] British policy in Iran in the early 1950s was 'to get rid of [Iranian Prime Minister] Mosaddeq as soon as possible' and to reverse the government's nationalisation of the oil industry, which had previously been under British control. British planners advised the Shah that the 'only solution' was 'a strong government under martial law' and where 'a dictator ... would carry out the necessary administrative and economic reforms and settle the oil question on reasonable terms'.[53] The British vision prevailed, with help from the US, and the Shah ruled the country with an iron hand, and consistent US and British support, until the revolution of 1978/9.

Britain engaged in many other interventions in this period. The most famous was the invasion of Egypt in 1956, a disaster which was a turning point for British power globally. The invasion has often been explained away as the fault of one ill man, Prime Minister Anthony Eden. However, documentary minutes show that 'the cabinet agreed that ... in the last resort, this political pressure [against Egypt] be backed by the threat – and, if need be, the use – of force'. It was believed that 'failure to hold the Suez Canal would lead inevitably to the loss one by one of all our interests and assets in the Middle East', an early example of the domino theory.[54] The then Chancellor, Harold Macmillan, was a key supporter of British policy, and succeeded Eden as Prime Minister. The Foreign Secretary, Selwyn Lloyd, also remained in post following his role in the secret collusion with Israel to attack Egypt. He had lied to Parliament, saying that there had been no such collusion. Meanwhile, British plots to assassinate Egyptian leader Nasser continued.[55] The US application of economic and political pressure on Britain was the key to halting the invasion. However, President Eisenhower said later that if Britain had 'done it quickly, we would have accepted it'.[56]

British involvement in Oman was at least as horrendous as in Egypt, and longer lasting, though it remains largely unknown to the British public. Virtually a colony in the 1950s to 1970s, due to the extent of British influence over the Omani government and the oil business, the Omani regime was also one of the world's most repressive, then or since. Even by 1970 it was forbidden to smoke in public, to play football, to wear glasses or to speak to anyone for more than 15 minutes. Britain fought wars in defence of the Omani regime in the late 1950s and 1960s and British officers remained as commanders of the Omani military until the 1980s.[57] Oman today remains the closest British ally in the Gulf (see also Chapter 6).

Two further interventions are of particular interest. The declassified documents suggest that the alleged threats to the Jordanian regime in 1958 and the Kuwaiti regime in 1961 were deliberately fabricated by British planners to serve as pretexts for intervention. In the case of Jordan, Britain was worried about the spread of nationalism in the region following the 1958 revolution in Iraq, which overthrew the pro-British monarch. Thus Britain intervened to bolster the regime of King Hussein, for which political support in Jordan was 'extremely meagre', British planners recognised. The State Department noted that it was not 'practicable to maintain the regime against the wishes of probably 90 per cent of the country's inhabitants'. The files also show that British planners considered an invasion of Iraq from Jordanian territory at this time but decided against it.[58]

In Kuwait, the British fear was that the oil-rich state would eschew its dependence on Britain for military protection and threaten the huge British economic stake in the regime. Two months before the intervention, one memorandum read:

> It is clear that, as the international personality of Kuwait grows, she will wish in various ways to show that she is no longer dependent upon us ... We must continue to use the opportunities which our protective role will afford to ensure as far as we can that Kuwait does not materially upset the existing financial arrangements or cease to be a good holder of sterling.

The files strongly indicate that the alleged Iraqi threat to Kuwait – which has always been promoted as the reason for the British military intervention – was deliberately fabricated in order to ensure continued Kuwaiti dependence on Britain.[59]

The 1960s continued to witness strong support for US foreign policy, including the war against Vietnam. Labour policy was not as effusive in its backing as the opposition Conservatives, but the Wilson government provided consistent basic support to the US ally. In March 1965, well after the US had significantly escalated the war into large-scale bombing, Prime Minister Wilson stated that 'we fully support the US action in *resisting* aggression in Vietnam'.[60] A British role in the war has always been officially denied. However, according to one study of British covert operations, the SAS fought in Vietnam attached to Australian and New Zealand SAS squads. The British signals base in Hong Kong also supplied US forces with intelligence and, with the US National Security Council, helped target US bombing strikes in North Vietnam.[61]

The special relationship was also important in determining British policy towards the Indian Ocean island of Diego Garcia. From 1965–73 Britain expelled the population of 1800 people from the territory to make way for a military base, doing so with minimal compensation for the indigenous inhabitants, most of whom ended up living in abject poverty in the slums of the Mauritian capital, St Louis. A Ministry of Defence spokesperson stated soon after the expulsions were complete that 'there is nothing in our files about inhabitants or about an evacuation'.[62] It would be wrong to say that this episode has been forgotten in histories of British foreign policy since it has hardly ever been mentioned at all. Britain retains formal sovereignty and Diego Garcia is now a major US military base, part of its intervention capability in the Middle East, and was used as a refuelling point for US bombers during the Gulf War of 1991.

As regards South Africa under apartheid, Britain remained the primary international supporter – in terms of investments, trade and military relations – of the regimes from the 1940s to the 1990s, as the historical record makes clear. Prime Minister Edward Heath noted that South Africa was not 'a country hostile to our own interests', reflecting a US official's later comments on Ronald Reagan to the extent that 'all he knows about southern Africa is that he is on the side of the whites'.[63]

The accession to the European Community (EC) in 1973 and the withdrawal from some major military bases in the Gulf in 1971 marked other turning points in British policy. In the latter half of the postwar era the British ability to engage unilaterally in furthering its interests has been undermined, with reliance on the US the preferred option. Britain's lending diplomatic and sometimes military support to the US, especially for the latter's aggression abroad, has provided a key pillar of international order (see below).

Britain was the only major state to support the US invasion of Panama in 1989 and unstintingly to support the belligerent US stance towards Iraq in the 1991 war, playing second fiddle to US power in the slaughter, just as it has done more generally throughout the postwar period. It has also continued to engage in joint covert actions with the US, such as in the training of Cambodian guerrillas allied to the Khmer Rouge (and evidently the Khmer Rouge itself) in the 1980s.

In the current era, the same foreign policy priorities as outlined at the end of the Second World War largely prevail but these are generally pursued, if not in the special relationship with the US, then in international fora where Britain retains key influence. Britain has been a leading architect of the new international trading regime – the WTO – plays a leading role in the World Bank and has been a strong supporter of structural adjustment, the modern equivalent of traditional Western economic policies in the Third World. Certainly, Britain has been able to continue many of its own particular policies and continues to enjoy strong bilateral relationships with some of the world's most repressive regimes, notably Indonesia, Saudi Arabia and Turkey.

The expanded process of European integration in the 1990s – which Britain has always wanted to prevent – as well as the extension of the North Atlantic Treaty Organisation (NATO), and proposed extension of the European Union (EU), into Eastern Europe – which Britain has firmly supported – focus current British attention on Europe. British policy in the past was consistently to prevent the emergence of a dominant power in Europe that would threaten British power (Napoleon; the Nazis). Nowadays, the priority is to champion a 'free trade' Europe with minimal social provisions and to prevent the further consolidation of a European entity that is beyond Britain's ability to control, and that offers a threat to the traditional source of postwar British power – the special relationship with the United States. Indeed, explaining British opposition to a more integrated Europe as being due to concern about 'sovereignty' is clearly misplaced. Britain is quite happy to give up sovereignty in the international economy and in NATO, 'whose war plans effectively place decisions concerning war and peace in American hands', conservative analyst Anthony Hartley comments.[64] British concerns are not over sovereignty as such but over the threat to traditional 'national interests'.

All in all, the basic priorities are remarkably similar to those of 50 years ago.

## The special relationship

There are two dominant views on the special relationship. The first is that it no longer exists and did not really survive the wartime and early postwar experience. The second is that it does exist and principally involves intelligence and nuclear collaboration. If we glance, again briefly, at the historical record, we see a fuller picture.

One view on the importance of the special relationship was outlined in 1993 by Raymond Seitz, US Ambassador to Britain. He noted that 'a critical component in the long, successful saga of the Cold War was the relationship between the United Kingdom and the United States' and that 'while our focus was in Europe, we both also recognised this was a global business'. Britain was 'our closest ally', Seitz noted, and the relationship 'would remain undisturbed regardless of which political party came to power in London or Washington'. A key aspect 'is the degree to which our two nations find their respective international interests to be parallel' and the vigour of the relationship 'depends on the perception of strategic coincidence'. The US 'saw Britain as its strategic forward post, and Britain regarded America as its own strategic hinterland'. While the US supports a central British role in the EU, the US remains 'anxious that Britain should preserve its capacity for independent action, within Europe and beyond the continent as well' in a military role. Seitz concluded by noting that 'our priorities will not match with quite the same frequency as they once did' but that 'there is so much content and body in this relationship that will carry through the passing of an old era'.[65]

The special relationship is rooted in much more than simply the wartime alliance. As Gabriel Kolko wrote in his landmark study of US planning for the postwar world:

> The key to the attainment of American postwar objectives for the world economy was Great Britain, for prior to the war the sterling bloc and North America accounted for about one half of the total world trade. If the two nations could agree, then the rest of the world would be unable to resist their power and would inevitably fall into line.[66]

The situation had reversed from 1917, when Sir Robert Cecil wrote to the British War Cabinet to the effect that 'if America accepts our point of view ... it will mean the dominance of that point of view in all international affairs'.[67]

US plans for the international economy also meant Britain playing a key role in the reconstruction of Europe. Underlying this was the policy of supporting British colonialism but also one of gradually replacing British power with its own and securing British dependence on US power. This had been a long-standing intention. As early as 1942, the President of the Council on Foreign Relations, an academic think-tank that, especially during the war years, was responsible for helping develop the broad contours of US foreign policy, stated that 'the British empire as it existed in the past will never reappear and ... the United States will have to take its place'.[68]

However, the US also looked to Britain to dampen down the more radical political forces in the Third World that were seen as threats to its basic design, especially in the Middle East. The Policy Planning Staff of the State Department outlined in 1948, for example:

> We must do what we can to support the maintenance of the British of their strategic position in that area [sic]. That does not mean that we must support them in every individual instance ... It *does* mean that any policy on our part which tends to strain British relations with the Arab world and to whittle down the British position in the Arab countries is only a policy directed against ourselves and against the immediate strategic interests of our country.[69]

The State Department noted in another memo that Britain was the 'outstanding example' of 'like-minded nations' and that Britain and its empire 'form a worldwide network of strategically located territories of great military value, which have served as defensive outposts and as bridgeheads for operations'. US planners also recognised the importance of 'strategic materials for which British colonies and dependencies constitute important sources of supply'.[70]

The argument has sometimes been made that Britain, the process of decolonisation, was more benevolent than other colonial powers such as France or Portugal, who engaged in large-scale massacres to maintain colonial control. Journalist Christopher Hitchens notes, however, in a study of the US–British relationship that 'there was no bloody, drawn-out torture of the Algerian or Angolan variety' but 'this was not just because ... the Empire was wound up with relative humanity and dispatch ... It was because Britain, unlike her European imperial rivals, had the option of a partial merger with another empire', that is, the US.[71]

Britain has long been understood by US leaders as 'a fortified outpost of the Anglo-Saxon race', as Henry Adams' brother Brooks noted.[72] 'You may be sure that we shall stand by you on fundamentals', Churchill wrote to Eisenhower in 1953,[73] having described himself as Roosevelt's 'loyal lieutenant' during the Second World War.[74] The British Ambassador in Washington correctly perceived as early as 1945 that US policy towards Britain 'expected her to take her place as junior partner in an orbit of power predominantly under American aegis'.[75] Britain opted for, and largely accepted, the subordinate role to the Americans. Policy in the Far East in the late 1940s would be 'best played by a combination of British experience and United States resources', one Foreign Office memo read.[76] By the 1960s the Kennedy administration noted that Britain would 'act as our lieutenant (the fashionable word is partner)'.[77]

The postwar beginnings of joint covert action included operations by the CIA and Britain's MI6 in the Baltic states of the Soviet Union. Operations were mounted from West Germany, some training and preparations were carried out in Britain and teams of agents were dispatched to support resistance groups until 1956. Other joint operations occurred in the Ukraine, beginning in 1949, whereby MI6 took the lead in the infiltration of agents. These operations involved members of the Gehlen organisation – after Reinhard Gehlen, a leading Nazi intelligence officer – and the training in the US of at least 200 men with Nazi connections.[78]

Four policy areas above all explain the importance of the special relationship. The first concerns nuclear proliferation. Since the 1960s the US has supplied Polaris and now Trident missile systems to Britain. This is the world's leading case of proliferation – making a mockery of professed interest by the US and Britain in curbing such proliferation – and the only case whereby one state has transferred a functioning nuclear system to another state (although Britain makes the actual warheads). The emplacement of US nuclear bases in Britain (the last US nuclear weapons left Britain in 1996) was a quid pro quo for nuclear collaboration with Britain in the early postwar years.

The second area is joint intelligence and covert operations, some of which have been noted above. US intelligence support was vital to Britain in the Falklands War. Intelligence expert Christopher Andrew notes that 'the SIGINT [signals intelligence] attack on Argentinian communications, which yielded the best intelligence of the Falklands war, was conducted virtually as a combined operation by GCHQ [Government Communications Headquarters – the British SIGINT agency] and NSA [the US National Security Agency]'. The CIA is also thought to have provided SIS with intelligence from its Buenos Aires station.[79] The extent of links in intelligence and covert operations was revealed in Duncan Campbell's landmark 1984 study which showed that there were 130 US military bases and facilities in Britain, comprising virtually the full range of US military-related equipment deployed worldwide.[80] Many of these facilities remain in Britain in the post-Cold War world, and remain subject to almost complete secrecy outside of democratic scrutiny.

The third area is the extent to which the British and US propaganda systems are mutually supportive in their reporting of the other's actions. The study I conducted on British press reporting of the US war in Nicaragua showed how both the same general frame of reference as well as the more detailed aspects of the war were conveyed in virtually identical ways on both sides of the Atlantic, drawing largely uncritically from the often quite explicit disinformation then emanating from the Reagan White House.[81] A similar study I conducted on the Gulf War of 1991 produced similar conclusions.[82]

The fourth area, and the most important pillar of the special relationship, in my view – indeed, the chief indicator of the existence of such a special relationship – is mutual support for aggression. Throughout the postwar period there have been a couple of cases of major US and British actions that have not been supported by the other. Suez is a major example, whereby US power was instrumental in halting the Anglo-French invasion; the 1983 US intervention in Grenada was privately opposed by Britain although public utterances were generally more supportive and often apologetic. Cases of mutual support are far more common, however, amounting to a clear pattern and part of what Seitz, noted above, calls 'strategic coincidence'. 'Whenever we want to subvert any place', leading US intelligence figure Frank Wisner once commented, 'we find the British own an island within easy reach.'[83] Wisner could have been referring to Diego Garcia – a support base for intervention in the Middle East – or Hong Kong which, as noted above, was used for the exchange of intelligence during the Vietnam War.

The US firmly supported the British overthrow of the Jagan government in British Guiana in 1953 and the two collaborated to overthrow Musaddiq in Iran in the same year; the following year Britain played a key role in the UN to prevent UN action against US aggression in Guatemala. The 1950s also saw strong US support for the British wars in Kenya and Malaya, the latter involving some policies – notably 'villageisation' – subsequently taken up by the US in the Vietnam War, in which British advisers, as well as the SAS, also served. As regards Castro's Cuba, Prime Minister Macmillan told Eisenhower that 'he is your Nasser' and 'I feel sure Castro has got to be got rid of, but it is a tricky operation for you to contrive and I only hope you will succeed.'[84] The British intervention in Jordan in 1958 was planned to coincide with the US intervention in Lebanon, with both countries fearing the rise of Nasser-inspired nationalism throughout the Middle East.

One of the more horrendous episodes of collaboration concerned the overthrow of the Sukarno regime and the support for the Generals' campaign of slaughter in Indonesia in 1965. This campaign was ostensibly against the PKI – the Indonesian Communist Party – but was in reality against all opposition, including ordinary peasants. The declassified US and British files show clear complicity in this mass slaughter, in which up to a million people may have been killed. The US provided arms to the Generals and a 'hit list' of thousands of opponents who were subsequently hunted down and killed. Diplomatic exchanges show that the US was 'generally sympathetic with and admiring of what [the] army [is] doing'.[85] Less well known is the British role, which was also significant. 'I have never concealed from you my belief that a little shooting in Indonesia would be an essential preliminary to effective change', Britain's Ambassador in Jakarta noted a few days after the killings began. The Foreign Office stated that:

> It seems pretty clear that the Generals are going to need all the help they can get and accept without being tagged as hopelessly

> pro-Western, if they are going to be able to gain ascendancy over the Communists. In the short run, we can hardly go wrong by tacitly backing the Generals.

The files show that Britain conducted covert operations in Indonesia in order 'surreptitiously to blacken the PKI in the eyes of the army and the people of Indonesia'. This involved the distribution of 'certain unattributable material' organised from Britain's intelligence and propaganda centre in Singapore. Moreover, British planners facilitated the Generals' campaign in another way. At the time, Britain was engaged in a war of 'confrontation' with the Sukarno regime, mainly in the territory of Borneo, which Indonesia claimed from Malaysia, a British ally. Once the Generals began their move against Sukarno, and the killings had begun, the Foreign Office stated that British policy 'did not want to distract the Indonesian army by getting them engaged in fighting in Borneo and so discourage them from attempts which they now seem to be making to deal with the PKI'. The Ambassador therefore delivered 'a carefully phrased oral message [to the Generals] about not biting the Generals in the rear for the present'.[86] These events marked the beginning of the close US and British relationship with the leader of the Generals – Suharto – that continues to this day.

The 1970s saw decreasing British ability to act militarily in support of world order and Britain's increasing turn towards Europe, resulting in fewer cases of overt joint action. It was under Thatcher and Reagan that the relationship took a turn back towards the earlier period. The SAS operation to train Cambodian guerrillas allied to the Khmer Rouge – and the British policy of de facto support for the Khmer Rouge at the UN – was closely coordinated with the US. Britain was the only major ally to offer full support for the US bombing of Libya in 1986, with Thatcher allowing US warplanes the use of British bases. The latter were not required for military reasons, since other aircraft could have undertaken the attack, but for political reasons to show that the US was not acting alone. Britain's agreement was partly in return for US intelligence support for Britain during the Falklands War, which Britain could probably not have undertaken unilaterally. Here, the US initially wavered and found itself in the difficult position of having to choose between one ally – the neo-Nazi military junta under Galtieri, which had worked with the CIA and helped in the proxy terrorist war in Nicaragua – and another, eventually deciding to back Britain. Reagan's consistent support for terrorism, military adventurism and abuse of international law (over the refusal to abide by the World Court's ruling against the mining of Nicaraguan ports, for example) did not prevent Queen Elizabeth II bestowing upon Reagan an honorary knighthood in recognition of the United States' backing of Britain. Her husband, Prince Philip, praised Reagan for his 'outstanding gifts of leadership, which helped the nation to regain its confidence, vigour and sense of purpose and to recapture the respect of foreign friend and adversary alike' and for his policy of advocating 'peace through strength'.[87] Caspar Weinberger, Reagan's Secretary of State for Defense who presided over the US's massive military arms build-up, was also given a knighthood, largely for services rendered during the Falklands War.[88]

The 1991 war against Iraq demonstrated the continuing British willingness to act as the 'junior partner', a role it had opted for nearly half a century previously. The Commander of the British forces, Peter de la Billiere, congratulated his US counterpart Norman Schwarzkopf, by saying that 'I just want you to know how proud we are to have served with the US troops and to have played a small part in what is *your* great victory.'[89] Britain also strongly supported the US cruise missile attacks against Iraq in 1993 and in 1996. Following the attack by 44 missiles in September 1996, which Britain was virtually alone in backing, Secretary of State Warren Christopher noted that 'we are very grateful' to the British government for 'their unstinting support'.[90]

There have been recent major policy differences, however; most notably over what London has regarded as US interference (and basic support for the nationalist side) in Northern Ireland, and British opposition (shared by the EU generally) over US attempts to pressure European business into stopping trade with Cuba. With regard to the former Yugoslavia, Britain's basic policy of conciliation towards the (Serbian) aggression in the region and opposition to lifting the arms embargo against Bosnia contrasted with the US policy of strong support for Croatia, the other main aggressor, and limited backing for the independent state of Bosnia. These tensions sometimes placed the relationship at great strain. The closest ally to the US apart from Britain has been Israel, and this US–Israel special relationship has traditionally been the only major US policy area that Britain has not actively supported.

The current British focus on Europe does not necessarily detract from the special relationship since the US has always firmly supported the British role in European integration and defines much of Britain's importance to it in terms of Britain's influence in Europe. However, the major service that Britain has provided the US over the last 50 years has been global, involving support for US policies outside of Europe and as a critical player in maintaining world order more generally. Indeed, despite the policy differences between the US and Britain, on the one hand, and the primary attention accorded by British planners to Europe, on the other, the fact remains that Britain still plays a critical role in support of US foreign policy and world order, usually independently from its role in the EU. Prime Minister John Major correctly suggested in 1995 that 'you have to look at the huge range of things in which the instinctive outlook between the United Kingdom and the United States government is exactly the same', and stated:

> If you run down most of the great issues of the moment – relationship with Russia, relationship on terrorism, relationship with Iran, relationship with Iraq – you won't find a scintilla of difference ... between the British government and the United States government [sic].

Major also noted that 'I hope very soon in the future that you'll be able to see Tomahawk cruise missiles in the United Kingdom armoury'. He was also correct in saying that these two nations were the 'foremost in propounding a free trade agreement, the GATT agreement' [General Agreement on Tariffs and Trade] (which, evolving into the WTO, owed much to Anglo-American power and which is likely to spell greater impoverishment for the South).

Clinton, in turn, noted that the 'extraordinary relationship' between the two countries was 'as important as ever' and also the 'commonality of interests that exists', especially as regards 'agreements that we have in terms of policy towards Russia, Iran, Iraq, the Middle East, Bosnia and a range of other areas'. He also declared – correctly – that 'I think that in foreign policy the differences are not easily discernible by party' in Britain.[91]

With regard to Iraq, the US and Britain see eye to eye on the need to maintain the sanctions against the country, which have resulted in great human misery, an alliance that has been powerful enough to prevent other UN members forcing a change in the 'UN' policy. Regarding Russia, both leaders are also correct in seeing general commonality of interests; both backing Yeltsin's increasingly draconian and corrupt regime and – through the variety of aid, trade and International Monetary Fund (IMF) loan instruments – seeking to turn Russia into a Third World-style source of investment profits for Western business. Britain also remains the de facto number two power to the US in NATO and commands the Allied Rapid Reaction Corps. It plays the lead role in the EU – with strong US support – in opposing the establishment of any EU military organisation likely to rival NATO and thus in stalling considerable European support for developing a more independent political and military identity.

In the three areas with which this book is primarily concerned – development, the Middle East and the United Nations – Anglo-American power is hugely significant and often decisive in shaping events. Overall, British planners regard it as an overriding priority to maintain the special relationship with the US, especially on military, intelligence and 'global order' matters. This is partly for the traditional reason that the alliance is deemed to protect and sustain Britain's global power, and partly because planners believe it allows Britain to influence the policies of the world's sole superpower. US planners continue to regard Britain as primarily important in terms of its influence in Europe, its strong support for NATO, the 'strategic coincidence' on policies associated with maintaining world order and its role as a key ally in times of a crises affecting that order (such as over Iraq in 1991).

# 2

# Foreign Policy Under the Democrats and Labour

## The aims of US foreign policy

In the years following the demise of the Soviet Union there have been a huge number of analyses by American academics as to the purposes and goals of current US foreign policy. This is not surprising given that establishment discourse routinely posited containment of the Soviet Union as the overarching objective of US foreign policy. A number of differences in perspectives can be detected in these analyses; however, what is more remarkable is the degree of consensus on fundamental US goals and priorities. Before considering government policies and thinking, and in recognition of the close links between establishment academia and policy makers in the US, it is worth initially considering some prominent mainstream US academic thinking, to help gauge current US foreign policy priorities.

In a study for the Council on Foreign Relations, Robert Tucker and David Hendrickson note that 'the United States is today the dominant military power in the world', and in the reach and effectiveness of its military forces 'America compares favourably with some of the greatest empires known to history'. Compared to the Roman and British empires, 'the United States has an altogether more formidable collection of forces than its predecessors among the world's great powers'. Tucker and Hendrickson also note that the end of the Cold War has 'dramatically broadened the area of freedom for the nation's foreign policy'. Since the 'postwar international order was an order inseparable from containment', and this order has disappeared, the US role is 'no longer that of freedom's champion and defender against totalitarianism' and its 'policy would have to change accordingly'. The principal thesis of this book is a warning against the US succumbing to an 'imperial temptation' in which, inspired by its role in the war against Iraq, the US engages in occasional massive uses of military power in an imperial role and a general overreliance on military power to secure its objectives. The US role should rather be to cooperate among 'the great representative democracies to preserve an open global trading system and to contend with a host of other functional problems', and should be a policy of 'devolution of substantial responsibilities to alliance partners'. In this, the US should not withdraw from its 'security commitments' around the globe. 'Power does entail responsibility', the authors note.[1]

At the other, 'conservative' end of the establishment spectrum is the view of William Kristol and Robert Kagan, writing in the house journal of US foreign policy, *Foreign Affairs*. They argue that the US role in world affairs should be 'benevolent global hegemony', which involves preserving and enhancing the US's 'strategic and ideological predominance'. They note that 'a hegemon is nothing more or less than a leader with preponderant influence and authority over all others in its domain. That is America's position in the world today.' The main threat to the US is 'its own weakness' and:

> American hegemony is the only reliable defence against a breakdown of peace and international order. The appropriate goal of American foreign policy, therefore, is to preserve that hegemony as far into the future as possible. To achieve this goal, the United States needs a neo-Reaganite foreign policy of military supremacy and moral confidence.

Kristol and Kagan call for increases in the US military budget, lamenting the fact that 'these days, some critics complain about the fact that the United States spends more on defence than the next six major powers combined'. They also note that 'the more Washington is able to make clear that it is futile to compete with American power, either in size of forces or in technological capabilities, the less chance there is that countries like China or Iran will entertain ambitions of upsetting the present world order'. US policy should be informed by 'a clear moral purpose' and foreign aid programmes should be maintained since they are 'a useful way of exerting American influence abroad'.[2]

Leading academic Michael Mandelbaum has castigated the Clinton administration for pursuing 'foreign policy as social work'. He cites the three failed interventions in the first few months of the Clinton administration: in Bosnia – where the US announced its intention, and then failed, to lift the arms embargo against the Bosnian government; in Somalia – with the deaths of 18 soldiers in October 1993; and in Haiti – with the turning back of a US ship carrying military trainers in response to demonstrations in Haiti. Clinton's foreign policy has not been 'centred on American interests', Mandelbaum argues, but has been 'intended to promote American values'. He notes that 'Mother Teresa ... is in the business of saving lives' which is what the Clinton administration was trying to make 'the cornerstone of American foreign policy' by turning it into 'a branch of social work'. To Mandelbaum, US foreign policy should have three objectives. The first involves the maintenance of a US military presence in Europe and the Asia-Pacific region in order to 'reassure all countries in both regions that there will be no sudden change in the military balance'. This is especially important regarding Germany and Japan, who 'without the assurance of American protection' might 'feel the need for stronger military forces, ultimately including nuclear weapons'. The second objective is to prevent the spread of nuclear weapons. The third is trade and to follow up on GATT and the North American Free Trade Agreement (NAFTA), both of which 'expanded the international trading system that has contributed mightily to global economic growth for five decades'.[3]

These various academic perspectives have a lot in common. Mainstream US academics as well as US leaders are unanimous in asserting that the US has unprecedented opportunities to shape international affairs in its own interest. Thus Clinton's former National Security Adviser Anthony Lake notes that 'we have arrived at ... a moment of immense democratic and entrepreneurial opportunity' in a world in which 'we are its dominant power'. 'Around the world', Lake notes, 'America's power, authority and example provide unparalleled opportunities to lead.'[4] Former Secretary of State Warren Christopher stressed that 'as the sole remaining superpower, we have an unprecedented opportunity to shape the world we seek' and that the US needed to 'protect our interests as the world's most powerful nation'.[5] Academic Tony Smith declares that 'the current era represents the closest the United States has ever come to seeing the international system reflect its traditional foreign policy agenda'. Smith manages to convince himself that 'world order' is 'opposed to imperialism' and composed of states 'promoting ... basic human rights'.[6]

There is consensus around the view that the US needs to assert its 'leadership' in world affairs. Only the means to achieve such 'leadership' are disputed. It is Americans' 'responsibility to lead the world', Kristol and Kagan note (apparently echoing their British imperialist predecessors in their moral certainty).[7] In fact, 'leadership' is barely distinguishable from supremacy or hegemony, involving the use of US power to secure basic objectives. Anthony Lake affirms that 'one old truth in this new era' is that 'power still matters'. 'Our power', Lake continues, 'will make the critical difference', and 'at the heart of American power lies the threat or use of military force ...

When we use force, we must be prepared to use it unflinchingly.'[8] Leading commentator Charles Maynes stresses that US 'leadership' should be used to maintain world order:

> The current international order is uniquely favourable to the United States and other major powers, including Russia and China. None of these powers is threatening the others and all have need for a period of external calm in order to attend to domestic deficiencies. Thus the common goal should be the defence of that benign order.

'Leadership' means influencing and controlling allies and it is widely accepted in US establishment thinking that the need is for the US not so much to assert its power unilaterally as to assert its power though its allies, and to devolve power to them as part of its policy of functional control over world order. Warren Christopher notes that 'American international leadership ... gives us unparalleled opportunities to influence their [that is, other countries] conduct.'[9] Central to US strategy is 'constructive relations with the world's most powerful nations' such as the Western European states, Japan, China and Russia: 'we must revitalise our alliances with this democratic core'.[10] The US has served warning that US security cooperation with Europe depends on Europe toeing the US line on trade. 'I want to remind our allies and trading partners in Europe once again', Christopher noted in November 1993, 'that advancing transatlantic security requires us not only to focus on reviewing the NATO alliance but also on successfully concluding the GATT negotiations.'[11]

Control over 'allies' was the general thrust of a leaked draft Pentagon document of 1992, which noted that the US should prevent 'the emergence of European-only security arrangements which would undermine NATO'. The US mission should be to convince 'potential competitors that they need not aspire to a greater role or pursue a more aggressive posture to protect their legitimate interests'. The essence of US strategy is to 'establish and protect a new order' that accounts 'sufficiently for the interests of the advanced industrial nations to discourage them from challenging our leadership', whilst maintaining a military dominance capable of 'deterring potential competitors from even aspiring to a larger regional or global role'.[12]

Alvin Bernstein, director of the Marshall Center, a study centre that is part of the US European Command of NATO, similarly declares that 'the Western alliance will have to remain together and committed to safeguarding common interests in order to deflect the rise of an alternative centre of power'. The main threat comes from the 'Asian arc' which contains 'formidable powers' such as Japan, Russia and China. 'Any power or coalition of powers that dominates the area will possess the ability to extend that domination globally, if it so chooses', Bernstein notes.[13]

Arch-'conservative' Alexander Haig, Reagan's Secretary of State, notes that the world needs 'American leadership backed by American military power, but that leadership can be exercised best in concert with a coalition of free peoples'.[14] Leading academic and former official Richard Haass declares that US leadership means 'the United States acting as the head of formal alliances and, increasingly, informal coalitions to protect a range of interests from countering classical aggression to stemming destabilising developments within states'. 'What defines this approach to the world', Haass notes, 'is that the United States pushes hard for its priorities, works to bring others around to them and retains national control over critical matters.' 'In today's deregulated world', he continues, 'Washington is first among equals and should act accordingly', including on the need to harness 'its power to its purpose'.[15]

The US policy of attempting to assert its supremacy over its Western allies/competitors has been a customary feature of the postwar world, the 'Soviet threat' often serving the useful role of helping to reinforce such US 'leadership'. The Soviet exercise of control over Eastern Europe was facilitated by reference to a similar threat from an enemy, and the two superpowers – in Europe as in most of the Third World – enjoyed a tacit understanding of respective spheres of influence.

The 1991 war against Iraq gave some comfort to many US planners, highlighting the degree to which the key US rivals of Japan and Germany were still dependent on US military power for maintaining international order. However, as two US analysts comment, the removal of the Soviet threat and a 'change in security dependence' means that 'when differences, particularly economic differences' arise between the Western 'allies', they will 'no longer be conditioned by the security protection' the US extends. 'A major source of American power and leadership' can be 'relied upon no longer'.[16]

This fear partly explains the US support for the expansion of NATO into Eastern Europe and the latter's new-found mission for 'out of area' operations. The former NATO Secretary-General Manfred Woerner has noted that the US needs NATO as 'the most important vehicle of US influence in Europe and the main instrument of US leadership'. As former British Defence Secretary Malcolm Rifkind has noted: NATO 'provides not just the military foundation for coalition operations but the one and only forum where the US is in constant consultation with European powers is at the NATO HQ in Brussels'.[17]

US foreign policy has two basic aims, one economic and one political. The economic aim is the maintenance of an international economic order in which US and international business flourishes. Joan Spero, Under-Secretary for Economic, Business and Agricultural Affairs, states that this involves getting 'our own economic house in order' with the need 'to open markets around the world'. 'We intend to open up new worlds of opportunity for our businesses overseas.'[18] The US Defense Intelligence Agency states that 'we must have fair market access to the resources and markets of the world. In some cases, such as the need for oil, the denial of such access carries with it unacceptable consequences.'[19] Similarly, US Trade Representative Carla Hills explained in 1989: 'I would like you to think of me as the US Trade Representative with a crowbar, where we are prying open markets, keeping them open so that our private sector can take advantage of them.'[20]

This current basic US aim is essentially the same as that consistently repeated by US leaders during and following the Second World War, entailing, as far as possible, US control over the international economy. Multinational firms are a cornerstone of the strategy (though their interests do not necessarily coincide with the government at all times). As Anthony Lake has noted, 'private firms are natural allies in our efforts to strengthen market economies'.[21]

The second goal is referred to as 'democracy promotion' and has also been constantly stressed by US leaders. Taken seriously in the overwhelming majority of academic circles, 'democracy promotion' essentially means putting in place or maintaining conditions conducive to achieving the first goal. A leading independent academic analyst of this policy is William Robinson, who notes that 'talk of living standards, human rights and democratisation – especially the promotion of the democratic ideals that become useful ... has replaced anti-communism as the ideological justification for what is in fact the self-interest of a rapacious elite'.[22] Robinson's major study of the issue stresses that the US is actually interested in promoting 'polyarchy', a form of elite political and economic organisation that aims at 'mitigating the social and political tensions produced by elite-based and undemocratic status quos' and also at 'suppressing popular and mass aspirations for more thoroughgoing democratisation of social life'. Thus the US is promoting 'democracy' as a strategy 'as a way to relieve pressure from subordinate groups for more fundamental political, social and economic change', and this is aimed at 'maintaining essentially undemocratic societies inserted into an unjust international system'. Polyarchy is a 'structural feature of the emergent global society'. Now, 'promoting "low intensity democracies" in the Third World is emerging as a cornerstone of a new era in US foreign policy'. The strategy can be achieved through holding elections, which are usually merely a formal mechanism allowing for little or no popular participation in decision making and which prevent the prospects for meaningful social change.

'Democracy' is thus synonymous with 'the stability of the capitalist social order' worldwide – in fact, a long-standing equation in US (and British) foreign policy. An important element in Robinson's thesis is that the US 'has taken the lead in developing policies and strategies on behalf of the agenda of the transnational elite' (which he defines as 'class fractions drawn around the world that are integrated into fully transnationalised circuits of production and whose outlook and political behaviour is guided by the logic of global rather than local accumulation'). Here, polyarchy is the necessary political accompaniment to economic globalisation, precisely required for the latter to proceed. US policy seeks to advance the agenda of the transnational elite by consolidating polyarchic social systems and neoliberal restructuring. It does this by developing 'technocratic elites' and 'transnational kernels' who will advance this agenda through the state apparatus as well as through civil society organisations. Robinson cites the Philippines, Chile, Haiti, Nicaragua, Eastern Europe and South Africa as among the main examples of such US policy.[23]

One example of the US conception of 'democracy' is the Philippines, where the US smoothed the way for the ouster of the Marcos dictatorship (after years of full support) towards support for Corazon Aquino, who headed a nominally democratic regime later ratified in elections, but which preserved the traditional political and social order in the country. A declassified White House policy statement of 1985, one year before the successful transition, noted that 'our goal is ... to preserve the stability of a key ally by working with the Philippine government and moderate elements of Philippine society' in order to 'assure both a smooth transition when President Marcos does pass from the scene and longer-term stability'. This would also involve 'restoring professional, apolitical leadership to the Philippine military'.[24] (Another document of 1986, when the country was in open revolt against the Marcos regime, notes that the US 'should strive in this situation to preserve the dignity of President Marcos as much as possible'.[25])

Former CIA Director William Colby has stated, with regard to the programme of the National Endowment for Democracy, a mainly US government-funded agency at the forefront of the 'democracy promotion' strategy:

> It is not necessary to turn to the covert approach. Many of the programmes which ... were conducted as covert operations [can now be] conducted quite openly and, consequently, without controversy.[26]

Strobe Talbott, former academic and later Deputy Secretary of Defense explains the utility of the concept:

> The American people have never accepted traditional geo-politics or pure balance of power calculations as sufficient reason to expend national treasure or to dispatch American soldiers to foreign lands. Throughout this century the US government has explained its decisions to send troops 'over there' with some invocation of democracy and its defence.

Thus Talbott stresses that US policy is now based on support for 'democratic' governments although, he notes, 'support for democracy is not an absolute imperative that automatically takes precedence over competing goals'. It is rather 'a strong thread' to be woven into foreign policy.[27]

Lisa Anderson, Professor of Political Science at Columbia University, draws attention, in a House of Representatives hearing, to a drawback of US support for democracy (as commonly understood) by noting that 'we run the risk in [sic] encouraging democratic political competition of giving voice and eventually power to positions and groups with whom we disagree'. 'After all', Anderson told the Committee, 'there was a strong and, to the United States, disturbing correlation in the Arab world between the extent of domestic political liberalisation and the level of opposition to American policy in the recent Gulf War.' 'From the point of view of the United States', she concludes, 'democratic politics may well produce undesirable foreign policy results.'[28] This helps to explain the permanent opposition on the part of the US to forms of meaningful democracy in the South, as opposed to the formal, elite type of polyarchy now officially promoted.

The two US aims are to be achieved in the strategy of 'enlargement', the centrepiece of the Clinton administration's foreign policy. 'The successor to a doctrine of containment must be a strategy of enlargement', Lake stated on numerous occasions. This involves 'strengthening the community of major market democracies – including our own – which constitutes the core from which enlargement is proceeding', fostering 'new democracies and market economies', and countering 'states hostile to democracy and markets'. These goals should be achieved not only by government officials and the state but also by 'private and non-governmental groups'. Lake noted:

> A strategy of enlargement suggests our principal concerns should be strengthening our democratic core in North America, Europe and Japan; consolidating and enlarging democracy and markets in key places; and addressing backlash states such as Iran and Iraq.[29]

The goals are thus US supremacy over capitalist allies/competitors, expansion into other areas by US interests and control over key regions. The key objects of the expansion aspect of the policy are viewed as Russia and the former Soviet Union, Eastern Europe, the Asia-Pacific region and Latin America, plus key states in sub-Saharan Africa, such as South Africa and Nigeria. The official 'rogue states' are the objects of the third aspect of the policy, insubordinate regimes which pose the main threat to traditional US control over the Middle East.

A key role in the 'community of major market democracies' is to be played by NATO, a military arm of enlargement. The enlargement of NATO into Eastern Europe, justified by references to enhancing 'peace and stability' on the continent, will happen to require new members to drastically increase substantially their military spending and re-equip their militaries with (mainly US) arms. Isabel Hilton, writing in the *Guardian*, correctly notes that 'there was another route' to the alleged aim of promoting peace in Eastern Europe: 'NATO could have stayed the size it is and the Clinton administration could have focused on the still dangerous nuclear issue, a matter which it has comprehensively neglected.' Hilton notes that the West rejected proposals by both Gorbachev and Yeltsin for five-power talks on nuclear safety and on the reduction of missiles below the numbers agreed in the Start negotiations. However, with the expansion of NATO bolstering hardliners in the Kremlin, the Russian Parliament may not be even able to ratify Start-2. However, there is 'one powerful argument' against the strategy that the US administration decided not to pursue: 'it does little or nothing for the industries of the US that face the challenge of finding markets for advanced fighter aircraft'.[30]

## Threats and military policy

It is instructive to consider the perceived threats to US goals in order to gauge some of the policy priorities. A primary threat has always been to Western control of raw materials. As outlined by Alexander Haig in 1981, 'disruption from abroad threatens a more vulnerable West as we draw energy and raw materials from regions in which the throes of rapid change and conflict prevail'. Twelve years later British Foreign Secretary Douglas Hurd referred to a 'new disorder' that 'would threaten our supplies of raw materials, our markets, our investments, our values'.[31] *The Economist* has noted the need for Western armies to gear themselves to this task:

> The democracies will want to make sure that they can keep getting the raw materials their economies need ... To this end, soldiers must change. For the most part, their attention will be turned further afield, South and East, to wars they may have to fight in distant places ... The one country to which this will come as no surprise is Britain, whose armed forces spent the 19th century largely on non-European business.[32]

The US Defense Intelligence Agency notes that in the 1990s 'the paradigm has shifted from Cold War "enemies" to global competitors and adversaries'. There are three categories:

1. Compliant competitors – Nation states or transnational entities who generally conform to US values and interests and who can be viewed as military allies.
2. Non-compliant competitors – Nation states or transnational entities who do not generally conform to US values and interests but who are not military adversaries. They may be in opposition to the US political, economic and strategic goals but do not engage in violence. Circumstantially, they may engage in policies or acts which compromise or endanger US security interests.
3. Renegade adversaries – Nation states or transnational entities who engage in unacceptable behaviour, frequently involving military force and violence and are potential or actual enemies of the US, against whom we must consider the active use of military force.[33]

The public is now routinely told by US and British leaders that 'since the end of the Cold War the world has become more unpredictable, less stable and in some ways probably more dangerous'.[34] British planners see two 'arcs of crisis' impacting on British 'security', namely North Africa and the Middle East/Central Asia.[35] The previous risk of global war has been replaced by the risk of 'smaller-scale conflict and suffering' in response to which 'we can expect to see growing calls on the United Kingdom to support conflict prevention, conflict resolution, peacekeeping and humanitarian aid missions'. 'We will need the ability to respond', says the Ministry of Defence, 'especially where our national interests are placed under serious threat.'[36] Fortunately for the US and British military industrial complexes, all this requires continued high military spending and the development of new weapons, although the demise of a global adversary presents serious public relations problems. Steve Schofield, of the Project on Demilitarisation, notes that:

> Military preparations will continue to make excessive demands on scarce industrial and technological resources and the UK will make no real contribution to disarmament and common security, despite the unprecedented opportunity offered by the end of the cold war. On the contrary, the UK represents a major force in the new militarism underpinning the new world order.[37]

'One of the big problems facing the United States', academic Michael Cox notes, 'will be to find a suitable alternative to national security (if indeed there is one) as a means of generating economic activity.'[38] ('National security' is, of course, the massive diversion of domestic resources into the arms industry, at the taxpayers' expense.) The public on both sides of the Atlantic is being asked to fund new military programmes to match a 'new strategic environment'. NATO Defence Ministers jointly noted in 1994, for example, the need for 'continuing equipment modernisation, improvements in mobility, sustainability and command and control and the establishment of effective arrangements for training and mobilisation'. 'We therefore agreed on the importance of making efforts to stabilise defence expenditure to provide this investment', they stated.[39]

The list of new 'threats' is daunting. The following have been variously outlined by British leaders: nuclear, chemical and biological proliferation; ballistic missiles; regional wars; 'high technology weaponry' and countries 'equipped with up-to-date tanks and artillery' and 'offensive aircraft'; 'the build up by some countries of excessive stockpiles of conventional arms'; terrorism; famine; natural disasters; migration; organised crime; drug trafficking; 'extremism, xenophobic nationalism, [and] a resurgence of ethnic, religious and border disputes'.[40] A review of the US literature elicits additional perceived threats: environmental degradation; rapid urbanisation; 'an increase in deadly diseases'; 'unconstrained population growth'; and 'unique forms of conflict such as information warfare'.[41] Some specific states are also threats: For Britain, 'Russia remains the UK's greatest potential direct enemy'; for the US, 'rogue states' such as Iran, Libya, Iraq, Sudan and Cuba, as well as, due to their nuclear capabilities, India and Pakistan. The world is clearly a mighty dangerous place.

So useful is the concept of a 'threat' that US leaders are able to use the most appropriate according to the circumstances and audience. To Madeleine Albright, then Ambassador to the UN, speaking to the National War College in Washington, 'the possible aggressive use' of nuclear weapons is 'perhaps the greatest threat to international peace and our security'.[42] To National Security Adviser Anthony Lake, speaking to the Council on Foreign Relations, population growth is 'perhaps the most important underlying transnational threat before us'.[43] Speaking to Johns Hopkins University, however, Lake declares that 'above all, we are threatened by sluggish economic growth' in the US.[44]

There are, however, a number of threats that leaders are somewhat less eager to publicise than those that serve public relations purposes. Academic Curt Gasteyger, for example, notes the problem of 'how to preserve the legitimacy of armed forces in an international environment without foes'. He also notes:

> A predominant role of the armed forces in controlling or quelling internal disturbances is hardly imaginable in parliamentary democracies, but we cannot totally exclude the possibility that our armies may be called upon once immigration reaches massive proportions, mass rioting gets out of control or ecological disaster strikes entire regions.[45]

George Joffe, now Deputy Director of Chatham House, also highlights the threat to state 'security' potentially posed by the public:

> As the ecological movement gains renewed impetus within most European states, there is every likelihood that protest on ecological grounds will extend beyond the normally accepted legal limits. Although such illegal protest is likely to be confined to the margins, it may well pose a security issue for the states concerned, reminiscent to that posed by some kinds of low intensity conflict in the 1970s and 1980s.[46]

Another problem is that people may increasingly refuse to want to die for their country. Leading British international relations academic Christopher Coker has reportedly explained that 'initially you need to motivate people to risk their lives and you do so by telling them that they are doing something significant for their country'. Now, however, 'the state can no longer require the citizen to fight and that is bound to be reflected eventually in a certain demoralisation and psychological debilitation within the armed forces'. Coker 'did not see how the issue could be resolved, given that in a post ideological age it is not easy to motivate people to do anything, particularly if the element of sacrifice is demanded' and 'one can see this extremely depressing reality in a non-military setting'.[47]

There remains the traditional domestic threat of 'subversion'. Before becoming an EU Commissioner, Leon Brittan, as British Home Secretary, once noted that subversives included people engaging in political activities 'who, for tactical reasons or other reasons choose to keep (either in the long or the short term) within the letter of the law in what they do'. His successor, Douglas Hurd, also affirmed that subversives in Britain were not only 'those who breach criminal law'. This was the context in which MI5, the domestic 'security' service, officially monitored groups such as the Anti-Apartheid Movement, Greenpeace, Friends of the Earth, certain trade unions, as well as leftwingers in the Labour Party, whose phones were tapped.[48]

Military policy remains central to securing foreign policy goals and US war-fighting strategy is concentrated on regional wars along the lines of the war against Iraq – 'regional contingencies against foes well armed with advanced conventional and unconventional weaponry', according to former Defense Secretary, Richard Cheney. But in addition to the Middle East:

> We have important interests in Europe, Asia, the Pacific and Central and Latin America. In each of these regions there are opportunities and potential future threats to our interests. We must configure our policies and our forces to effectively deter, or quickly defeat, such future regional threats.[49]

If such regional threats are not dealt with, establishment academic Michael Cox states in a study for Chatham House, they could present a challenge to 'America's control over vital economic resources', the balance of power in some regions and to 'US credibility'.[50] US leaders and academics are therefore agreed on the need for significant intervention capabilities. 'So long as the United States seeks to remain a world power', one academic notes, 'it must retain a robust interventionary capability to dissuade countries from seeking superpower status and to deter those who attain it from threatening US interests.'[51]

Overall, US military forces are intended to ensure dominance in conflicts. 'We don't want to engage in a fair fight', Defense Secretary William Cohen noted in 1997. 'We want to dominate across the full spectrum of conflict, so if we ever have to fight, we will win on our terms.'[52]

US academics have articulated a number of scenarios for the use of US military force. According to former official Richard Haass, 'there will be many opportunities to intervene in the future'. Such scenarios begin with classic interstate aggression, as with a North Korean invasion of the South, Iraq on Kuwait or another Gulf state. 'At the other end of the spectrum', however, possible uses of military force include 'limited punitive reprisals against terrorists or states supporting them' and 'interdiction ... for the purposes of regulating immigration'. 'Preventive strikes by the United States against terrorist facilities or, more likely, against the unconventional military capabilities of another state', Haass notes, might apply to North Korea, Iran, Iraq or Libya. 'Punitive actions are quintessentially political in nature', he notes. 'They are designed to make a point, not change the situation created by the adversary's provocation.'[53]

Charles Maynes recognises that there are certain deterrents to the US use of force (although they cannot be labelled 'deterrents' as such, since the idea of anyone deterring the United States is heretical in the propaganda system). Along the Russian rim, for example, the US 'has to worry about' the reaction of the Kremlin and in Northeast Asia the reaction of Japan or China. Indeed, 'in most parts of the world except the Western hemisphere and perhaps the Persian Gulf, there is a regional power whose opposition to US intervention could make the exercise of force much more difficult to carry out successfully unless one assumes that air power alone will be sufficient'.[54]

Anthony Lake outlined, in March 1996, seven circumstances which 'may call for the use of force or military forces': to defend US territory and its allies; to counter aggression; 'to defend our key economic interests'; 'to preserve, promote and defend democracy'; to prevent the spread of nuclear weapons and terrorism; 'to maintain our reliability, because when our partnerships are strong and confidence in our leadership is high, it is easier to get others to work with us'; and for 'humanitarian purposes'. Lake noted that 'threatening to use force can achieve the same results as actually using it'. The US military 'has a unique ability to concentrate the minds of our adversaries without firing a shot'.[55] One can only wonder how the academic community in the West would react if policy makers and academics from, say, Mexico or Algeria – not to mention Iran or Libya – outlined the use of force as justified in so many ways.

Indeed, aside from regional deterrents, the main deterrent to the US use of force is recognised as being the US public. Two analysts write that the 'external constraints' on the US use of military force 'have become weaker and weaker' but that 'internal domestic constraints, however, have increased'.[56]

Another acceptable use of force is fomenting coups. 'Backing coups can be defended on ethical grounds', Steven David asserts (without debating whether such reasoning also applies to any other country in the world apart from the US). 'If the regimes that are toppled are truly despotic and abusive ... and if they are replaced by governments that are democratic' then 'there is strong moral justification for the coup backing effort'.[57]

One former CIA official has noted that 'trends in international relations are disquieting' and challenges to the US 'are increasing and becoming more dangerous'. These challenges are 'becoming less tractable and less amenable to solution by traditional instruments as diplomacy and overt military operations'. The US will therefore 'have to rely on covert military operations if it is to ensure its security and uphold the international system which it inspired and for which it is in large measure responsible'.[58]

The particular emphasis in British, as well as US, military planning is now on 'power projection' in the light of the 'changed strategic environment' whereby the Third World is the designated threat. Britain has developed a triservice Joint Rapid Deployment Force (JRDF) 'to strengthen our existing capability to project power quickly and potentially worldwide in support of British interests'. 'In particular', the Ministry of Defence (MoD) notes, 'we are looking at how we can develop the capabilities of our rapidly-deployable forces, such as the Airborne and Commando Brigades and appropriate maritime and air forces, to intervene even more effectively and speedily together'.[59] Indeed, it is possible that this role for the British military will become the official *primary* one over the coming decade or so.[60] Field Marshal Sir Peter Inge, Chief of the Defence Staff, for example, asserts that:

> I sense the Armed Forces which I shall be leaving behind when I retire are moving back towards the kind of worldwide role conducted by the Armed Forces that I joined. They are going to be involved in places around the world that we believed unthinkable a few years ago.[61]

New, improved weapons systems will continue to be developed and procured to support this role. An important one for Britain is the introduction of the new Apache attack helicopter. 'For the army', Air Vice-Marshal Black Robertson comments, the new weapon 'will arguably have as radical an effect on its war fighting capability as did the tank'.[62] Another example is British procurement from the US of the cruise missile which, according to former Defence Secretary Malcolm Rifkind, would be of value 'in the coercive use of force as an instrument of policy'.[63] Having already demonstrated its utility in strikes against Iraq, it is one of the current ultimate weapons for power projection. These are the equivalents of the nineteenth-century role of the British Royal Marines, which involved their 'free use in "backward countries" on the more defenceless peoples'.[64]

## British foreign policy under Labour

The election of a Labour government in May 1997 after 18 years of Conservative rule was greeted with great anticipation, even euphoria, in many circles in Britain. This deepened as Labour declared that it would 'put human rights at the heart of our foreign policy' and that foreign policy 'must support the demands of other people for the democratic rights on which we insist for ourselves'. The Labour government also announced a 'new' policy on arms exports, stating that it would not supply regimes 'that might use them for repression or international aggression'.[65] 'Labour is ready to make Britain once again a force for good in the world community', the government declared.[66]

At the time of writing – just six months into the new government – it is not possible to assess properly the record of policy. However, from policy statements and some of the decisions that have already been taken, it is very apparent that Labour policy will be marked by continuity with the Conservatives rather than any significant change, which is fully consistent with the historical record. Indeed, such continuity appears to be the case with all areas of the government's external relations.

Labour's foreign policy agenda was very explicitly outlined in a major speech by Tony Blair in Manchester ten days before the election victory. Blair completely embraced the foreign policy agenda pursued over the past two decades. Britain should use its assets 'to make ourselves once again a force that can stand comparison with other great powers', and 'to promote Britain's interest firmly, persistently and toughly', he noted. 'Britain has been a major force in world affairs for several centuries', Blair noted without a trace of embarrassment, and 'no British patriot should be willing to give up that status'. He boasted of the fact that Britain 'led the way in setting up the institutions that dominate international life' 50 years after the end of the Second World War, presumably referring to such institutions as the World Bank and the UN Security Council.

Continuing, Blair noted that Britain's armed forces 'are rightly admired throughout the world' and 'we believe in strong defence' and 'strong and effective armed forces'. He then lamented that 'the Conservatives have presided over the largest reduction in our military capability since the war' before telling his audience that Labour would retain British nuclear weapons, maintain the British military-industrial complex ('an internationally competitive defence industry') and promote arms exports. Also, 'we have our especially close links with the US' and 'the cornerstone of our security will remain the North Atlantic Alliance [NATO] and our relationship with the US'. Blair also noted that 'we strongly support NATO enlargement to help underpin the hard won democracies in Central and Eastern Europe'. He also declared that 'we intend to play a leading role in the world-wide effort to achieve further trade liberalisation' to be pursued 'through the World Trade Organisation'.[67] Thus all of the major policy areas would remain intact. On the crucial question of policy towards Europe – the only foreign policy issue that figured in the election – Blair confirmed there were basically no differences in policy between his party and the then government: 'The real dividing line is between success and failure. The fundamental differences lie in party management, attitude and leadership.' In effect, this was official acknowledgement of the irrelevance of the election in terms of distinguishing between foreign policies.

It was therefore consistent that, after the election, when Michael Portillo – one of the most rightwing Conservative Defence Ministers – was being proposed for the post of international mediator in Bosnia (whose war Portillo and his party had effectively fanned for the previous six years) the press reported that 'there were no objections from Tony Blair or the Foreign Secretary Robin Cook'. Blair's spokesperson said: 'we were aware that Mr Portillo was interested and we would have been very happy to see a British candidate'.[68] It was also consistent that the top posting in the British diplomatic service – Ambassador to Washington – went to 'a former spokesman for John Major' and former head of the Foreign Office's news department under Geoffrey Howe, a man who formed 'a double act' at international summits with Bernard Ingham, Margaret Thatcher's Press Secretary.[69]

The new government also appointed the former Conservative Defence Secretary Tom King – who led Britain's arms export drive to Indonesia – as head of the new House of Commons Intelligence and Security Committee which is meant to scrutinise the 'security services'.[70]

Additionally, it appointed the Chairman of British Petroleum (BP), David Simon, as Minister in both the Department of Trade and Industry (DTI) and the Treasury. Simon had been a key supporter of the Thatcher government's economic reforms, especially privatisation. Since he was unelected, the government arranged a peerage for him so that he could speak in the House of Lords. One of the country's rare independent voices on social affairs who manages to get published in the mainstream press, George Monbiot, notes that 'people who could scarcely have done more to demonstrate their contempt for democratic processes are set to rule over us'. Monbiot notes that as Chairman of BP, Simon 'was one of the most influential members of the European Round Table of Industrialists' which met in secret, 'taking pains to avoid public scrutiny', and drafted the EC's Single European Act – basically a charter for big business in Europe – and 'some of the EC's most portentous directives'.[71] His responsibilities in government also included DTI relations with the City of London and 'specific responsibility for corporate governance'.[72]

In the area of 'development' policy, many were hoping that Labour would embark on fundamentally more progressive policies, especially since the Ministry responsible (the renamed Department for International Development) was elevated to Cabinet representation and headed by the government's most progressive minister, Clare Short. However, while some reforms have been proposed or introduced, the more noticeable feature of policy is that the basic strategic framework of traditional British policy towards 'development' has been accepted by the Labour government.

It is as strong a supporter as the previous government of the WTO and is committed to deepening the WTO by also negotiating liberalisation in the areas of services and agriculture ('The last thing we want is protectionism in any shape or form', Tony Blair has stated[73]). It strongly supports the WTO's intellectual property rights regime (TRIPS), one of its more insidious aspects, which allows transnational corporations (TNCs) to exercise even greater control over the international economy through product patenting: 'we must ensure the strengthening and protection of intellectual property rights, not least to ensure the enforcement of existing agreements', the Trade and Industry Secretary notes.[74] The only relent in the government's fierce pursuit of the WTO is its support for a 'social clause' which would 'ensure that all countries in the world trading system uphold the human rights standards enshrined in the UN Convention on Human Rights'.[75] This is, however, a minimalist stance – designed to ensure only 'minimum standards'[76] – and a very limited step in promoting the basics of social welfare in comparison with the giant leap represented by the WTO (see also Chapter 4).

Indeed, it appears that Labour's agenda is at least as favourable to promoting TNCs' de facto control over the international economy as the previous government's. Before the election, Labour's major policy statement's only reference to TNCs stated that they 'are a major source of investment for developing countries, and provide employment as well as transferring skills and technology' and called for 'an international code of conduct for TNCs', which is merely voluntary. The government also firmly supports the proposed Multilateral Agreement on Investment – designed largely to open up Southern economies still further to penetration by TNCs – and which, according to the government, is 'based on the principles of non-discrimination against foreign investors, open investment regimes and investor protection'.[77]

Labour's pledges suggest that government support for British business interests through the aid programme and development policy will be stepped up rather than reined in. The Aid and Trade Provision (ATP) element of the aid programme – which acted as a direct subsidy to business – has been abolished, but 'that does not preclude deploying development assistance in association with private finance, including in the form of mixed credits'. The 'new partnership between relevant government departments and the private sector' includes:

> new measures to consult British business on country and other development strategies; to improve the information available to business on trade and investment opportunities in developing countries; to see whether ways can be found to reduce the initial costs and perceived risks for investments which support the aim of poverty elimination; and to ensure that multilateral development projects make full use of the skills of UK business.[78]

Labour is also committed to promoting World Bank/IMF structural adjustment programmes (SAPs), another vehicle for ensuring that Northern interests are accommodated in economic policy in the South and which, a wealth of evidence shows, have exacerbated poverty. Rather than being opposed to SAPs in principle, 'we have been critical of the way these adjustment programmes have been *imposed in practice*', the Labour Party states, an important difference which apparently signals its intention merely to promote mild reforms. The government has continued the Conservative policy of offering only modest relief to some Third World countries' debt burdens, but its position is that debt relief is 'conditional on recipients adopting balanced economic reform programmes' (that is, continuing to implement SAPs).[79] Labour is also a strong supporter of the economic 'reforms' in Eastern Europe, designed to integrate their economies into a system controlled principally by Western European economic and financial interests. Reports produced under the previous government hardly hide the fact that Britain's 'aid' to Eastern Europe – the 'Know How' funds – is principally a subsidy for British business seeking to invest in the region, aimed at deepening the privatisation process and the use of British advisers in the process. In this wider context, Labour's pledges to focus the aid programme on the reduction of poverty appear hollow and of marginal importance.

The government's policy towards human rights has been the subject of substantial press comment, much of it quite surreal given evidence of actual policies. Foreign Secretary Robin Cook's speech outlining an 'ethical' dimension to foreign policy in July 1997 noted – quite honestly – that the government was seeking to promote only 'modest advances' in this area. Cook simply said that:

> If we and our allies maintain international criticism, some regimes will refrain from the excesses of violent repression. But if we and others encourage reform, some countries will improve their police and justice systems ... If we promise solidarity, some local NGOs [non-governmental organisations] and the media will have greater courage to insist on their freedom of expression.

The 'twelve-point plan' outlined by Cook stated that Britain would condemn gross abusers (naming only Nigeria), continue to support sanctions against some countries (Iraq), refuse to supply military equipment to some regimes, support the introduction of a human rights clause in the WTO (both considered in this chapter) and review the British military training policy. The other policies were even more modest than these very limited steps – as Cook himself suggested, these policies do not amount to a significant change in policy.[80]

Labour is an active champion of the sanctions against Iraq which have contributed to horrendous human suffering in the country. These are now being maintained with hardly even the pretence of any hope of success in forcing compliance with UN resolutions – the regime may even have been strengthened by them – but have the main effect of punishing the Iraqi people. Also being maintained is the previous government's operation to place the blame for the Lockerbie bomb on to Libya, when much evidence points to Iran.[81] The government continues to support the sanctions against Libya; the accusation of Libyan involvement in the bombing serving as a pretext for their implementation.[82] The Iraq and Libya policies remain closely coordinated with the United States, a relationship which remains key to Labour. The government spokesperson in the House of Lords states that 'our very close relationship with the United States' is one 'which could not be substituted in any way by our relationships with our European allies'.[83] The government has also made much publicly of its commitment to see a return to democracy in Nigeria but rejects implementation of the one serious measure available to it to put real pressure on the military regime – oil sanctions. This is because of the interests of companies like Shell, whose de facto alliance with the Nigerian military and economic elite has been significantly responsible for the impoverishment of the Nigerian people, a state of affairs presided over by successive British governments.[84]

In the government's first months in power there was no evidence whatever that Britain's close relations with the oppressive regimes in Turkey, Colombia and the Gulf states would change significantly. An indicative aspect of Labour's policy is the backing shown for the regime in Bahrain. A Foreign Office Minister has stated that Britain does not seek to impose specific forms of democracy and the *shura* system practised in Bahrain is a 'respected and accepted' form of consultation in the Gulf region: Bahrain's '*shura* council is not perfect but we should not write it off', the Minister noted.[85] The increasingly repressive Bahraini regime, which has consistently put down protests and movements for greater democracy in the country (see Chapter 6), could be expected to take great heart from this statement. It may also have been intended to reassure Britain's other major friends in the region, principally Saudi Arabia, which has a similar system but for whom it is more politically difficult to express public support.

Labour's military ('defence') policy bears striking similarity to the Conservatives'. Indeed, in 'defence' planning throughout the postwar period, one would be hard pushed to find any major differences, apart from Labour's official policy of supporting nuclear disarmament for a brief period in the 1980s. While in opposition in 1996, Labour's Shadow Defence spokesperson told the House of Commons that:

> We have, of course, supported the government in almost every operational decision that they have taken over the past decade,

not because it has been expedient to do so, but because it has been right.[86]

The current government promoted the Strategic Defence Review as a long overdue reassessment of policy in the light of the changes brought about by the end of the Cold War. The *Guardian*'s Jonathan Steele noted, however, that many of the outside experts who attended the meetings under this process believed that the meetings 'were either for show or that the review would miraculously end up by endorsing the policies and programmes already in force'.[87] The 'review' took place while the government had already announced no change in its commitment to the very policies that might have been up for review, such as the commitment to NATO, the Trident nuclear system, the Eurofighter project and a global role. Trident is an obvious candidate for a change in policy – even some arch-conservative figures, such as 60 generals and admirals, including two former NATO supreme commanders and the former Chief of the Defence Staff, Lord Carver, recently called for the elimination of nuclear weapons on the grounds that keeping them is more risky over the long term than destroying them.[88]

Britain's military-industrial complex is also safe in Labour's hands, from the evidence. Labour leaders have stated on numerous occasions that they are committed to maintaining a strong 'defence' industry. An example is the Eurofighter project, a joint development between Britain and other countries of a next-generation fighter, of which the government plans to order 232 at a cost of £15.9 billion.[89] 'Our commitment to the Eurofighter is as strong as the last government's', the Defence Secretary stated at a time when he was imploring the German government not to withhold funding from the project, which would have caused it to fold.[90] The government also notes that 'as concerns export orders' for the Eurofighter, there have been 'quite firm enquiries' from 'major Middle Eastern countries'.[91] Britain also agreed to be part of a six-nation consortium developing a new Future Large Aircraft, a £14 billion project to provide militaries with enhanced strategic lift capability. British Aerospace was reported to be 'delighted' with Whitehall's agreement to take part.[92]

To great fanfare in May 1997, the media reported that the government announced a 'ban' on the use and export of landmines. The 'ban' was no such thing, however. The government stated that landmines would continue to be used if 'for a specific operation the security of our armed forces would be jeopardised without the possibility of the use of landmines'. Moreover, the existing stocks of landmines would be destroyed in 2005, which, the *Guardian* noted, was 'a concession to the military', meaning that it would allow enough time to develop 'alternatives, such as better surveillance techniques and more advanced conventional bombs, including mortars and shells', which already 'were being developed'.[93]

Labour's policy on arms exports is especially worthy of consideration. The media has widely reported the government's 'new' policy of 'restrictions' on arms exports which might be used for internal repression or international aggression and has occasionally commented on how policy towards, for example, Indonesia doesn't exactly appear to match supposed Labour rhetoric. However, Labour is not guilty of such double standards: actual policy statements clearly show unequivocal commitment to a strong promotion of arms exports as well as British military industry while the references to human rights are so qualified as to be virtually meaningless. A few weeks before the policy was announced, the government told Parliament that the Defence Export Sales Organisation, the body responsible for promoting arms sales, 'will continue to provide the strongest possible government support' for arms exports.[94] Labour's policy was outlined by its spokesperson in the House of Lords, Baroness Symons, in July 1997. She began by confirming that:

> The government are committed to the maintenance of a strong defence industry which is a strategic part of our industrial base, as well as our defence effort. Defence exports can also contribute to international stability by strengthening bilateral and collective defence relationships in accordance with the right of self-defence recognised by the UN charter. But arms transfers must be managed sensibly, in particular so as to avoid their use for internal repression and international aggression.

She continued:

> *Full weight* should be given to the UK's national interests when considering applications for licences, including: the potential effect on the UK's defence and security interests ...; the potential effect on the UK's economic, financial and commercial interests ...; the potential effect on the UK's relations with the recipient country; the potential effect on any collaborative defence production or procurement project with allies or EU partners; the protection of the UK's essential strategic industrial base.

She then outlined the criteria determining government arms exports, but said that 'the criteria will constitute broad guidance. They will not be applied mechanistically and judgement will always be required.' The criteria could therefore be ignored when required and are anyway heavily qualified. For example, the criteria regarding 'human rights and internal repression' are worth quoting at length:

> The government: will *take into account* respect for human rights and fundamental freedoms in the recipient country; will not issue an export licence if there is *clearly identifiable* risk [sic] that the proposed export *might* be used for internal repression. For these purposes equipment which might be used for internal repression will include: equipment where there is *clear evidence* of the *recent* use of *similar* equipment for internal repression by the proposed end-user ...; equipment which has *obvious* application for internal repression, in cases where the recipient country has a significant and continuing record of such repression, *unless the end-use of the equipment is judged to be legitimate*, such as protection of members of security forces from violence.

Similar reasoning applies to the criteria concerning 'international aggression': 'The government will not issue an export licence if there is a *clearly identifiable risk* that the intended recipient would use the proposed export aggressively against another country, or to assert by force a territorial claim.' And, 'when considering the risk that the country for which arms are destined might use them for international aggression, the government will *take into account*' a range of factors such as the existence or likelihood of armed conflict between the recipient and another country.[95]

In announcing the policy, Foreign Secretary Robin Cook noted that 'Britain is one of the largest arms exporters in the world. That leading position obliges us to take seriously the reputation of the arms trade. Success and responsibility go hand in hand.'[96] At the same time, the Royal Navy was conducting an eight-month tour of the Asia-Pacific region – the biggest naval task force to go beyond the Middle East since the 1991 Gulf War – as part of a huge British arms exports effort in the region.[97]

In these circumstances, it is clear that Labour has no intention of affecting the worst aspects of Britain's military exports. The £2 billion a year contract with Saudi Arabia (considered in Chapter 6) will be unaffected. The *Guardian* noted that 'other Arab countries where there are human rights concerns, including Bahrain, have been told by the Foreign Office to expect no change'. It quoted a well placed source as saying that 'there'll be differences at the margins, but little more'.[98] The government has repeatedly refused to say who exactly will be affected by the arms exports policy. In a question in a House of Lords debate the Foreign Office Minister was asked to give 'one concrete example' of where the government's policy would differ from the previous government's, although he did not do so.[99] It followed, therefore, that the government permitted the sale – arranged under the Conservatives – of Hawk jets and armoured cars to Indonesia, and invited the Indonesian military's Commander in Chief to an arms fair, at the same time as announcing the 'new' policy. This is understandable since, on the evidence, the policy is not intended to affect seriously – or usually, affect at all – any arms exports.

If the British role in internal repression in the Third World were really of serious concern, there would be a halt to military training, much aid and arms exports to numerous countries simply as a first step. Even the pinpointing of a few worst offenders – like Saudi Arabia and Indonesia – is in many ways misleading, serving to give the impression of a few exceptional cases. As I try to show below, and especially in Chapters 5 and 6, which outline British (and US) priorities in the Middle East, aiding internal repression (usually termed 'internal security') is precisely what much of British foreign policy, including arms exports, is for. Fomenting close relations with Southern elites, which are often repressive and military dominated, is a key underlying principle of basic British foreign policy through which priorities and aims are pursued. The criticism of alleged double standards when the government supplies arms to a repressive government shows a particular mindset of thinking that accords a basic benevolence to general British policy.

Thus two myths have accompanied the discussion on Labour's arms exports policy. The first is the widespread belief that the main, or sometimes only, problem is whether exported weapons are *used*. The second is that it is a question of 'morality versus jobs'. Underlying both myths is the view that the only or major motivation for arms exports is commercial.

On the first myth, Britain's MoD stated under the Conservatives that 'military assistance takes place in support of wider foreign policy aims' and 'are a key part of our wider diplomatic relationships with our friends and allies throughout the world'.[100] Britain has the same basic posture on arms exports as the US, which 'views the transfer of conventional arms ... as an indispensable component of its foreign policy'.[101] The utility of arms exports and military aid and training to Third World states is well revealed in the declassified planning record and has hardly changed over time. According to a US government report of 1947, military aid:

> is ... a powerful influence in orienting the recipient nations toward US policy. Foreign armed forces which are supplied with US equipment will look to the US for replacement and maintenance. In addition to contributing to the internal order and integrity of the countries concerned, moderate security forces maintained by those nations offer several benefits to the US against the contingency of war.[102]

An important role for arms exports is in 'contributing to the internal order and integrity of the countries concerned' or 'maintaining internal security'.[103] This is closely linked to the policy of cementing alliances with power brokers, who are often military figures. The US Joint Chiefs of Staff once noted, for example, that 'most of the Latin American governments are dependent upon the military for stability. In consequence, contact with Latin American military men would in reality mean contact with very strong domestic political leaders'.[104]

British policy towards Indonesia is a good current example of this long-standing policy. The Indonesian military is the principal and ultimate guarantor of the domestic status quo and, according to the US State Department, 'the maintenance of internal security' is the 'primary mission' of the Indonesian military.[105] The armed forces have intervened regularly in labour disputes: according to the Indonesian Human Rights Campaign, TAPOL, 'military involvement in labour affairs is structural and has been the main obstacle to the emergence of independent unions'.[106] Dissent has been severely suppressed: according to Amnesty International, 'elderly women and teenagers have been shot dead by soldiers, because they lived in a rebel stronghold, or because they protested against eviction from their land'.[107] The army also clamps down on domestic dissent in 'anti-crime' campaigns, where the targets have included academics, journalists, independent labour organisers and human rights activists.[108] This often involves 'extrajudicial execution of criminal suspects', the US-based organisation Human Rights Watch notes.[109] In the mid-1980s 5000 alleged criminals were killed by government death squads.[110]

Indeed, the armed forces dominate the political (and much of the economic) life of the country. According to a report by the US-based Project on Demilitarisation and Democracy:

> Indonesia's armed forces dominate the politics of the country, not only at the national level through a military dictatorship, but at the village level through what independent experts call a 'skeleton structure' or 'shadow government' that parallels and controls civilian institutions; the armed forces are far larger than necessary for Indonesia's external security threats, and are in fact configured primarily to control dissent, both in Indonesia and in occupied areas such as East Timor.

Furthermore, the report notes:

> The armed forces control over Indonesia is nearly impossible for citizens to challenge, despite the existence of an elected legislature. According to the State Department, the Indonesian electoral apparatus and legislature are controlled by Suharto's Golkar party to such an extent that 'citizens do not have the ability to change their government'.[111]

Thus, as Amnesty International has correctly pointed out, 'systematic human rights abuse is inextricably linked to the structure of political power in Indonesia', in which 'the extensive political power of the military' is a key factor. Further, 'the legal system reflects and reinforces executive and military power, and the judiciary is neither independent nor impartial'.[112]

It follows that (for example, British) arms exports to, and high-level military relations with, the Jakarta regime are likely to have the effect of increasing the domestic legitimacy and political power of the military and its ability to conduct repression. Britain has provided military training to Indonesia since 1983, including in combat methods, with one such trainee having been a platoon commander in President Suharto's special security force.[113] According to leaked application forms cited by TAPOL, the British Embassy in Jakarta saw the need for training thus:

> the position of the armed forces in Indonesian society is such that its members are important decision-makers and opinion formers ... Up to 40% of the participants in Indonesia's political fora are drawn from the armed forces and they are a target for support under FCO [Foreign and Commonwealth Office] schemes in Indonesia.[114]

There are other general advantages of arms exports and training. One is that such military aid helps to 'augment our own military potential by improvements of our armaments industry'.[115] Another is that military aid helps to 'develop facilities in the recipient nation for possible use by US forces in the event of local aggression'.[116]

A further advantage, highlighted by Britain's Chiefs of Staff in 1956, concerns the recognition that 'the British serviceman on foreign soil is often repugnant to the local inhabitants'. In the key area of the Middle East, therefore, the Chiefs of Staff noted that the expansion of training of the local military and police forces would offer 'great advantages', especially by 'thereby reducing the need for military intervention'.[117] Forty years later, the MoD states that 'training overseas students and deploying military training and assistance teams support long term diplomatic objectives' such as the promotion of 'stability' (which might be regarded as the same as 'internal order') and 'help foster cordial relationships'.[118] Training and arms exports are closely related. The Armed Forces Minister under the Conservatives once stated that 'much of the training we provide leads to export sales and the whole business of training for the armed forces cements relationships with a number of countries'.[119]

Military training is routinely given to, and specifically helps, some of the world's most repressive regimes. For the US, the infamous School of the Americas in Georgia has trained numerous assassins and torturers throughout Latin America, including former Argentinian dictator Galtieri, dozens of Colombian and Salvadoran army officers accused of war crimes, and members of death squads in Peru and Honduras, to name but a few.[120] Each year, Britain trains thousands of military students from around the world and provides loan service personnel (395 in 1995[121]) to foreign militaries. In 1997, British forces were serving in 71 countries, including such regimes as those in Bahrain, Brunei, Colombia, Indonesia, Kuwait, Oman and Saudi Arabia.[122] In 1995–96 over 90 countries received police or military training from Britain, including the regimes in China, Guatemala, Indonesia and Kenya.[123]

The standard defence for training military officers from repressive regimes is that by receiving such training their behaviour will improve, a simply hysterical proposition in the light of the precise reasons for such military relationships. This argument recalls the case of a visitor to the army training centre at Sandhurst who asked a Sri Lankan army officer what he was going to do on his return, and who replied: 'kill Tamils'.[124]

On the second myth, it is customary to discuss arms exports (training is rarely discussed) in the context of 'morality versus jobs', a framing of the issue that avoids the important aspects noted above. It is certainly true that tens of thousands of jobs currently depend on British military industry, since such militarisation of the economy has been overtly promoted by past Labour and Conservative governments, and this has become the standard argument for continuing to promote arms exports. However, various studies show that military spending is wasteful and unlikely to promote the kinds of social welfare that accrue from other forms of government spending. One analysis by three British analysts stated that 'there is no evidence that cuts in military spending in conjunction with sensible macro-economic policies would cause an increase in total unemployment'. A reduction in military spending by half, they estimated, could create half a million jobs and increase economic growth by 2 per cent, because it would free-up spending in areas that create more jobs.[125]

Neil Cooper of the University of Plymouth notes that:

> There is a significant body of literature which suggests that the British [military-industrial base] has had a negative impact on economic growth by variously depressing investment, diverting scarce R&D [research and development] resources, and/or by imbuing key economic sectors with a corporate culture antipathetic to innovation, low-cost production and competitive marketing.

He continues by noting that using arms exports to maintain British military industry 'undermines the balance of payments advantages that accrue from British arms sales'. Thus 'not only is the notion of an independent defence [sic] production capacity a chimera' but using arms exports 'to maintain such capacity actually implies a weakening of the UK's economic security'. Cooper concludes that 'far from promoting a virtuous circle of benefits based upon the efficiency of the British defence [sic] industry and enjoyed by all, UK defence exports arguably promote a vicious circle of disadvantage from which only the arms traders benefit'.[126] In Britain military spending and arms exports do have the advantage of benefiting individual important companies, such as British Aerospace and GEC-Marconi, principally in whose interest the military-industrial complex functions.

Overall, the historical record shows that Labour's foreign policy has always been geared to the priority of maintaining the current international order and the pursuit of traditional 'national interests' within that order. Labour has traditionally promoted this same strategic agenda by adopting a few usually minor reforms that deviate from orthodox Conservative policy. This has sometimes included adopting slightly less belligerent stances than the Conservatives, such as over support for the US in the Vietnam war and for apartheid regimes in South Africa. However, although Labour governments have in general pursued better (in the sense of less immoral) policies, there is a sense in which Labour policy can have a worse effect than the Conservatives, by serving to convince many that the internationalist and egalitarian rhetoric is being pursued in practice. Labour governments, because they represent the acceptable alternative to the Conservatives, have also been able to convey the false impression that their policies are at the outer limits of what can realistically be pursued and therefore help set the parameters of mainstream debate. This is not to deny that there have been genuinely progressive and radical voices in the party who have often been vocal in proposing alternatives to official policy – and there still are – but these have now been systematically undermined and marginalised by Blairite 'modernisation'.

It is no exaggeration to say that in all the areas of the current government's external relations – military, economic, diplomatic – there are no indications of any major changes from the previous government's, or any other postwar government's policies. The media have also often recognised that there are no differences in foreign policy but one will search in vain for references to the threat this poses to democracy. Rather, such Labour positioning is seen as a sign of its *strength* and the entire political class has acquiesced in and is actively supporting such totalitarianism. Thus *The Times* notes:

> Foreign policy is largely bipartisan and Labour has supported the government in the global issues that have preoccupied Britain, the wars in Bosnia and the Gulf, political and economic reform in Russia and Eastern Europe, enlargement of the European Union and NATO, Hong Kong, the Middle East and the environment. In large swaths of foreign affairs Labour policy needed no wrenching modernisation. Neither was there partisan advantage to be gained by harrying the government.[127]

Overall, it needs to be emphasised that Labour's policy is not one of double standards on the ethical question. The evidence hitherto clearly shows that Labour's foreign policy is wholly consistent in its pursuit of an unethical policy, in the tradition of the most basic standards of British foreign policy.

# Part II

# Development

# 3

# The 'Development' System

The 1990s have been marked by increasing poverty and inequality in many countries of both the North and South, making these surely the most significant human concerns of our times. The majority of people on the planet live in poverty, with the poorest three-quarters of the world's population – over four billion people – having an average income of just $750 a year.[1] Yet poverty as an everyday reality in the Third World is barely ever mentioned in the mainstream media, for example, except in stories of conflicts or famines, where people are portrayed as helpless victims of forces unconnected with the North. At the same time, wide debate on poverty and development is non-existent. What discussion there is, is confined to a very small specialist development circle, consisting of academics, international institutions such as the World Bank and the UN, government departments responsible for 'development' and NGOs. Yet here it is important to realise that discussion usually takes place within very narrow parameters where the framework of analysis offered by the powerful sets the agenda, with criticism of current policies usually falling within this establishment framework.

There are barely any studies in mainstream development academia that consider in any depth the role of US and British foreign policy in international development. The interests and motivations of the states which control the development agenda including, largely, the international financial institutions, are usually barely even entertained, let alone analysed. This lack of proper critical analysis gives rise to a great deal of naivety about the role of these states and even allows for analyses which see them as genuine 'partners' for 'development cooperation' in poverty eradication. This view is completely at odds with the historical and contemporary record, which clearly shows a permanent opposition to meaningful development on the part of the leading Northern powers and their Southern allies.

The basic fact is that Britain and the United States are two of the leading states responsible for the maintenance and deepening of poverty in the Third World as a product of their fundamental domestic and foreign policy priorities. Indeed, the US and Britain are the leading historical architects of the international economic order as well as its current champions, witnessed in the recently established WTO. Yet when Britain's former 'Development' Minister Lynda Chalker noted in the House of Lords that 'by common consent, the United Kingdom makes one of the most significant contributions to the alleviation of poverty in the developing world',[2] no howls of laughter followed. There is simply no common framework for understanding that, in fact, the opposite is the case.

This chapter and Chapter 4 attempt to understand the current crisis of poverty and development in the context of the foreign policy of the United States and Britain. They also look at the historical record and consult the formerly secret government files of both Britain and the US, mostly for the first time, hoping to shed light on the reality of the development system.

## Establishing the postwar system

The US design for the postwar international order was, as noted in Chapter 1, one in which its business interests would be pre-eminent and in which the international economy be subject to an 'open door' in trade and investment, a goal tirelessly repeated by US leaders during and after the war and now well documented in various studies.[3] Given the extent of US power, this was understood to amount to achieving global economic supremacy. British postwar planners were keen above all to re-establish the economic control they exercised over their colonial territories and other regions of key economic importance, principally the Middle East. This, as with the US, involved a mix of covert action, military intervention and a range of international economic instruments, especially the Bretton Woods institutions (described below).

The Commonwealth was of particular significance. A British Cabinet memorandum of 1954 noted that the UK should admit colonial territories 'to a status of nominal equality' in the Commonwealth and ensure that 'they will remain within our sphere of influence'. Thus Britain's maintaining its role as 'primus inter pares' in the Commonwealth would help to 'maintain [Britain's] influence as a world power'.[4] Similarly, a paper in 1956 by the Commonwealth Relations Office stated that over the next ten to fifteen years the countries of the colonial empire would probably become independent members of the Commonwealth. This 'will reduce the area under direct United Kingdom control and will necessitate still greater concentration by the United Kingdom on maintaining its political influence and its markets throughout the Commonwealth'.[5]

Overall British priorities in the international economy were highlighted in a Treasury memorandum of 1945. Britain must ensure 'a rapid and non-autarkic economic growth in the middle and low-income countries', it read, since this would help to expand world trade. The 'real difficulty' with this, however, was that these goals depend on 'decisions on internal policy in the countries concerned'. Therefore, 'we have to devise techniques for bringing influence to bear upon other countries' internal decisions'. Thus 'we could usefully begin with parts of the world in which we already have great influence – the Colonial Empire, the Middle East and India'. It continued:

> If we accept the principle that we want to see rapid economic development there we should be able to exert a very great influence upon the structure of that development. We need not overtly use the sterling balances as a weapon; but the fact remains that if those countries want to be repaid in goods they will be very well advised to accept our advice on the general course of their development.

The memorandum also noted that 'we should tend to deprecate industrialisation for its own sake where adequate world capacity already exists ... One need hardly stress the danger to us of autarkic industrialisation undertaken for its own sake and the advantage to the terms of trade of a real growth in agricultural efficiency'. Countries should therefore 'develop' for the benefit not so much of themselves but for the international system (understood as the interests of the leading powers). Finally, it notes:

> We might have fruitful cooperation with the Dutch, the Belgians and the French on such development as they seek to organise in their Colonial Empires. Similar considerations should be taken into account in the Bretton Woods Bank loans. What I am suggesting is that we should take a definite line on the desirable course of economic development of backward areas, that we should press this strongly in those areas where we have great influence and that we should press the same ideas upon others who will become responsible for such development elsewhere. If we can develop a view which is genuinely and obviously in the interests of the undeveloped countries as well as in our own and if we can build up the batteries of advisers and experts which these countries need, the dividends to British trade can be very large indeed. This is, indeed, a natural development from our 19th century position.[6]

British priorities have a long history. Joseph Chamberlain, for example, believed that the task of the Foreign Office and Colonial Office was to 'find new markets and defend old ones', while the War Office and the Admiralty protected the flow of commerce. 'Abroad', imperial historian Jan Morris comments, 'national power was properly used to further private trade and investment – by forcing other countries to reduce their tariffs and abolish their monopolies'.[7] Another historian of the empire, Lawrence James, comments that in the seventeenth century, 'although keeping the title Royal Navy, the British fleet was now a national force at the disposal of those subjects with foreign and colonial business interests'. Thus 'henceforward, the navy would be an instrument of commercial and colonial policy'.[8]

US documents reveal similar priorities. A State Department report of 1955 declared:

> Our foreign policy is aimed at achieving the kind of world community in which trade and investment can move with a minimum of restrictions and a maximum of security and confidence. Thus, almost every aspect of our foreign policy has some ultimate effect, directly or indirectly, upon the flow of private investment abroad.[9]

A 1956 report by the US government's Council on Foreign Economic Policy stated: 'Foreign economic policy is part of our overall foreign policy' and US policy should be to 'assist and encourage the orderly economic evolution' of the Third World, 'not only as markets and sources of raw materials but for the desired effect on their attitudes and orientation toward the free world'. In this, 'efforts should be continued to develop climates attractive to private investment'.[10] A US goal in Latin America was the 'creation of suitable climate for US private investment. Primary responsibility for this on LA governments' [sic].[11] As regards Southeast Asia, the State Department pointed out in 1950 that 'the US is feared throughout the whole area, and much of the fear is based upon the notion that our interest in the area originates in large part from conscious programs of economic imperialism'.[12]

As with Britain, US strategy was essentially to prevent the prospects for independent nationalist economic development. One State Department Adviser commented, in reference to Latin America, that 'economic nationalism is the common denominator of the new aspirations for industrialization. Latin Americans are convinced that the first beneficiaries of the development of a country's resources should be the people of that country.' These were the wrong priorities since development in Latin America, and elsewhere, was to complement and not compete with the US economy, and US policy set itself to oppose them. A 1949 study for the NSC stated that the US should find ways of 'exerting economic pressures' on countries that do not accept their role as suppliers of 'strategic commodities and other basic materials'.[13] Much of US foreign policy and military intervention throughout the postwar era – especially in Latin America – is explicable in these terms, and remains so today.

A good example of US priorities is revealed in 1961 files concerning proposals for a UN Development Decade. One report lamented:

> The US was unable to avoid the inclusion of two items in the resolution which may cause concern in the future. The most hotly debated issue was the proposal by the representative of Iraq that an increasing share of the profit from the exploitation and marketing of natural resources by foreign capital be made available to the host country. After several days of intense negotiations, agreement was reached on wording calling on member countries 'to pursue policies designed to ensure to the developing countries an equitable share of earnings from the extraction and marketing of their natural resources by foreign capital in accordance with the generally accepted reasonable earnings on invested capital'.[14]

The primary obstacle to the pursuit of these Anglo-American priorities was nationalism. (The modern variant is national sovereignty [of others], which is to be defeated through 'globalisation', essentially meaning the control of the international economy by the North and its corporations.) An interesting paper by the British Foreign Office is from 1952, entitled 'The Problem of Nationalism', which notes that there are essentially two types of nationalism – that which is friendly towards British interests (called 'intelligent and satisfied nationalism') and that which is not (called 'exploited and dissatisfied nationalism'). The wrong kind of nationalism is likely to 'undermine us politically' and to 'encourage worldwide speculation as to our ability and readiness to maintain our position as a world power'. It also means:

> (i) insistence on managing their own affairs without the means or ability to do so, including the dismissal of British advisers; (ii) expropriation of British assets; (iii) unilateral denunciation of treaties with the UK; (iv) claims on British possessions; (v) ganging up against the UK (and the Western powers) in the United Nations.[15]

This was referred to elsewhere as 'the severe blow which confidence in overseas investment has suffered as a result of the actions of certain foreign governments in expropriating investments created by overseas capital in return for compensation often equal to only a fraction of their true worth'.[16] One problem in the British policy to combat and subdue these nationalist forces was that 'British public opinion is in the main largely in sympathy with nationalist trends in the colonies'.[17]

In defeating unacceptable nationalism and achieving its priorities Britain and the United States would work through – as they do today – elites in the Third World. They were cultivated after independence to ensure 'stability', and responsible leaders ('moderates') were juxtaposed with 'irresponsible nationalism' ('extremists').[18] As one Colonial Office minute stated, 'it is at least a very plausible social hypothesis that a major civilising influence comes from the action of the elite among a community, but only if the social structure permits the natural elite to emerge from the average ruck'.[19]

For Britain, Africa was of particular importance. Labour Foreign Secretary Ernest Bevin noted in 1948, for example, that the basic need was 'to develop the African continent and to make its resources available to all'.[20] The Governor of Kenya, Phillip Mitchell, noted in 1947 that Africa south of a line drawn from the Gambia to Somalia was faced with a 'strategic problem' similar to which the US Monroe Doctrine in Latin America was proclaimed: 'there is a strategic unity which is as essential to the safety of all the parts, as the whole is to the survival of the Commonwealth and of the nations of Western Europe who share the responsibility with us'. Britain was in Africa 'to develop and civilise this continent as part of what I may call Western European civilisation and economics'.[21]

Similarly, Field Marshal Montgomery outlined in December 1947 'the immense possibilities that exist in British Africa for development' and 'the use to which such development could be put to enable Great Britain to maintain her standard of living, and to survive'. 'These lands contain everything we need', he noted, such as minerals, raw materials, labour and food but he lamented the 'lack of a grand design', stating that 'there must be a grand design for African development as a whole'. Britain needed to develop the continent since the African 'is a complete savage and is quite incapable of developing the country [sic] himself'.[22] The Colonial Office replied to Montgomery and refuted his suggestion of a 'grand design', at the same time noting agreement with his 'main contention regarding the importance of a quick and vigorous development of our African territories'. 'Politically', the reply continued, 'our long term aim must be to secure that when the African territories attain self-government they do so as part of the Western world.' Meanwhile, Western Europe's position could be strengthened by 'building up the economy of Africa and linking Africa more closely with this country and the other countries of Western Europe'.[23] This, it should be noted, was to be promoted under a Labour government.

The Foreign Office was correct to point out in a memo of 1950 that 'the United States realises the importance to her own economy, in peace and war, of many British colonial resources and the possibilities of their further development'.[24] Further, 'the United States agrees with the basic aims of British colonial policy ... The United Kingdom and the United States are basically agreed on long term objectives in Africa'.[25]

The documents show that it was US policy to leave Africa essentially to the Europeans. The State Department had noted in 1947 that 'we believe that our economic goals in Africa should be achieved through coordination and cooperation with the colonial powers'.[26] In tripartite talks over a decade later, the US Representative Robert Murphy told the British and French that 'the US regards the European powers as best equipped for the leading role' in the 'development' of Africa. 'The Africans were on the whole immature and unsophisticated', he added.[27] A Department of Defense paper from 1963, entitled 'The Strategic Importance of Africa', stated that 'from a global perspective Africa is not an area of primary strategic importance to the US and we therefore have a strong interest in restricting our involvement in Africa. Nonetheless, we have a considerable number of specific interests and commitments.'[28]

A US National Security Council report on Africa of 1957 declared that the US wanted sub-Saharan Africa to develop 'in an orderly manner' towards independence 'in cooperation with the European powers now in control of large areas of the continent'. This transition should occur in a manner which 'will preserve the essential ties that bind Europe and Africa – which are fundamentally complementary areas'. It continued by noting that the US wished 'to avoid the deprivation of African markets and sources of supply to Western Europe'.[29] If, however, African countries aligned themselves with Moscow, then, President Eisenhower noted, 'we would not wish to undertake programs for their orderly development and political progress'.[30] An NSC report of 1960 similarly noted that it was important that the 'traditional economic ties' between Europe and Africa be maintained and that efforts be taken to encourage the Europeans 'to continue economic and technical assistance'.[31]

The control of raw material supplies was central in the pursuit of these policies. Both the US and British documents contain numerous studies of key raw materials in the colonies and elsewhere. This was in keeping with the long-standing view, expressed by the philosopher John Stuart Mill, that 'colonies should not be thought of as civilizations or countries at all, but as agricultural establishments whose sole purpose was to supply the larger community to which they belong'.[32] In May 1950 British planners noted that Africa provided over half the world's cocoa; Northern Rhodesia (now Zambia) was one of the world's most important producers of copper and cobalt; the Gold Coast (now Ghana) accounted for 15 per cent of the world's output of manganese; Nigeria was one of the leading producers of oil-bearing nuts and seeds; Malaya grew half the world's natural rubber; and British Guiana (now Guyana) produced nearly a quarter of the world's bauxite.[33] The UK's Deputy Permanent Representative on NATO's North Atlantic Council noted in 1956 that 'we ourselves and the sterling area depend vitally on Africa for raw materials, eg, gold, uranium and copper'.[34]

Southeast Asia was also crucial. A 1950 British government report noted that South and Southeast Asia 'is a major source of the food and raw materials consumed throughout the industrialised world' and a provider of almost half the world's jute and rubber, more than three-quarters of its tea and almost half its tin.[35] A Foreign Office minute of 1950 noted that 'it is important for the economy of Western Europe that Western European trading and business interests in Southeast Asia should be maintained'.[36] US files show that 'in the UK view, the economic development of South and Southeast Asia should contribute not only to the welfare of Southeast Asia but also to the balance of world trade by developing sources of raw material for the United States and Europe'.[37] Britain's interests in Southeast Asia centred on Malaya, with its rubber and tin, but Indonesia was also important. US files from 1947 state that British investments in Indonesia were substantial and that it 'relies on the Indies as a major source of certain commodities which are in short supply all over the world'. 'British interests in Indonesia', the report continued, 'are overwhelmingly economic in character and not influenced by imperial considerations.'[38]

A Cabinet memo from June 1947 called for the creation of new sources of supply for raw materials: 'there are great opportunities which we should use of whipping up production of vital materials and foodstuffs overseas through worldwide propaganda and through United Nations agencies'.[39] The Colonial Development Corporation (CDC) – the forerunner of the current British aid programme – was recommended to be established so as to help achieve this objective – 'to promote and undertake the expansion of supplies of colonial foodstuffs, raw materials and other commodities'.[40] A Colonial Office paper from 1950 declared that the 'development of those areas at present underdeveloped, and higher standards of living in those areas, means additions to the world's resources and new markets for the products of Europe and America'.[41] Expansion of raw material production in the colonies was a policy which continued to be promoted by the subsequent Churchill government. This was described as involving 'an expanded contribution to the sterling area's viability' and would promote 'the production of the commodities the Colonies already produce'.[42] British plans in this period – the late 1940s and early 1950s under both Labour and Conservative governments – all emphasised concentration on commodities the colonies were already producing, helping to reinforce the colonial economic pattern of dependence on one or two exports.

The US was also interested in increasing supplies of raw materials from the British domains. The State Department noted in 1948, for example, that 'we have a direct interest in increased availability of strategic materials for which British colonies and dependencies constitute important sources of supply'. Among these were manganese, chrome and copper produced in Southern Rhodesia (now Zimbabwe), tin produced in Malaya, and industrial diamonds produced elsewhere.[43] The US also believed it should have access to these raw materials on the same terms as the businesses of the host nation itself.[44]

There is ample evidence in the files of the recognition by planners of the human costs of these policies: the direct exploitation of the people of the Third World. The Colonial Office noted in 1955:

> Most of the colonies are primitive communities in which the people enjoy only a low standard of living, many indeed barely surviving in a life-long struggle against the chances of pests, disease, soil erosion or adverse weather.[45]

Then – as now – they also had to struggle against the policies of the British government. The system of bulk-buying of commodities produced in the colonies by the UK government at prices below market prices was the subject of some interesting exchanges. This system involved almost all the agricultural and some non-agricultural products produced in the colonies. It led to the Colonial Office arguing against the Treasury to pay the colonial producers the market rate and the Treasury apparently holding out for the lower one. One document read: 'There have been many complaints, the justice of which it is impossible to deny, that His Majesty's Government's policy of avoiding high prices operates one-sidedly. Although Colonial exports are sold to the United Kingdom at less than world prices, the Colonies have to pay fully competitive prices for the manufactured goods they import in return.' This is clearly reminiscent of the contemporary situation of worsening terms of trade for Third World countries through long-term declining commodity prices and rising manufactures prices. Another similarity with the current era is the gross mismatch between these low export prices and the level of 'aid'. In a 1947 document it was estimated that Nigeria lost over £8 million through low prices for its exports, while it received £2.5 million under the British government's Colonial Development and Welfare allocation.

One 1947 Colonial Office memo confirmed that such a system of exploitation existed. It noted that:

> We have previously been at pains to deny recently that there is an element of exploitation in our Colonial economic policy. There is prima facie evidence of exploitation if we subscribe to any marketing arrangement which does not, all things considered, constitute a good business deal for the Colonial producers concerned.

The memo had just in fact noted the latter. The Treasury, however, was 'refusing to accept our claim that their buying price should be based on a fair world valuation'.[46] By 1951 a Cabinet memorandum stated that the marketing boards in West Africa and Uganda 'have already accumulated very large surpluses indeed and are under sharp criticism for holding down unduly the standard of living of the producers whose interests they are meant to represent'.[47] A document from 1951 simply noted that 'the Colonial territories are helping so much on [Britain's] balance of payments'.[48]

During 1948 colonial net dollar earnings were around $150 million.[49] By 1951 a Cabinet memo noted that the sterling assets of the colonies in London topped the £1 billion mark.[50] At the end of 1952 the Colonies' sterling balances amounted to £1.2 billion, of which £1.06 billion was held in UK securities, which had risen over 90 per cent in three and a half years, the main reason being the 'high level of Colonial export earnings'. A Treasury report of 1953 noted that this recent rise in the Colonial balances 'has aroused, both in the United Kingdom and in the Colonies, the accusation that HM Government is "exploiting" or "living on the backs of" the Colonies'. This was untrue, the report noted.[51] A Colonial Office memorandum of 1948 noted that present plans to develop the Colonial empire were 'obviously subject to wholesale misrepresentation on the grounds that they are merely an attempt by the United Kingdom to suck the colonies dry'.[52]

The reasoning behind exploitation was explained by the Under-Secretary of State at the Colonial Office, Lord Lloyd, in February 1956:

> We do not believe it is realistic to consider colonial economies as being entirely external to that of the United Kingdom ... London is their banking centre where they both keep their reserves and raise loan capital ... These close links mean that any surpluses earned by the Colonies which are banked here in fact relieve the strain on the UK economy.

The sterling balances of the colonies were then rising at around £100 million a year and their net dollar earnings in 1954 were also around £100 million. 'These figures suggest that it is to the United Kingdom's advantage that she should act as a banker to the Colonies.'[53]

It was not surprising that in this situation the need for propaganda was recognised by officials, and this is another recurring theme in the documentary record. A Colonial Office memorandum from 1948 noted that:

> Considering the great difference which as yet exists between the average standard of living of the British people and that of the vast majority of Colonial peoples, it is not easy for the latter to understand why the former regard themselves as making any sacrifice at all. There are here obvious seeds of discontent and unhappy relations if public pronouncements are not very carefully considered and handled.[54]

Foreign Secretary Bevin wrote to Prime Minister Attlee in October 1947 on the subject developing the colonies: we must ensure that 'in their presentation there is no possible suggestion of exploitation of the colonial populations'. 'The possibilities in this field', Bevin noted, 'are almost endless.'[55] The Cabinet Secretary noted in 1948 that in recent meetings of the Labour Cabinet there had been 'general support for the view that the development of Africa's economic resources should be pushed forward rapidly in order to support the political and economic position of the United Kingdom'. He noted, however, the 'difficulties of defending this policy against the criticisms and misrepresentations' since the policy 'could, I suppose, be said to fall within the ordinary definition of "imperialism"' and it could be represented as 'exploiting native peoples'. The answer was that 'care and preparation' would be needed to put the argument that 'the more rapid development of Africa's resources will bring social and economic advantages to the native peoples in addition to buttressing the political and economic influence of the United Kingdom'.[56]

Consistent with basic foreign policy priorities were the early policies towards the multilateral development institutions. An early US success in securing control over the development system concerned the International Trade Organisation (ITO), whose charter was signed in Havana in 1948. Former UN official Nassau Adams notes in his study of postwar development that whereas in the case of the Bretton Woods institutions the US 'so dominated the scene that it could virtually dictate the terms of the final outcome', in the case of the ITO 'the US had to be more accommodating, allowing other countries greater scope to make their voices heard and have their points of view taken into account'. The ITO was also to have far-reaching powers of decision making and enforcement, making it less easy to be dominated by one country, and therefore 'seemed to offer the possibility of a rule-based international trading system'.

The ITO, however, never saw the light of day. According to Adams, 'the UK announced that it would not ratify until the US had done so, and the US took no action, and that was the end of the ITO'. The GATT was established in the ITO's place and, since mostly industrial, and not agricultural, goods would benefit from it, would be of almost exclusive interest to the industrial countries. It also meant that, in Adams' words, 'other important elements in the ITO charter going beyond the narrow issues of commercial policy found no place in the newly established world economic order' and that 'the special concerns and interests of the less developed countries in the area of international trade and development were simply ignored'. Summing up, Adams notes:

> The reason why the ITO never saw the light of day is that in its conception it was too universalist in scope, too democratic in outlook, to serve the needs of the elitist mentality which could not contemplate an institutional setting in which the rich countries might mingle on equal terms with the poor.[57]

A second early success for the leading Western powers was the defeat of the proposal for a Special United Nations Fund for Economic Development (SUNFED). First put forward in 1953, SUNFED, although fairly modest in scope, aimed at providing finance to less developed countries largely on soft loan terms and, in contrast to existing multilateral institutions, control would be shared equally between the major contributors of capital and other members. The proposal was debated in the UN for over five years and had wide support in the South but was 'vigorously opposed', Adams comments, by the US and, to a lesser extent, Britain. The proposal to provide capital on soft loan terms was deflected by the United States to the World Bank, an institution over which it had greater control, and the Bank's soft loan window, the International Development Association (IDA), was set up in 1960 largely in place of SUNFED.

US documents reveal its stance towards SUNFED. The US noted in 1956 that 'the underdeveloped countries want SUNFED. They want it urgently and persistently' and 'by withholding support for SUNFED, we have been thwarting the underdeveloped countries in the realization of an important aspiration'. The US position, however, was that:

> We prefer to provide aid on a bilateral basis. We control the funds; we determine the priorities. The recipient knows that we are the source of aid. When our funds are merged in the common pool ... such good will as the aid creates is directed toward the United Nations rather than to us.[58]

Similarly, the US Treasury Secretary, George Humphrey, noted in 1956 that 'we are far better off to handle our own economic assistance throughout the world in the way that will best serve our interests and preserve whatever credit there is in it for ourselves, rather than to turn the use of our money over to SUNFED management'.[59]

A much watered-down version of SUNFED survived (the UN Special Fund) and eventually evolved into the United Nations Development Programme. Initially called the United Nations Development Authority (UNDA), US files show major concerns about this new proposal. One problem, the Under-Secretary of State for Economic Affairs, George Ball, noted in 1961, was that 'there is no assurance that the plans proposed by UNDA would be consistent with the more precise requirements of our foreign policy'.[60]

The establishment of the International Finance Corporation (IFC), an affiliate of the World Bank which promotes the private sector in developing countries, revealed the same US goals. The IFC was established by bypassing the United Nations and giving the Security Council and General Assembly no opportunity to discuss its statutes. Adams comments that 'the US had made its point. The UN, where the underdeveloped countries had such influence, was not to be allowed to dabble in the fashioning of the development financing institutions.'[61]

Such control and undermining of Southern views and demands for changes in the international system continued in the negotiations surrounding the establishment of the United Nations Conference on Trade and Development (UNCTAD),[62] whose 'functioning was blocked by continuous efforts by the North to deny it any negotiating or binding authority'.[63] It also continued in the debate over a New International Economic Order in the 1970s[64] and in the undermining of the prospects for international commodity agreements among Third World producers throughout the postwar period.[65]

## An instrument of control: the World Bank

The foremost of the world's 'development' institutions US and British planners have always explicitly regarded the World Bank as a vehicle for exerting influence over the international economy and as an instrument of their foreign policies. A study published in 1994 by the liberal US think-tank, the Brookings Institution, noted, for example, that 'the United States has viewed all multilateral organisations, including the World Bank, as instruments of foreign policy to be used in support of specific US aims and objectives ... US views regarding how the world economy should be organised, how resources should be allocated and how investment decisions should be reached were enshrined in the Charter and the operational policies of the Bank.'[66]

The original purpose of the World Bank – the control of which was proportionate to the capital invested, and therefore a US-dominated agency – was to accord with the primary US foreign economic objective: 'to promote private foreign investment by means of guarantees or participations [sic] in loans and other investments made by private investors'. The US Senate noted in 1945 that 'the Bretton Woods proposals give us the opportunity to decide whether international trade and investment will be carried on through private enterprise on the basis of fair currency rules or through governments on the basis of bilateral agreements'. US officials noted that 'willingness on our part to subordinate the independent use of our financial power to joint decision must be limited and kept in step with the willingness of other countries to act likewise in other matters'. The leading historian of US planning in this period, Gabriel Kolko, comments that 'this would require an acceptance of the

American program for world economic reconstruction not only in principle but in fact'.[67]

US Treasury Secretary Hans Morgenthau noted that the aim of postwar US planning was 'to move the financial centre of the world from London and Wall Street to the United States Treasury'. The establishment of the Bretton Woods institutions was 'the first practical test of our willingness to cooperate in the work of world reconstruction [and] one very important step towards the orderly, expanding foreign trade on which our agriculture and industry depends'.[68]

In 1946, soon after the World Bank was created, the US State Department noted the 'important diplomatic weapon of loans' and that the Department's Office of Near Eastern Affairs (NEA) 'is convinced that under certain conditions NEA could gain important US diplomatic objectives through the judicious use of credits to countries deserving the goodwill and support of the US and UN'. A memo to the NEA's Director noted that 'the proper agency for the longer range development of Near Eastern countries is the International Bank' (that is, the World Bank).[69]

Important to the US in the 1950s was the Bank's philosophy of 'promoting the right kinds of decisions' (World Bank President Eugene Black). This amounted, Gabriel Kolko notes, to 'directing poorer countries to specialise in exporting primary materials that could earn hard currencies with which to pay back loans and create the international division of labour that US development planners, both in and out of government, so enthusiastically endorsed'.[70]

Later, US plans envisaged the development of a 'consortium' under US/World Bank leadership for the pursuit of US foreign economic objectives. The US 'must develop consortium arrangements', one 1961 memo by an adviser to President Kennedy read, in order to 'bring as many nations as authentically qualify under long term aid arrangements of the kind we now have with India'. The possible candidates were Pakistan, Nigeria, Tanganyika, Iran, Egypt, Formosa (later Taiwan), Tunisia, Brazil and other Latin American states. The President of the World Bank, Eugene Black, 'must cooperate to the hilt' in this policy, 'as father of the consortia'.[71] 'Anything which suited Mr. Black would also suit the United States', noted US Under-Secretary of State, Douglas Dillon, two years earlier.[72]

The World Bank, and the development banks more generally, have had specific utility in promoting the private sector. One 1963 US government meeting on foreign economic policy noted, for example, that 'one mechanism that gets around some of the difficulties in programming for the private sector is the Development

Bank ... Use of Development Banks removes from our people the onus and responsibility for direct judgment on particular investments.'[73]

An official US report from 1974 similarly noted the function of development banks to:

> use their loans as leverage to encourage positive economic performance and acceptance of market economy principles in recipient countries. Thus the banks perform the difficult task of requiring performance standards of their borrowers, a task which the United States and other lenders may be reluctant to impose on a bilateral basis.

These included a strong export orientation, especially for 'increased supplies of raw materials and other products needed by the US economy'. The report also noted that 'the [World] Bank's reputation as an instrument of the developed economies seems justified'. Further, the development banks:

> serve as vehicles for assisting countries favoured by the United States and for influencing the economic affairs of countries with which the US government has international disagreements.

(The World Bank's ability to achieve US objectives that the US finds difficult to achieve bilaterally was outlined by the US Deputy Treasury Secretary in the case of the Philippines in the 1980s: 'We have not been particularly successful ourselves in winning policy reforms from the Philippines. Because it is something of a disinterested party, however, the World Bank has been enormously successful in negotiating important policy changes which we strongly support.'[74])

An important role of the development banks is for their policy advice to be seen as impartial and technical rather than political. By using what it purported to be 'relatively apolitical economic policy expertise', a US Treasury report of 1982 noted, the development banks were 'acting as a catalyst for private investment'. This occurred by 'encouraging rational LDC [less developed country] economic policies under free market concepts and global economic efficiency'.[75] The report also noted that the development banks overall had been 'most effective in contributing to the achievement of our global economic and financial objectives and thereby also helping us in our long term political/strategic interests'. They 'encourage developing countries to participate more fully in an international system based on liberalised trade and capital flows', which 'means expanding opportunities for US exports'. The policies and programmes of the

World Bank specifically had also been 'consistent with US interests', which was 'particularly true in terms of general country allocation questions and sensitive policy issues'.[76]

The 'soft lending' arm of the World Bank – the IDA – is currently the main source of World Bank loans to the poorest developing countries. The 1959 declassified files show US government proposals for the establishment of the IDA. This capital from the IDA was seen as needing to supplement the 'bilateral and regional programs of Western governments'. Indeed, 'the US believes that Western interests can be enhanced effectively in the field of multilateral aid to underdeveloped countries through cooperative Western arrangements such as the proposed International Development Association'.[77] US intentions in establishing the IDA were made explicit by the US Treasury Secretary in a memo to President Eisenhower in December 1959:

> The first draft of an IDA charter now under consideration demonstrates clearly the broad agreement among industrialised as well as less developed countries that an IDA can become an important new source of capital for *promoting economic development within a framework which would safeguard existing institutions and traditional forms of private finance*.[78]

By the mid-1990s US Treasury Secretary Robert Rubin continued to emphasise the utility of the IDA and the IMF's Enhanced Structural Adjustment Facility (ESAF) by describing them as 'among our most important foreign policy tools for integrating the world's poorest nations into the global economy'.[79]

Given their important function as instruments of foreign policy, it is not surprising that both the World Bank and the IMF are closely controlled by Washington. This is manifest in a number of ways: in the US-dominated origins of the Bank's charter and guiding principles; in the US position as the largest shareholder in the Bank with the largest voting power (the G7 states account for over 40 per cent of voting power, compared to just over 4 per cent for the whole of sub-Saharan Africa[80]); in the importance of its financial market as a source of capital for the Bank; and in its hold on the Bank's President, senior management and other staff positions. According to former Chairman of the US Federal Reserve, Paul Volcker, for example, the US Treasury and Federal Reserve Board 'directed' World Bank lending in the 1980s, the source of the Third World debt crisis.[81] Extension of World Bank credits to countries favoured by the US and withholding of credits to unfavoured countries has been standard policy throughout the postwar period.

The British government views the World Bank similarly, as generally acting as an instrument for pursuing Western economic policies and, especially in the colonial period, as facilitating the extraction of Third World raw materials. In the early postwar period the British government looked to the new bank to provide capital to support its exploitation of colonial resources. Foreign Secretary Bevin stated that World Bank financing would be especially useful in Rhodesia, whose raw materials 'must be made available to the members of the Organisation for European Economic Co-operation (OEEC) [the forerunner of the Organisation for Economic Co-operation and Development (OECD) and the main body for Western European reconstruction] for not only were they badly needed but they would enable us all to affect an important saving of dollars'. This policy was described by the Labour government as one 'to develop the African continent and to make its resources available to all'.[82]

In 1995 the Overseas Development Administration (ODA) noted: 'There is a high degree of congruence between Bank and [International Monetary] Fund objectives and ODA's aims ... This congruence of objectives allows ODA to wield considerable influence in the Bank.'[83] Thus Britain has been a chief supporter of the Bank's promotion of 'liberalisation' and encouragement of economic climates favourable to foreign investment in Southern countries throughout the 1980s and 1990s. Having become a major supporter of World Bank/IMF SAPs – the promotion of which was seen as a central aim of the aid programme under the Conservatives – one British academic study notes that 'broadly speaking, the conditionality attached to British programme assistance [the part of the aid programme that directly supports structural adjustment] is simply a photocopy of whatever policy advice has already been offered by the Bank'.[84] Britain's former Minister for Overseas Development under the Conservatives noted that countries 'must not be allowed to stop adjustment. Make no mistake – there is no alternative.'[85] In principle, support for basic World Bank objectives is continuing under Labour, as noted in Chapter 2.

## The aid system

A crucial aspect of the development system is that the Northern public is expected to pay the costs of exploiting the South. One major way in which this has occurred has been by Northern taxpayers subsidising governments bailing out private banks exposed to Third World debt. In the decade from 1982, it is estimated that Northern taxpayers paid between $44 billion and $50 billion in tax relief on bank provisions and losses and on disguised subsidies from public bodies to private banks. (Over a somewhat shorter period, banks received over $600 million in debt service as many made healthy profits on their loans during the 'crisis').[86] British government figures show that British banks were granted £2.7 billion in tax relief from 1986 to 1995.[87]

Another public subsidy is aid money returning to the 'donor' in debt service payments. The OECD notes, for example, that 'a central element of the overall success of the debt strategy is the need to ensure adequate flows' of aid in order 'to permit them [that is, aid recipients] to service their debt' (as well as to promote 'sustainable development').[88] In 1994, of the $2.9 billion lent by the World Bank's IDA, $2 billion returned to the World Bank in the form of debt repayments. Similar to IDA, loans from the IMF's ESAF also come from aid budgets: between 1987 and 1993, the IMF received around $4 billion more in repayments from sub-Saharan Africa than it provided in new loans. Around one-fifth of all aid is now transferred to multilateral creditors, mostly via balance of payments support under the auspices of SAPs. This state of affairs has been described by Oxfam as an 'intra-donor affair' in which 'what passes for assistance ... is in fact an accounting operation which transfers resources from one side of 19th Street in Washington to the other' (that is, from the World Bank to the IMF).[89]

Official aid is part of this development system in a more general sense, however. The evidence shows that aid is in reality largely a corporate and foreign policy welfare programme in which the Northern public subsidises domestic private companies and reinforces economic conditions in the South favourable to foreign investment, as well as facilitating the pursuit of Northern states' foreign policy objectives in the South. This occurs under the guise of 'humanitarianism' and 'moral obligation'. One reason why aid is in decline is that these objectives can now be more openly pursued in the South, through the near-global remit of SAPs and the WTO, aided by the collapse of the Soviet Union.

This issue is important since the promotion of official aid helps convince the Northern public that something significant is being done by their governments about Third World poverty. This, along with individuals' own giving to charities, which is surely sincere, provides a comforting but false reassurance that poverty in the Third World can be addressed without major (political and structural) upheavals in the North. However, the usual parameters of the debate are, at one end, that 'aid works' (that is, it helps to promote development/reduce poverty) and, at the other, that 'aid doesn't work' (that is, it fails to reduce poverty). Let us, though, look briefly at the declassified record and current evidence.

The British aid programme was begun in 1948 by the establishment of a Colonial Development Corporation (CDC) with the power to borrow money from the Treasury 'for schemes of a specifically economic nature, ie, schemes which over a period of years can reasonably be expected to pay their way but which for various reasons are not attractive to private capital'.[90] The reasoning behind such an 'aid' programme was explained a year earlier: the CDC 'should be set up with adequate powers to promote and undertake the expansion of supplies of colonial foodstuffs, raw materials and other commodities'. The CDC's functions were also 'to develop other industries where these show promise of being remunerative and of benefiting the Colonies or the United Kingdom'. It was important to take account 'of the needs of this country for physical supplies and of the possibilities of improving the balance of payments position of the sterling area as a whole by developing new production'. This was part of the 'task of economic development in the Colonial Empire'.[91]

One problem was of presenting such schemes to the public as acts of benevolence. This was difficult, one memo from 1947 read, since welfare contributions by the government to the colonies 'hardly balance in amount what colonies [sic] are losing by not receiving world prices for their products'. Therefore:

> His Majesty's Government could not keep the moral lead which it has given to the world in laying down principles and developing the practice of sound Colonial administration if it could be shown that welfare expenditure in the Colonies was not, as had been claimed, an act of benevolence but was an investment calculated to yield substantial returns in the shape of supplies of Colonial produce for the United Kingdom at below market prices.[92]

A Colonial Office memorandum noted four years later that the CDC 'may well be criticised for exploitation if and when it makes substantial profits in any colonial territory; for that territory is not likely to find much consolation in the fact that these profits are being used to offset losses incurred in other territories'.[93] Colonial Secretary Oliver Lyttleton noted bluntly: 'I cannot offhand recall any exploitation company of this kind that has won through in this century. We must therefore recognise that the Corporation is unlikely to succeed.'[94]

Aid was also intended to provide other functions. British technical skill provided through the aid programme, for example, would help to 'guide the energies and abilities of nationalist leaders towards cooperation with British interests in the economic field', something that would be especially useful 'in the oil-producing countries of the Middle East'.[95]

By 1953 British planners were noting that 'the underdeveloped countries seem to be coming to the view that they have a right to assistance' and that a recent resolution passed at the UN on 'the right to nationalise foreign enterprises' was 'typical of this state of mind'.[96] In this situation, the British view 'attaches very great importance to getting Colonial governments and peoples to take a closer interest in the prosperity of overseas enterprises operating in their territories'.[97]

The demand for 'funds for undeveloped territories' was part of the 'general rise of the under-privileged against the privilege[d]' – something which necessarily had to be avoided.[98]

The aims of US aid outlined at the beginning of the postwar era were 'to support economic stability' throughout the world, to prevent the growth of 'national or international power which constitutes a substantial threat to US security and well-being' and 'to orient foreign nations toward the US'. This meant applying assistance 'where it will do the most good from the standpoint of promoting US security and national interest'. One objective was described thus:

> It is important to maintain in friendly hands areas which contain or protect sources of metals, oil and other national resources which contain strategic objectives or areas strategically located which contain a substantial industrial potential, which possess manpower and organised military forces in important quantities or which for political or psychological reasons enable the US to exert a greater influence for world stability, security and peace.[99]

Secretary of State John Foster Dulles correctly pointed out in 1956: 'Our so-called foreign aid program, which is not really foreign aid because it isn't to foreigners but aid to us, is an indispensable factor in carrying out our foreign policy.'[100] Also, 'maximum use should be made of our assistance programs ... in stimulating those conditions under which private investment and enterprise can develop and operate effectively'.[101]

Thus 'aid and other [government] programmes ... constitute the tools of US foreign policy':[102] 'our purpose is to put the resources that go beyond our borders in the service of our national aims', memos from the early 1960s read.[103] One of President Kennedy's National Security Advisers noted in 1961:

> In my view our general rule should be that we use our aid program to achieve the three major strategic objectives to which aid might contribute: viable independence; an increased concentration on domestic affairs; and a long term dependence on the West.[104]

By 1963, it was noted that bilateral aid 'has proven to be a valuable instrumentality of US diplomacy and a primary leverage in influencing countries toward cooperative activities and sound development programs'. It was also noted that:

> There are also advantages to our continuing small US aid presences and programs in areas, such as the former colonial areas, since modest diffusions of aid in these areas make it easier politically for the recipient country to continue to accept aid under self-help criteria from a dominant donor. Similarly, multinational mechanisms may for the same reason assist us in pressing our objectives in areas of primary US aid responsibility, ie, Latin America.

Also, 'the search for new markets and sources of raw materials, as well as political and strategic considerations, leads naturally to diffusion rather than concentration of aid'. Small aid programmes provide the 'most effective way' to 'maintain some active presence in a great many countries'.[105]

Aid also, crucially, helps to cement relations with elites:

> A judicious mixture of military and economic aid is a way of carrying on a continuing relation with two groups that are powerful and important in nearly every underdeveloped country: the would-be economic planners and the military.[106]

(Similarly, the minutes from an NSC meeting in 1960 show President Eisenhower saying that 'he had heard from some of our South American friends that all our aid merely perpetuates the ruling class of many countries and intensifies the tremendous differences between the rich and poor'.[107])

A policy to extend 'deep tying of US aid' to US goods and services was recommended by Kennedy adviser J. K. Galbraith in 1963:

> We must begin to extend aid tying to include dollars which, in the absence of such assistance, would have to be spent in the United States ... Countries thus would have an inducement to direct purchases now going to other countries to the United States and to use dollars for this purpose. Our aid would thus become a direct inducement to dollar trade; our aid, if you will, becomes a massive but quite legitimate subsidy to our dollar trade.[108]

The implications of such deep tying of aid, one of Kennedy's National Security advisers pointed out, was that 'the new development program can be honestly presented as a measure which would increase American domestic production and exports'.[109]

Britain's (Labour) Minister for Overseas Development from 1967–69, Reg Prentice, similarly noted in 1970:

> Our aid programme can be seen as an investment in our own overseas markets. This applies to all donor countries ... We provide at the moment about 7.5 per cent of the global flow of aid, but we get about 12 per cent of the orders for goods imported by the developing countries from the developed countries. Our aid programme, being a part of an international aid flow, is almost certainly a help to our balance of payments ... Taking into account the indirect effects ('trade follows aid') and the orders we get from other countries' aid programmes, the total result is in our favour.[110]

The same priorities are firmly in evidence today. OECD countries' bilateral aid is often tied to purchasing goods and services of the 'aiding' state; Britain's ATP (see also Chapter 2) was a special form of tied aid, acting as a direct subsidy to companies and helping to 'develop markets for British goods and exports', Britain's former Overseas Development Minister, Lynda Chalker, noted.[111] Between 1978 and 1984, each £1 million of aid under ATP generated £3.2 million in exports, the huge majority of which went to 15 companies.[112] Northern business also receives good returns from multilateral aid programmes, which are technically untied. In the ten years from 1982–91, for every £1.00 in 'aid' provided by Britain to the multilateral agencies, British companies received £1.20.[113] The United Nations Development Programme (UNDP) is more profitable: for every £1.00 that Britain 'gives', British companies receive £1.90 in return.[114] The system works similarly with the World Bank's IDA. In 1992 net IDA disbursements were $4.4 billion, of which $2.3 billion was paid out again in procurement contracts associated with IDA credits. IDA disbursed more money back to Britain ($285 million) than to Bangladesh ($253 million) and more to Switzerland than to numerous African countries.[115]

US companies also profit from the Asian Development Bank (ADB). The latter's Vice-President has noted that US companies benefited from contracts amounting to $2.3 billion by the end of 1994 – 'a sum roughly equivalent to the total paid-in capital contributed by the US government to the ADB'. This figure would be larger 'if American services and equipment provided through non-American firms which win contracts from the bank are included'.[116] According to the US Treasury, the multilateral development banks provide 'one of the largest and most important sources of finance now available for US firms doing business internationally'.[117] As Andrew Young, former US Representative to the UN, noted in February 1995: 'we get a five to one return on investment in Africa, through our trade, investment, finance and aid ... We're not aiding Africa by sending them aid. Africa's aiding us.'[118]

The case of 'aid' to Russia is also instructive. World leaders have trumpeted huge sums in support of Russian 'reforms' but, the *Guardian* notes, 'although these were often described as "aid" packages, they were made up almost entirely of insurance for Western companies exporting to Russia, debt relief and loans which added to the country's huge debt burden'. Russian governments have been happy to receive this 'support' but, the paper reports, the policy has alienated ordinary Russians, 'who believed the West has broken promises to provide capital', as well as Western taxpayers, 'who think they are subsidising Russia to a greater extent than they are'.[119]

USAID's openly proclaimed objectives are 'support for free markets and broad-based economic growth'.[120] The current priorities were also clearly articulated by Britain's Minister for Overseas Development under the Conservatives, Lynda Chalker. Overall, she noted, 'our aid programme is a vital part of the British government's foreign policy, complementing our defence and diplomatic activities'.[121] Thus 'we use our aid to improve the environment for private sector development', which includes attracting foreign investment and liberalising trade.[122]

In a speech to the Confederation of British Industry (CBI) in January 1995, Chalker boasted that 'British aid has done a great deal to assist structural adjustment in recent years' and that aid 'helps recipient countries to make reforms relevant to investors', something which has contributed to 'the much improved climate for investment'. Chalker continued by noting that 'the most important thing we [that is, the ODA] can do for British business to encourage these [Third World] countries to adopt reform, sound government and competent institutions; [is] to make them better and more profitable trading and investment partners'. Finally, she asked her business audience 'what more we might do to improve the climate for investment' and what plans they had 'for taking advantage of the much improved policy environment for which we have striven so hard'.[123] Elsewhere, she declared that aid should be used 'as a catalyst for the development of free markets'.[124]

Overall, then, aid plays a key role in maintaining the international economic order. Chalker noted that 'we use the aid programme to support the kind of international economic system which serves our interest'.[125] The British government has also noted that 'aid has helped to sustain the post-1945 liberal international economic and political system. All OECD countries have a collective interest in using aid to maintain and extend this system.'[126]

# 4

# The Prevention of Development

## Post-Cold War euphoria

If recent years have been ones of celebration for Western political and business leaders – with their victory in the Cold War, the defeat of Iraq in the 1991 war and the prospects offered by economic globalisation – they have been ones of grim recognition for many people in the South. This was shown in the report of the South Commission, a group of leading individuals in the South, under the chairmanship of the former President of Tanzania, Julius Nyerere. Released in 1990, the report remains very relevant today. It noted that the people of the South have been 'largely bypassed by the benefits of prosperity and progress' and that 'they exist on the periphery of the developed countries of the North ... While the economies of the North are generally strong and resilient, those of the South are mostly weak and defenceless.' The report stated that 'the decision-making processes that govern the international flows of trade, capital and technology are controlled by the major developed countries of the North and by the international institutions they dominate'. The North–South divide 'is worsening, not improving' and these widening disparities 'are attributable not merely to differences in economic progress, but also to an enlargement of the North's power vis-a-vis the rest of the world'.

> The fate of the South is increasingly dictated by the perceptions and policies of governments in the North, of the multilateral institutions which a few of those governments control, and of the network of private institutions that are increasingly prominent. Domination has been reinforced where partnership was needed and hoped for by the South.

The report continued by noting that:

> A network of relationships has been built up among private entities – banks, investment houses, transnational companies – in the leading developed countries. This has served to strengthen the

> influence of decisions made by private bodies on world economic activity and to that extent to limit the effectiveness of governmental policy decisions. For the South the result is even further marginalization and greater powerlessness.

'By the late 1980s', the report continued, 'it could be seen that the achievements of the South during that period [of independence] had not fundamentally changed the status of most Third World countries in relation to the world economic system. They remained poor, subordinate and powerless.'[1]

The human consequences of this state of affairs are staggering, with increasing inequality between rich and poor an important indicator. The richest fifth of the world's population account for 84.7 per cent of world gross national product (GNP), while the poorest fifth have only 1.4 per cent;[2] the richest ten people in Britain have as much wealth as 23 poor countries with 174 million people.[3] Indeed, estimates suggest that inequalities have massively increased in the past centuries. In 1750, GNP per head is estimated to be around the same in North and South; now it is around 60 times higher in the North.[4]

The current era is in many ways one of the grossest exploitation, perhaps on an unprecedented scale. The barriers to Northern commercial penetration of the Third World are virtually as negligible now as under colonialism, as Third World economic policies (through SAPs), their trading environment (through the WTO) and investment regulations (through the proposed Multilateral Agreement on Investment) are brought under the de facto control of the North and its elite Southern allies. While Northern countries preach so-called 'free trade', Northern trade protectionism costs developing countries around $500 billion a year in lost income.[5] It is only a few years since UNICEF (the United Nation's Children's Fund) noted that half a million children a year were dying from Third World attempts to meet debt repayments. The debt crisis has actually intensified with the total debt of developing countries (at around $2 trillion) increasing – though this is a crisis only for Third World countries, not Northern banks, therefore the issue is currently being addressed without any urgency and with extremely limited debt relief proposals on the international agenda. Recent years have witnessed, in much of the Third World, but especially Africa, a reversal of the gains made since independence. The UN Economic Commission for Africa, for example, has noted that 'Africa may begin the next millennium with a greater proportion of its population being illiterate and unskilled than it did at the beginning of the post-independence era in the 1960s'.[6]

A UN report of 1994 worth consulting at length highlights the links between the processes causing poverty in the South and in the North, noting:

> We live at a time when the vast majority of people around the world are being integrated into a single global economy and culture, organised around the principles of individualism, liberal democracy and faith in the market. This is a revolutionary development, comparable in scope to the industrial revolution of the late eighteenth and early nineteenth centuries, and in many ways a logical extension of that process.

It continued by noting that 'increasing reliance on a liberalisation of markets has profoundly altered the economic and political context for social integration'. This:

> has contributed to major changes in the configuration of power relations among different social groups and countries. For instance, it seems clear that the organised working class has been greatly weakened, while transnational enterprises, owners of capital and some managerial and professional groups have been significantly strengthened.

Economic liberalisation 'has also driven down wages and contributed to increases in unemployment, poverty and inequalities'. 'Recent years have been marked by a clear trend towards intensification of poverty and inequality in most regions of the world', in which 'in general, the global processes already outlined have played a central role'. 'Ironically', the report declares, 'the impoverishment of increasing numbers of people throughout the world – and often their growing inability to meet even the most basic requirements for food, water, shelter, education and medical attention – occurs during a period when the incomes of the very rich have risen markedly.'

The report notes that 'transnational enterprises are the predominant actors in the continuing process of global economic integration, controlling almost 75 per cent of all world trade in commodities, manufactured goods and services'. At the same time national governments, 'forced by liberalization and deregulation to strengthen the competitive position of their economies in the global arena, must ... increasingly adopt measures which attract foreign capital and which furthermore cheapen production for export'. This means 'a growing inability to protect the national industrial sector, to sustain wages at levels considered to be adequate by organised labour and to maintain social security provisions which symbolise the hard-won gains of working people'. In turn, the worldwide tendency is 'for national governments to lose their authority to regulate some of the most important variables in the national economy ... Governments are often perceived as having abdicated their responsibility to defend national projects, preferring to ally themselves with powerful foreign patrons than with their own political supporters.'[7]

It is instructive, therefore, that the reversal of gains made since independence in the South is occurring alongside a reversal of the gains made by people in the North in the postwar era.

## Return to the great empires

A hundred years ago British Colonial Secretary Joseph Chamberlain noted that 'the days are for great Empires, not little states'.[8] Recent years have witnessed the disappearance of one such empire – the Soviet, though not Russian, one – and the emergence of the undisputed reign supreme of those of the other Northern powers, their business corporations and the international financial institutions (such as the World Bank and the IMF) under their control. The world economy is firmly organised for the benefit of these empires, though disputes occur between them and between states and firms. The 'little states' of the modern era (but not only them), such as the Burundis or the Bosnias (or the East Timors and the Kurdistans), are the objects of the same processes of exploitation and impoverishment as in Chamberlain's day, with tremendous human consequences.

Current control is being exercised through a nexus of TNCs, multilateral banks and the trading regime of the WTO. The G7 states act as the global directorate; US Under-Secretary of State Joan Spero notes that 'our goal is to strengthen the G7 as a coordinating mechanism for the world economy'.[9] It has been argued that the only places where this control is not being exercised are where there are strong governments, where there is civil strife which has disrupted the economy or where religious fundamentalism is acting as a bulwark against imperialist forces.[10] An OECD report refers to 'the emergence of a tri-polar world'[11] from which these forces are controlled. Nobuo Matsunaga, Adviser to Japan's Minister for Foreign Affairs, poses the question: 'what kind of system is the most appropriate one in managing world affairs after the East–West confrontation is over?' He answers that what is required is 'policy consultation and coordination' among the 'three pillars of the global economy' –

Japan, the EU and North America. 'We should strengthen the trilateral policy consultation process for the management of global issues in the future', he adds.[12]

Michel Camdessus, the Managing Director of the IMF, suggests that the 'four pillars of the institutional structure of multilateral cooperation for global development' (that is, control by the Northern states) should be the IMF, the World Bank, GATT/WTO and the UN system. The division of labour is that 'structural and development policies' are the responsibility of the World Bank, trade policy of the GATT/WTO, 'humanitarian missions, human development and social policies more generally' the responsibility of the UN, and macroeconomic policy of the IMF.[13]

TNCs are the real power brokers in the world economy. Of the world's 100 largest economies, 50 are private companies; the aggregate sales of the world's 10 largest companies exceed the aggregate GNP of the world's 100 smallest countries.[14] S. P. Shukla notes that the G7 states 'have more or less transformed themselves into a kind of wider conglomerate of transnational corporations and the state. The representatives of these nation states have been functioning as lobbyists for their trade and industry. International finance capital is controlling their territories.'[15]

Prominent US development analyst David Korten states:

> The widespread image is one of the corporate titans of Japan, North America and Europe battling it out toe-to-toe in international markets. This image is increasingly a fiction that obscures the extent to which a few core corporations are strengthening their collective monopoly market power through joint ventures and strategic alliances with their major rivals ... The world's corporate giants are creating a system of managed competition by which they actively limit competition among themselves while encouraging intensive competition among the smaller firms and localities that constitute their periphery.[16]

This has little to do with classical free enterprise:

> Corporate libertarians regularly proclaim that central economic planning does not work and is contrary to the broader public interest. Yet successful corporations maintain more control over the economies defined by their product networks than the central planners in Moscow ever achieved over the Soviet economy.[17]

Korten's concept of 'corporate libertarianism' means that 'corporations have emerged as the dominant governance institutions on the planet'.[18] Noam Chomsky has called this 'corporate mercantilism', where 'governance is increasingly in the hands of huge private institutions and their representatives'.[19]

The increasing power of private financial flows is well recognised. In 1990, the *Wall Street Journal* noted that the US central bank 'has lost much of its control over US interest rates' and that 'gradually, its power is slipping away to markets in Tokyo and Frankfurt'.[20] The size and volatility of private capital flows reduces stability in the international monetary system. However, the emergence of sophisticated financial management techniques, such as hedging, is increasing the ability of private companies to insulate themselves from this volatility.[21] Companies may be able to protect themselves, therefore, but states and peoples will not.

The power of TNCs is evidenced in the WTO, basically a charter and blueprint for virtually unadulterated control of international trade and the economy by TNCs. S. P Shukla notes that:

> We have in WTO a virtual emergence of a World Parliament enacting international laws on matters which have remained under national jurisdiction so far ... the continuing erosion of the authority and jurisdiction of nation states will work largely and decisively against the interest of the large, silent, deprived majorities in the polities of developing countries, particularly those where there is a functioning democratic apparatus. The minority elites who constitute the ruling establishments in the Third World are the ones who are extending a warm welcome to WTO in the name of globalisation and integration with the world economy. For them, even a secondary or tertiary role in the new world order symbolised by WTO is a welcome prospect.[22]

For British Foreign Secretary Douglas Hurd, however, 'the GATT agreement [which established the WTO] was a great success'.[23] As the World Bank's Chief Economist notes, the completion of the Uruguay Round 'marks the end of the beginning of the critical process of integrating the developing countries into the global economy'.[24]

At root, the WTO is about opening up Southern economies to Northern commercial penetration. The *Financial Times* reported in July 1997, for example, that India was coming under 'intense international pressure to show more flexibility in dismantling tariff walls and accelerating its integration into the global economy'.

Northern states were insisting on the removal of Indian controls that 'would have satisfied their central demand of swift access to the Indian consumer market'. The US was reported to be considering taking the complaint to a WTO panel, 'which would almost certainly rule against India', the paper noted.[25]

India is a prime example of how policy making in the Third World has in recent years been effectively transferred to the World Bank and the WTO. Previously a hold-out to traditional reforms promoted in the South by the North, in the 1990s India has adopted World Bank-guided 'reforms'. Indian writer Smitu Kothari notes that 'India is now pursuing a development path that even at the level of rhetoric has abandoned the commitment to national self-sufficiency and global justice. Global capital and multilateral institutions in collaboration with Indian capital and the present regime are increasingly controlling the Indian economy.'[26]

Regional trade agreements perform a similar function. An OECD study notes that the Mexican government saw a major motivation for signing the NAFTA treaty with the US to 'lock in' its 'market-oriented economic policy reforms' to 'ensure that future Mexican governments have little scope to reverse' them. The study states that 'while those reforms have enabled Mexico to become a major exporter of manufactures, they have not so far raised the income of most Mexicans ... The reforms have in fact been accompanied by a stagnation of real wages since 1989.'[27]

Structural adjustment promoted by the World Bank and IMF, meanwhile, is 'no instant cure', according to IMF Managing Director Michel Camdessus, but a 'permanent discipline'. 'How encouraging it is', he notes, 'that so many developing countries and countries in transition have been freeing their trade and exchange systems within the framework of our structural adjustment programmes!'[28]

> Countries that are unable to participate in the expansion of world trade or attract significant amounts of private investment run the risk of being left behind by the global economy ... This raises the prospect of a widening gulf between countries that are able to take advantage of globalisation and those that are left by the wayside.[29]

Britain's former 'Development' Minister Lynda Chalker – in a series of speeches in 1990–91, when the markets of Eastern Europe were reopening after having been largely closed to Western capitalism for 45 years – noted that 'developing countries will have to face the reality that they are now in competition with the emerging democracies and private sectors of Eastern Europe for other financial flows and markets'.[30] A month earlier, she had said:

> If Africa is to prosper and get its fair share of investment it must offer terms that are at least as good as its competitors. Foreign investment will go to the countries which offer the best prospect of stability, which welcome enterprise and which give a fair rate of return with the right to repatriate a reasonable proportion of profits.[31]

The formerly walled-off Eastern Europe and the recalcitrant Third World states could now be brought into line. Jacques Attali, President of the European Bank for Reconstruction and Development – basically the World Bank for Eastern Europe – has stated that 'today in Europe we have a unique opportunity to develop an under-exploited landmass, rich in natural resources; a well-educated workforce and a vast market on the doorstep of the Single Market itself'.[32]

An advertisement in the *Japan Times* by the five Central American governments of Costa Rica, El Salvador, Nicaragua, Honduras and Guatemala, typified the climate elsewhere. The Honduran Ambassador noted that in his country 'foreign investment is most welcome and receives very competitive treatment and protection' thanks to 'the combination of high productivity and low costs'. 'The people of El Salvador', its Ambassador commented, also 'now offer good opportunities to new investors'. Costa Rica's contribution went under the headline: 'Attractive business climate'.[33]

One US official once advised: 'We must counter, both in the UN and within the framework of the North–South dialogue, any discussion of global problems which questions the validity of the free market and of free enterprise in the countries of the Third World.'[34] To the heads of the IMF and the World Bank this has indeed been achieved: 'throughout much of the developing world, a "silent revolution" has brought increasing acceptance of the benefits of financially disciplined and outwardly directed economic policies'.[35] The prospects have been summarised by a British merchant banker who, referring to African leaders, notes that 'they really only have one place to go now and that's the World Bank and the IMF and he who pays the piper calls the tune. They are going to have to conform to Western-style, capitalist, open-market philosophies, which is hugely exciting.'[36]

In this situation, overall control of the Third World remains a clear imperative. One reason is because of what development analyst Claude Ake called its 'nuisance potential'[37] – how global stability and the pursuit of Northern policies might be upset through developments such as mass migration, population growth or conflicts. However, a major interest remains controlling raw material supplies and markets, which contradicts the currently vogue idea that the Third World is marginal to the North now that the Cold War has ended.

The view that Africa's major importance to the West in the postwar period was due to its strategic relevance in the Cold War is largely mythological (although widely promoted now) and part of the establishment framework of thinking that provided a convenient background to forging close relations with dictatorships. In reality, Africa's major importance, like most of the rest of the Third World, is primarily economic, serving as a source of raw materials. This continuing imperative has been well described by leading development scholar Samir Amin, worth quoting at length:

> It is said that the Third World is becoming increasingly marginal in the world system, whether as a supplier of raw materials or as a market for exports ... True, the revolution of technology, on the one hand, and the quantity of mineral resources of the North American and Australian continents, on the other, have diminished for the time being the importance of the contributions of the Third World. But this does not mean that the Third World is now marginal. This fashionable idea is simply wrong. The relative decrease in its contribution is largely due to the depression – prevailing since 1970 – but there would be a revival in a new, sustained and long expansion. And though – thanks to the enormous strategic stockpiles of raw materials built up by the United States – there is no danger of serious shortages in case of localised conflicts, it is by no means evident that this situation can continue once a new strong expansion is under way. There is every chance of an all-out race for raw materials once again.[38]

Several new frontiers for raw materials are being opened up. One academic noted in 1991 in reference to South Africa that 'some of those in business anticipate a substantial post-apartheid dividend, in which the removal of sanctions will revive old markets and open up fresh opportunities'. South Africa's 'great mineral resources are an asset that should continue to attract trade and investment'.[39] Conflict over resources is likely to remain an important issue. Paul Rogers of the University of Bradford notes that 'the mineral wealth of Central and Southern Africa, the High Andes, Amazonia and Eastern Asia' are possible areas where 'there will be a tendency towards conflict over the political control of strategic resources'.[40] The US Defense Secretary Richard Cheney noted in 1993 the importance of such supplies by stating that 'failure by the Western nations to promote stability in Africa could result in disruption in the production and distribution of strategically important resources and could reduce access to facilities important to regional contingencies'.[41]

There would be nothing new about such 'resource wars' ('development wars'); this is what much of history has been about, including in the postwar era, though the motives were shrouded in notions of defending the free world from communism. Intra-Northern competition over these new frontiers, and other matters, is increasingly likely in the current era. This is, again, not a new phenomenon: Many of the events of the postwar era have been the result of such competition among Northern states – for example over oil in the Middle East and power status in international relations more generally.

## Preventing development

The historical and contemporary record clearly suggests, in my view, that the currently dominant Northern-promoted 'development' policies in the South – especially structural adjustment and the trading regime of the WTO – are intended to promote Northern interests specifically, and entail the prevention of the prospects for meaningful development and reduction of poverty in the Third World. These policies have in many ways succeeded in these terms, often by achieving outcomes that those who criticise them for 'failing' would cite as evidence for their case. Three points illustrate this.

First, a prescient analysis is that by UNCTAD, in an illuminating quote from its annual *Trade and Development Report*:

> The dramatic increase in the level of discipline accepted by developing countries through their acceptance of all the multilateral trade agreements resulting from the Uruguay Round and the binding of their tariff schedules has significantly reduced the flexibility of governments in the use of trade and domestic policy instruments. Consequently, *many WTO members will not be able to emulate the development strategies pursued successfully by many countries in the past* and will need to adapt to the constraints and opportunities of the new system.[42]

The policies currently advocated by the North to achieve development in the South bear little resemblance to more successful cases of postwar development. There are now numerous studies of the East Asia experience and how these policies radically departed from the current prescriptions of the World Bank.[43] Indeed, even mainstream commentators are able to note that policies in East Asia 'owe little or nothing to Bretton Woods institution adjustment programmes. Indeed, in important and well-known ways, most of them departed from [their] orthodoxies.'[44] The Vice-President of Japan's Ministry of International Trade and Industry has noted that, had Japan adopted 'free trade', 'it would almost permanently have been unable to break away from the Asian pattern of stagnation and poverty'.[45]

An especially illuminating analysis is by Ajit Singh, of Cambridge University, who concludes that 'the experience of the East Asian countries ... runs totally contrary to a central thesis of mainstream economics, namely that free, flexible, competitive internal and external markets are necessary for achieving fast, long-term economic growth'. Singh argues that the virtues of openness, international competition and close integration into the world economy urged by the World Bank 'were not in fact practised by either Japan or the Republic of Korea, the two most successful East Asian countries'. From the 1950s to the 1970s the Japanese economy 'operated under a regime of draconian import controls' and was 'far from being open or closely integrated into the world economy'. Other key policies – also heretical to World Bank orthodoxy – were a highly protected internal market, 'discouragement of foreign direct investment' and heavy government intervention 'in all spheres of the economy'.[46]

Second, it is also well documented that a strong role for the state has been central to development successes: yet its virtual dismantling has been urged in some cases of structural adjustment and in effect continues to be, despite recent posturing by the World Bank. The IMF has noted, albeit cautiously, drawing on the East Asia experience: 'there is an interpretation that suggests that an interventionist stance in the early stages of development may be a necessary first ingredient for success'.[47] One international report noted that in Eastern Europe 'the reform programme involved the dismantling of most of the administrative mechanisms by which an economy can be monitored and controlled by government'. Thus 'many of these countries allowed the power and authority of their central governments to decline to the point where they could no longer enforce conditions needed for operation of either a command economy or a free market system'.[48] World Bank policies of severely reducing the role of the state in key areas have thereby opened the economy to private enterprise (largely meaning TNCs) – its basic objective, thus further undermining national political sovereignty but increasing the control over the economy by private foreign forces ('integration into the world economy'). Since the state – and its ability to regulate the economy – offers the only barrier to Northern economic intervention in the Third World, undermining that, perhaps for good, offers a win–win strategy for the North. At the same time, Southern domestic elites have generally acquiesced in such liberalisation for their own benefit and self-interest.

Third, World Bank prescriptions also usually require major promotion of exports, usually meaning primary commodities. At the same time, it is well known that increasing such exports, especially when several countries do so simultaneously, is akin to economic suicide for developing countries since it both reinforces dependency on those commodities at the same time as forcing prices down.[49] A World Bank report from 1989 noted that countries undergoing adjustment programmes increased their exports but that the benefits of so doing were almost entirely wiped out by a deterioration in their terms of trade. Countries that were not undergoing adjustment did not increase their exports and experienced an improvement in their terms of trade.[50]

Some independent academics have also expounded the view that Northern strategy is essentially one of preventing development. For Susan George the debt crisis afforded the North an ideal opportunity to pursue Northern objectives and discipline the Third World: 'whichever way you slice it', she notes, 'the debt crisis turns out to be the best opportunity for neo-colonialist pursuits ever invented'. Heavily indebted countries' economies become closely controlled from outside either directly through subordinating productive investment to servicing debt or indirectly through growing foreign investment in key sectors. According to George, the North is therefore waging a Financial Low-Intensity Conflict (a corollary to Reaganite military Low-Intensity Conflicts against the South) which helps 'to prevent the Third World from posing a threat, from dictating its terms, from changing the political balance of forces in the world'. It also 'allows the North to keep a check upon any pretensions to real independence on the part of the South and to ensure privileged access to the South's resources, and to its industrial capacity, on the cheapest possible terms'.[51] It follows that, in this scheme of things, the North is not overly interested in seeing an end to the Third World's debt burden. Indeed, a consistent policy would be to ensure debt service continues to be paid but with no end ever in sight.

The evidence supports this view. It is hardly open to question that the purpose of IMF and World Bank policy – and an underlying purpose of SAPs – is to get Third World countries to repay their debts through creating a balance of payments surplus. Only favoured clients of the US – such as Egypt, as a result of its supportive policies during the Gulf War – have had their debts substantially reduced. Debt relief elsewhere is invariably dependent on countries pursuing structural adjustment: it has been long-standing British (and US World Bank) policy, for example, that 'debt conversion measures are much more likely to be open to countries that have a sound record of economic adjustment'. Debtors must pursue 'the right policy. This must be a prerequisite for access to further finance', the British Treasury once noted in what it called 'the market-based approach to debt reduction'. The task at hand is not one of substantially writing off debt but of 'managing the debt that remains'.[52]

This total debt burden is increasing each year, with only around a third of current debt levels being original debt.[53] Oxfam points out in a 1995 report that while Africa has paid out over $100 billion in debt payments since 1987, its debt level has risen by a quarter. It comments that 'Northern donors have been at pains to publicise the generosity of their debt forgiveness schemes, yet such schemes have at best slowed the rate of arrears accumulation'. The poorest countries (severely indebted poor income countries) have in recent years repaid three times more debt than they have had forgiven or reduced.[54] In 1995 the British government alone (that is, not banks) received £262 million in debt service from developing countries.[55]

It is worth recalling that the US and Britain bear special responsibility for the debt crisis not only because their policies significantly influence the international debt regime, but also because their domestic policies helped to create the crisis in the first place. Reagan and Thatcher's domestic economic policies were a direct cause of the sudden rise in interest rates in 1981–82, forcing up borrowing charges for Third World countries and precipitating the world debt crisis of 1982. Another consequence of the deflationary economic policies pursued by the US, Britain and other Western governments was the collapse of world commodity prices.[56]

US development expert David Korten sees the debt crisis of 1982 as providing 'the opportunity to address the threat of prospective new NICs'. Thus the World Bank and IMF 'moved to restructure the economies of the debt-burdened Southern countries to open them to penetration by foreign corporations' (that is, structural adjustment). For Korten the two aims of structural adjustment are, first, to ensure that loans are repaid and, second, 'to advance the integration of domestic economies into the global economy'.[57] According to Korten, if one measures the record of the World Bank and the IMF in terms of their contribution to improving lives, they have been dramatic failures. But 'in terms of fulfilling the mandates set for them by their original architects – advancing economic globalisation under the domination of the economically powerful – they have both been a resounding success'. Together, these institutions have 'removed most consequential legal and institutional barriers to the recolonisation of Southern economies by transnational capital'.[58] SAPs, far from being failures, can therefore be seen to be fundamentally successful since they have drastically reduced the role of the state, privatised and sold off – often to foreigners – assets previously controlled by the state, eliminated protectionist barriers and lightened restrictions on foreign investment, while countries have become more firmly integrated into the global economy.

Leading analyst Walden Bello, considering US foreign and economic policy more generally, similarly concludes that the US 'seeks to reinforce a set of global economic practices whose observance would favour the continued dominance of the status quo powers'. US policy is directed at:

> those development strategies in which the state – through planning, industrial targeting, protecting markets, favouring local investors or engaging in production itself – spearheads the process of development and makes 'catching up with the North' a real possibility. It aims, in fact, to make it very difficult for new Japans, new South Koreas and new Taiwans to emerge from the South.[59]

British 'development' priorities should thus be viewed in this light. Lynda Chalker, for example, stated:

> The Government helps to stimulate investment [by providing aid] ... by promoting economic reforms which create a more favourable climate for inward investment. Industry does not develop in a competitive way when shielded by protective tariffs and quota systems. We need to get the barriers down so that the right economic circumstances can be created. The conclusion of the GATT Uruguay Round and the flow-up work is an important and encouraging step.[60]

The rich have often greatly benefited from these policies. Egypt, for example, has followed IMF prescriptions and has experienced a great rise in poverty from the 1980s and the 1990s, with the number of millionaires rising substantially. One economist was quoted in the press as noting that 'the IMF's basic objective is to reduce the consumption of the poor, not the rich, because the rich save and invest'. The Egyptian elite is estimated to have a portfolio of $87 billion invested in the West.[61] In Zambia, the President of the Inter-American Development Bank has noted that 'the bulk of the costs of adjustment fell disproportionately on the middle and low-income groups, while the top five per cent of the population retained or, in some cases even increased its standard of living'.[62]

Evidence that SAPs have resulted in increasing poverty is now legion.[63] But even with the massive resources available to the World Bank, with a proclaimed goal of poverty reduction and development, by the early 1990s it was still the case that World Bank country poverty assessments 'did not sufficiently analyse the impact of specific macro-economic and sectoral policies on the poor'. In Gambia, which has been undergoing adjustment since 1984 and has averaged economic growth of 4 per cent per year, 'substantial inroads' had yet to be made into the country's 'existing low living standards'.[64] In 1994, the World Bank's Vice-President for Africa even noted that in sub-Saharan Africa the reduction in poverty which he claimed had been achieved was 'maybe not enough to write home about'.[65] Research also shows that money from IDA, the Bank's soft loan arm, much of which is supposed to go to poverty reduction in the poorest countries, fails to reach poor communities or actually harms them. The financing of large dams through such means provides some examples.[66]

The strategy of preventing development is intrinsically related to that of preventing political upheaval threatening the status quo, which may also be a motivation for providing official aid. Before becoming World Bank President, Robert McNamara noted that 'the wealthy and secure nations of the world' should 'open their eyes and act' against poverty 'if only to preserve their own immunity from the infection'.[67] This view explains much of the World Bank's shift towards the focus on poverty and 'basic needs' when McNamara became President. Development specialist Ben Wisner similarly notes that in the 1960s 'the failure of trickle-down and the successes of a kind of basic needs approach in China and the liberated zones of a number of countries undergoing revolutionary change (Vietnam and Mozambique, for example) meant that great masses of unemployed and impoverished people in the Third World might take to revolution unless something was done'.[68] Similar thinking underlay the World Bank's advice to Northern creditor nations in 1988 that they should revise their debt strategy towards the Third World to avoid the 'erosion of political support for national governments ... and the radicalisation of attitudes to debt servicing'.[69]

The current promotion of 'good governance', especially by the World Bank, should be seen in this light (as well as in the light of the US strategy of 'democracy promotion' considered in Chapter 2). 'Good government' is being emphasised at a time of an unprecedented attack on democracy around the globe in the context of economic globalisation. It is not a new concept: the 1837 House of Commons Committee on Aborigines considered it Britain's national duty to 'carry civilisation and humanity, peace and good government and, above all, the knowledge of the true God, to the uttermost ends of the earth'.[70] The concept is interesting:

First, the Bank, whose own internal structure is fundamentally undemocratic and reflects the interests of a handful of powerful states, is funded by taxpayers who are kept unaware of its policies. The British public, and also the Mother of all Parliaments, have virtually no scrutiny over public spending on the World Bank of £1 billion over the last five years.

Second, this structure leads to decisions routinely negotiated in secret with a few officials in Southern countries on behalf of whole populations who may be denied even basic information about them.

Third, these decisions then result in policies further undermining what little democratic policy sovereignty remains in the Southern country. In this context it is perhaps remarkable that the concept of 'good governance' can be given serious attention at all.

The IMF states in its official journal:

> The IMF has sometimes been criticised because important population groups that may be significantly affected by policy measures under adjustment programmes do not normally participate in the policy dialogue between the member country and the IMF. The IMF's working assumption is that because the social and economic goals of an adjustment programme reflect the realities and aspirations of the adjusting country, population groups with interests in particular issues should make their views known to their governments through domestic channels.[71]

On the latter point, it would be interesting to know how ordinary Nigerians, for example, can make their views known to the government and have any impact (and stay alive). But the statement also confirms the policy of working through elites as standard practice. At the same time as admitting that 'important population groups' have no say, the IMF notes that adjustment reflects the 'realities and aspirations of the adjusting country'. The reality is that only the elites are consulted and these people are synonymous with 'the country'. Expressing an apparently similar view, World Bank Vice-President for Africa, Edward Jaycox, once noted that 'we don't impose a lot of conditionality. What we do is provide the ammunition and support for the tiny minority that starts a reform process.'[72] This basically accords with what is meant by 'good governance' and it is only, essentially, for these minority elites that the international economy is organised.

## Deciphering reality

Three key myths are, in my view, common to current discussions on development. The first is that the leading Northern powers – especially the United States and Britain, the two main objects of analysis here – fundamentally pursue (and are interested in, as a matter of high policy) meaningful development and the reduction of poverty in the Third World. It is amazing how such good faith is routinely ascribed to powerful institutions. This myth is rarely explicitly outlined in analyses but usually forms an implicit basic assumption. It does not preclude some criticism of current policies, or presenting evidence of how those policies occasionally can even exacerbate poverty, but it does this in the context of 'failed' or 'mistaken' strategies. The logic of this view points to supporting concepts such as the current possibility of meaningful 'development cooperation' between North and South, the need modestly to improve overseas aid programmes and calls for greater Northern engagement in the South based largely, again, on good faith in the policies of the powerful. Overall, this view is consistent with calls for improving and changing existing policies essentially within the current system, involving few changes in the structure of international power.

Related to this is the widespread acceptance (usually implicit) of the view that the policies promoted by the two key international financial institutions, the World Bank and the IMF, are seriously intended to promote (even if they do not always achieve) meaningful development and the reduction of poverty. There are currently three main views on World Bank/IMF SAPs, the dominant economic policy in the Third World. Proponents of SAPs argue that they have 'worked' in the sense of achieving economic growth and laying the groundwork for poverty reduction. Critics argue that they have 'failed' and have increased poverty and not even sometimes achieved the stated objective of growth. There are also many commentators in between these two parameters who believe that some SAPs have 'failed' and some 'worked'. Yet few analysts try to explore critically what the actual aims of such policies are, or question whether the professed goals are genuine, within a setting that outlines the fundamental priorities of the Bank's major shareholders – such as the US and Britain. Few therefore question whether such 'failures' of policies are actually sometimes successes when viewed through a different lens. In the 'failure' school, it is remarkable how publicly stated World Bank policy intentions are taken seriously, even if criticised. Unless the interests and motivations of the World Bank and others are exposed and studied for what they are, their overall framework of analysis is likely to continue to be the subject of good faith and set the parameters of the debate.

The second myth is the view that, given widespread poverty in the Third World, greater (improved) Northern involvement in the South is to be recommended. Thus aid volumes should be increased, or 'humanitarian interventions' undertaken, or improved SAPs devised (with Northern experts). Underlying this view is belief in the basic Northern interest in the reduction of poverty. The analysis above rejects this view and infers that the general withdrawal of the leading Northern states from the Third World would be more in the latter's interests than a greater involvement.

The third myth concerns the existence of a propaganda system in the media and academia which obscures the reality of poverty and the policies of those responsible for it. It goes without saying that Northern governments and international financial institutions (IFIs) do not recognise this system, yet the same is the case with academia. I am not aware of a single study in development academia which critically examines, or even recognises, this system, although it is easily documented. Most NGOs are little better – they recognise that the media is not on their side in the sense that it is difficult to get their (usually only mildly critical) stories of current policy published. But even though such a system severely obstructs their goals, none have provided any evidence that they are aware of the extent of media and academic complicity in the dominant 'development' agenda or its function as a *system*, partly perhaps since many NGOs, unwittingly or wittingly, are part of it; indeed, actively promote it.

The area of disinformation is probably the most underanalysed of all aspects of development – unsurprisingly since, simply, the huge majority of commentators fall within that propaganda system. It is so pervasive that an attempt will not be made to do justice to it here, but to provide some examples.

The common view that the North promotes 'free markets' has provided an important ideological pillar to its system of control. The so-called free market hardly exists in Northern domestic societies, where states – especially in the non-English-speaking countries, where social gains have been greater – play significantly interventionist roles in the economy as well as in social welfare provision. The trend towards mergers and acquisitions, rather than the encouragement of competitive markets, is also current evidence of this. Disinterest in 'market solutions' is also clearly seen in subsidies to agriculture: virtually the entire agricultural system of the Northern hemisphere is subsidised, by the EU's Common Agricultural Policy and similar support systems in North America. Total government aid in the EU amounted to £73 billion in 1993–94, half of which went to the manufacturing sector.[73]

This state of affairs coexists with severe Northern pressure to force Southern economies to 'liberalise' and dismantle state support to agriculture. 'The industrial countries have long aimed at agricultural self-sufficiency', the UNDP has noted, something now barred to the Third World.[74] Further, the international 'market' in almost all major commodities – such as beverages, minerals and grains – is controlled by a handful of Northern TNCs. The 'free market' really means Northern oligopoly or monopoly, both domestically and internationally. As a 1992 OECD study concluded: 'Oligopolistic competition and strategic interaction among firms and governments rather than the invisible hand of market forces condition today's competitive advantage and international division of labour in high technology industries' and, one might add, most others.[75]

The conventional belief that the North is pursuing 'free trade' is at odds with the policy of maintaining protectionist barriers against imports from the South (although Britain in particular has been a chief advocate of lowering these barriers). The cost to developing countries of unequal access to global markets of a staggering $500 billion has already been mentioned.[76] Free trade is understood to involve the South opening up its economies to the North – in the first seven years after the launch of the Uruguay Round, developing countries were responsible for 58 of the 72 autonomous liberalisation actions reported to the GATT.[77]

According to Indian analyst and activist Vandana Shiva, 'free trade offers precisely the opposite – freedom from social accountability and responsibility'.[78] Martin Khor, of the Third World Network, notes that free trade means:

> the vastly expanded freedom and powers of transnational corporations to trade and invest in most countries of the world, whilst correspondingly governments now have significantly reduced powers to restrict their operations; and at the same time, these corporations have 'freedom' from potential new competitors whose possibilities to develop technologically are now curbed by intellectual property provisions in TRIPS.[79]

Imperial historian Lawrence James notes that 'Britain's conversion to free trade in the 1840s ... coincided with a determined effort to open up new markets'. In this scramble for new markets, it was inevitable that British merchants would face local opposition and thus it was necessary for British governments to teach the rulers of such countries where their duty lay, including by the use of naval force. Foreign Secretary Lord Palmerston noted in 1895 that some 'half-civilised governments' 'all require a dressing down every eight or ten years to keep them in order'. Britain's 'anti-piracy' operations were, James notes, 'part of a wider effort to break into Far Eastern markets during the 1840s and 1850s'.[80] The WTO rules perform similar functions today.

'Population control' is now usually referred to in the more politically correct language of 'reproductive choice', 'family planning' or 'children by choice' (the latter phrase is that of Britain's Department for International Development). Past US policy in this area is evidenced in a declassified report which was adopted as national security policy in 1975 following preparation by the Departments of State, Defense and Agriculture and the CIA. One concern was the radicalisation of the Third World where 'younger people – who are more prevalent in high-fertility populations – can more readily be persuaded to attack such targets as multinational corporations'. Another problem concerned some Third World countries such as Bangladesh, 'whose positions on international issues will be likely to become radicalised ... as its problems grow ... inevitably in opposition to US interests'. It might then 'advocate a better distribution of the world's wealth'. The report also noted:

> In the absence of slow or zero population growth, concessions to foreign companies are likely to be expropriated or subject to arbitrary intervention. Whether through government action, labour conflicts, sabotage, civil disturbance, the smooth flow of needed materials will be jeopardised.

To prevent this, assistance for family planning and health was stepped up and integrated into the aid programme and foreign policy to 'help the US contend with the ideological charge that it is more interested in curbing the population of the Less Developed Countries than their future and well-being'.[81]

Considering briefly some examples of how official policies are supported by mainstream academia and the media, a standard role for academics is to parrot uncritically governments' allegedly benign intentions. For example, Peter Byrd, an analyst of British foreign policy from the University of Warwick, writes on the goals of the British government's aid programme:

> General political goals include the promotion of human rights, the promotion of democracy at the expense of non-democratic regimes (with a particular emphasis on communist-inclined non-democratic regimes) and the promotion of stable regional balances of power in order to minimise the risk of uncertainty which could threaten British economic interests.[82]

Another standard formulation, shared by the entire establishment spectrum, is that the Cold War made the West prop up appalling regimes. 'Human rights, sound economies and democratic policies came second to strategic advantage', the *Daily Telegraph* states. Now, the view goes, 'the cold war over, industrialised nations are taking a more "moralistic" view of Africa's performance. They can demand economic reforms and more democratic policies in return for aid.'[83] In reality however, the Cold War provided a cover for the West's pursuit of traditional policies in Africa, especially control over important raw material supplies, by allying with favoured elites. Now that the Cold War is over, with the Soviet Union and alternative models no longer available, this policy can be pursued largely without hindrance. Note how establishment formulation always accords benevolence to Western policy.

The *Independent* notes that 'the fact that every single government south of the Sahara has had to make some concessions to multi-party democracy is proof of the power of Western countries in Africa'. Then it notes that 'led by the United States, they have forced Africa to adopt free market economics and to hold real elections'.[84] That embracing 'free market economics' is a cause for celebration is surely an interesting notion for Africans who, as a result, have in recent years endured a rise in poverty and the virtual destruction of their social service systems. The *Independent* has also weighed in on the side of the greatness of British aid. In an editorial in 1995 it noted that British aid projects had 'improved enormously' over the last decade, were more efficient than the programmes of the EU, World Bank and UN

– which were subjected to 'political correctness and penchant for grandiose projects', something which Britain would presumably not entertain – and now British aid helps 'the poor to stand on their own feet'. Aid is now more important and 'there is a moral imperative upon those of us who are comparatively wealthy to help those who are so abjectly poor'.[85] Indeed there is, perhaps comparable to the moral imperative of communicating the actual reality of British policy – including on aid – to the public.

At the helm of Britain's aid programme, meanwhile, was previously a Minister who 'has turned the ODA from an instrument of Foreign Office policy to an aid agency in its own right', *The Economist*'s Richard Dowden writes. 'Out of the unrelenting ghastliness of Rwanda', he writes, 'has emerged one success story.' This is the 'British disaster relief operation' which, we are informed, was tried out in Iraq, developed in Bosnia and 'delivered in Rwanda'. 'The surge of concern in Britain', Dowden notes, 'pushed the government into greater involvement than British interests and historical connections might have merited.' Another element to the British relief system is 'the British armed forces' who 'are looking for a role and certain units are admirably suited to working in disaster zones'.[86]

A nice view was written by Ross Clark, in the *Sunday Telegraph* under the heading 'rights are wrong':

> The reason Western nations are richer than Third World ones is that their populations have been more effective in their efforts to create wealth. If the United Nations wishes to eradicate poverty, it ought to encourage poor nations to emulate rich ones, not pretend that the poor are having their human rights violated ... To repackage morality in a passive form and say that all men have a right to live and a right to eat is unnecessary and misleading. It leads people to expect others to pander to their needs.[87]

One of the media's failures is in *not* detailing the priorities and policies of Northern governments. Many policies are simply never reported. The British role in systematically exploiting the Third World is simply never mentioned. Public relations statements are invariably reported uncritically. Other aspects of propaganda are regularly promoted: seeing aid as an act of generosity; simply ignoring everyday mass poverty in the South; and seeing Northern-promoted 'development' programmes as technical solutions rather than as part of a political agenda.

If we take an independent look at current and past policies I believe a fairly clear picture emerges of the actual international development system. The basic *nature* of the system is that it is essentially controlled by, and organised in the interests of the leading Northern states, the transnational corporations based there (who are partly autonomous) and allied Southern elites (governments, business elites, the military). The framework of this system was soon established following the Second World War and marked above all by the dominant role of US foreign policy – a subject usually considered to be outside the scope of proper development studies. Since then the system has undergone some changes, notably the rise of other Northern actors, the NICs and the even more entrenched role of private corporations. Essentially, however, the overall structure of the system – if not the relative power of the actors within it – has changed remarkably little.

The fundamental *aim* of the most powerful Northern states and their allies has been clearly outlined in the planning documents of the postwar period: control over the international economy and the world's economically most important regions, including raw material supplies and markets, in a system which benefits their business elites and confers great power status, having the effect of subordinating the people and resources of the Third World to these basic priorities. The poor are also expected to bear the main burden of adjustment to global crises in the system such as low commodity prices, the debt crisis and devaluations. Such policies are pursued consciously, as the record – outlined above – shows.

The *means* by which the North attempts to achieve this aim include foreign policies (including military intervention and covert action, military training, arms exports and aid programmes) and the use of multilateral instruments largely under its control (especially the World Bank). The Northern public is, as noted in the previous section, expected to pay for these policies, including in subsidies to domestic business through the aid programme and by subsidising the creation of favourable investment climates in the South through World Bank/IMF-promoted SAPs.

The *threats* (or limits) to such a system have been principally nationalist movements in the Third World, often popular and democratic forces whose goals have been to secure resources for domestic use, thus confronting basic Northern policy. Currently, a more prominent role is played by independent civil society organisations who have the ability to garner significant public opposition to these policies and to construct alternatives. Another major threat has been the publics of these states themselves, who wield considerable power as consumers of Third World goods and protesters against immoral policies. The propaganda system plays a crucial role in shrouding the reality of policy from the public, thus severely restricting the latter's role.

The *pretext* for pursuing such policies was formerly the 'Soviet threat' – a reality, but often a minor one which obscured the primary threat of indigenous nationalism – which provided the standard official reason for intervention (military or otherwise) in the affairs of the Third World. Currently a variety of newer issues – drug trafficking, Islamic fundamentalism, the principled need to stand up to aggression – serve as pretexts for implementing the standard policies. The most effective current pretext is the existence of poverty and the failure of development itself – thus it is on this basis that SAPs, which promote the same basic Western policies as throughout the postwar period, have been promoted.

The *basic theme* of the system is a conflict not between East and West (as was assumed during the Cold War) nor between North and South (regarded as dominant in many development circles) but between rich and poor, and the powerful and the powerless, with both existing in North and South. The chief *consequence* is plain: the maintenance and deepening of poverty and insecurity in the North as well as South within a fundamentally unjust order. This conflict is increasing in the current era, with potential crisis implications even for those who hitherto believed they could wall themselves off from the poor majority and the implications of their policies.

# Part III

# The Middle East

# 5

# Controlling the Modern Middle East

The Middle East has in many senses been the fulcrum of world politics since the end of the Second World War. Oil's function as the world's most important commodity, the Arab–Israeli conflict and the powerful influence exerted over the region by the Western states – primarily the United States and Britain – have ensured that Middle Eastern affairs have been internationalised. The largest array of weaponry deployed in the 1990s has also occurred in the Middle East, during the war against Iraq in 1991. Many of the key aspects of current international affairs are more relevant to the Middle East than any other region – such as Islamic radicalism, nuclear proliferation and Western military planning for intervention. In short, making sense of international affairs in the 1990s – and especially the general foreign policies and priorities of Britain and the United States – requires close consideration of the Middle East. Moreover, understanding the roots of some of the everyday horrors in parts of the Middle East – human rights abuses, repression, poverty – requires an understanding of past and present US and British policy in the region since they share considerable responsibility for them.

## The need for control

The basic issue – of long-standing concern to the US and Britain – has been one of preserving the current order in the region and ensuring that major regional developments proceed within an overall Western framework of control. This is effected either directly through their own military power or through favoured regional clients and has taken place under several different US doctrines – the Eisenhower Doctrine, the Carter Doctrine and what one US energy analyst has called, in the light of the war against Iraq, the Bush Doctrine: 'pledging defence assistance to oil-rich conservative regimes against any force that threatens them'.[1] Both the Eisenhower and Carter Doctrines were justified as responses to the 'Soviet threat', but the real issue, however, has been control of oil.

In the first half of the postwar period – when Western oil companies produced and largely owned the oil resources in various Middle Eastern states – the aim was to maintain direct control of the production of that oil. This requirement led to military interventions and the sponsorship of various coups. In the second half of the period – as Middle Eastern regimes gradually displaced the oil companies and took over the production of oil themselves – the Western aim has been to maintain control over the non-production aspects of the oil industry and to ensure close relations with the main producers. In both periods, effective control of the world economy has been at stake, as has the issue of oil revenues, where the aim has been to ensure that the massive profits accruing to the Middle Eastern oil regimes are invested in the West. One of the threats of nationalism – recognised in the planning documents as always being much more important than communism in the region – was that such revenues would be directed towards the (impoverished) populations of the Middle Eastern countries themselves. Saudi Arabia invests 80 per cent of its oil revenues in the United States and, in the early 1990s, Saudi investment in the US and Western Europe was estimated at $200 billion.[2] As Iraq was occupying Kuwait in August 1990, it was estimated that Western banks owed Kuwait $8 billion and had $17.6 billion in Kuwaiti deposits.[3] A corollary is that the Gulf states have failed to invest the windfall from oil in the region – a World Bank study showed that only 5 per cent of the financial surplus of the oil-rich countries was invested in the region.[4] The West's regional clients understand these priorities and pursue them in their own interests but also as the local managers of resources under effective Western supervision.

The need to maintain control over Middle Eastern oil resources is usually described in public by Western leaders, as during the 1991 war against Iraq, as the need to maintain 'access' to that oil. However, a 1959 memorandum to the Director of the CIA outlined the real concern, stating:

> A change, gradual or sudden, in Kuwait's government will not necessarily threaten Western access to Kuwaiti oil. Even if nationalist-reformist elements gained full power, or if Kuwait fell wholly under UAR [United Arab Republic – comprising Syria and Egypt] hegemony, those in control would continue to want Western markets for the oil. However, *Western control over, and profits from, oil production would be reduced*, and eventually some form of nationalization would be likely.[5]

The danger posed by large segments of oil being under the control of a single Middle Eastern government was promoted during discussion of the 1991 Gulf War. The US State Department noted in 1962 that it would be 'undesirable to have oil resources of Kuwait and Iraq or Kuwait and Saudi Arabia under sway of any single government [sic]'. The reason was that the maintenance of 'Kuwait's independent status' was the 'best means of preserving Western stakes in this important segment of ME [Middle Eastern] oil'.[6] Preserving Kuwait has therefore always been bound up with effective Western control of the Middle East, a point masked during the 1991 war by professions about 'sovereignty', maintaining international law and standing up to aggression.

'We must at all costs maintain control of this oil', British Foreign Secretary Selwyn Lloyd noted in a letter to the US Secretary of State in 1956, referring to the Gulf states 'with which we have special relations'.[7] This reflected the US view, outlined in 1945:

> Our petroleum policy toward the United Kingdom is predicated upon a mutual recognition of a very extensive joint interest and upon a control, at least for the moment, of the great bulk of the free petroleum resources of the world ... Recognising these realities, it is the view of the United States government that US–UK agreement upon a broad, forward-looking pattern for the development and utilization of petroleum resources under the control of nationals of the two countries is of the highest strategic and commercial importance.[8]

'Control of this source of energy, important in peace and war, is a desirable goal in itself', the State Department declared in 1950. Added benefits were that 'oil operations of US companies in the area familiarizes [sic] large number of US technicians with strategic minerals in a strategic area; area intelligence is consequently excellent'. It was also recognised that 'oil companies are instrumental and can be more instrumental in contributing to the attainment of overall US policy objectives for the area'.[9]

Both collusion and rivalry between the Western powers marked their policies. In 1947, for example, Foreign Secretary Bevin proposed to the US a review of the situation in the Middle East 'for the purpose of arriving at a gentleman's understanding in regard to a common policy and joint responsibility throughout the area'.[10] The US State Department declared that 'the cornerstone of our thinking is to maintain the British position in the Middle East area to the greatest possible extent'.[11] This joint interest posed some public relations difficulties and one US government report noted the need 'to minimize publicity of Anglo-American collusion on oil in the Middle East while at the same time avoiding Anglo-American conflicts over oil, ie, no oil publicity mentioning the US and UK together'.[12]

However, Bevin's proposal to the US government for a 'gentleman's understanding' in the region was accompanied by the need, expressed in a purely British meeting, to 'keep the Middle East predominantly a British sphere and to exclude the United States militarily from the area'.[13] This rivalry and competition continued throughout the postwar period, most notably in the 1953 coup in Iran (leading to increased US involvement in Iranian oil production) and the failed 1956 British invasion of Egypt (which undermined the general British position in the Middle East and which the US refused to support). Collusion and competition continue into the present day: collusion in terms of working together to secure primary interests, as in the war against Iraq; and competition over, for example, arms markets.

A recurrent view of US and British planners was that of oil as a 'prize'. To give some examples:

> The oil of Saudi Arabia constitutes one of the world's greatest prizes ... (US Secretary of State, Cordell Hull, 1943)[14]

> ... this rich prize for American interests ... (Iranian oil: US Chargé d'Affaires in Iran, Richard Ford, 1944)[15]

> The oil in this region is the greatest single prize in all history ... (US Oilman Everette Lee DeGolyer, 1944)[16]

> ... a vital prize for any power interested in world influence or domination ... (Middle East: UK government memorandum, 1947)[17]

> ... probably the richest economic prize in the world in the field of foreign investment ... (US government official, 1948)[18]

> ... the biggest prize in the world ... (Middle Eastern oil: British Prime Minister Harold Macmillan, 1957)[19]

Western policies are only one of the major factors that explain conditions in the Middle East, but the pursuit of fundamental Western priorities – both in the region and globally – has significantly influenced the shape of Middle Eastern politics. The horrors of Western policy in the region are well understood and documented in the declassified planning record. The perspective from the 1940s, expressed in one Foreign Office memorandum, was: 'the untrammelled and outrageous exploitation of the workers by the capitalists throughout the Middle East area makes anyone from Europe astonished that the whole working class is not Communist'.[20] Similarly, a US government special representative in the Middle East stated that he associated the British presence there with 'the principles of imperialism, monopoly and exploitation'.[21]

The US State Department viewed British policy in the region through a similar lens by 1947. The long-time British protectorates (colonies in all but name) of Kuwait, Qatar, Muscat and Oman were 'so primitive that any industrial development in these areas, other than the development of oil, will have to wait for some time'. The State Department continued by correctly noting that 'it was long the British policy to keep the people flanking the sea route to India in a state of primitive economy'.[22] British planners correctly recognised in a top secret paper, also of 1947, that 'it cannot be pretended that our original motives in going to the Middle East were particularly noble and altruistic'.[23] One can only wonder with what similar lucidity about the effect of their policies, current planners are pursuing fundamental interests in the Middle East.

Straightforward racism also plays a part in facilitating the exercise of Western control over the region and the British documentary record is illuminating in this regard. 'A primitive mind finds it easier to embrace Islam with its five simple duties, one of which offers the fun and excitement and community feeling of the pilgrimage', the British Ambassador to Iran wrote to the Foreign Secretary in 1946.[24] Similarly, another official from the Teheran Embassy noted in 1952 that '99% of the Persian populace are mentally thorough-going asiatics – that is, what they understand most clearly is force and success. They have practically no social consciousness.'[25] Britain's special envoy to Beirut gave an illuminating picture of the people of the Middle East:

> Self-indulgence, heartlessness, complete indifference to social evils ... and a total incapacity to plan and execute, characterise the people. Owing to some defect of mental equipment, they are unable to see more than is immediately before them ... Their minds are fixed on the immediate present, though certain lobes of the brain are reserved for producing materialistic hallucinations of other worlds, including the hereafter.

Middle Easterners also demonstrated 'susceptibility to excitement and passion', while 'logic means nothing'.[26]

In similar vein, British planners also stated at various times that the Turks were 'backward and barbarous', the Egyptians were 'essentially a cowardly and underbred race', the Iraqis were 'crude, coarse and over-bearing'; and finally there were the 'fickle, self-seeking, hypocritical Syrians'.[27]

## The post-Gulf War era

The current order in the Middle East has arisen partly out of the most significant recent event in the region – the 1991 Gulf War. The war and its consequences are now favourable to the pursuit of Western policy in a number of senses. Indeed, the level of structural control over the region now exercised by the United States (and through its allies in the region) is in some ways greater than at any stage certainly over the past 20 years, and possibly throughout the entire postwar era. A number of points bear this out. First, the state that was previously an ally and that became an enemy on 2 August 1990 – the date of its invasion of Kuwait – was militarily defeated and its infrastructure largely destroyed, removing an immediate obstacle to Western control over the region.

Second, the war reinforced the dependency of the Gulf states on the West. Thus, the West has re-secured effective control over the defence policies of the Gulf states for the first time since the smaller Gulf states became independent from Britain in 1971. Saudi Arabia – the biggest single prize of all – is now also included into the bargain. Thus the (largely) Western military intervention of 1991 achieved the same basic end as the British one of 1961 in Kuwait (which was conducted ostensibly to defend Kuwait from Iraqi attack): reasserting Western power in the region and demonstrating the need for reliance on the West. Indeed, the Western military intervention of 1990–91 undermined the prospects for a regional solution and the ability of regional states and organisations to play a more meaningful role in the region's affairs.[28]

The British intervention in Kuwait in 1961 performed a similar function. Mustafa Alani, who has written an extensive account of the crisis, notes that in the days from when the Iraqi leader claimed Kuwait to the British intervention, there was 'intensive inter-Arab diplomatic activity, aimed at defusing the Iraq–Kuwait crisis and achieving a lasting political settlement'. Three separate initiatives were launched in the hope of reaching a settlement – by the Arab League and by the governments of Lebanon and Saudi Arabia – all three of which were scuppered by the landing of British troops. Alani, noting the 'threat of an "Arab solution"', states that 'there was a race between the British government's efforts to give the Iraq–Kuwait dispute the appearance of a military confrontation' and Arab efforts 'to keep the dispute within a political context and stress the possibility of solving it by political means'. The problem from the British perspective was that such Arab efforts 'might succeed in achieving a sort of political settlement by which Britain could be isolated and its interests undermined'.[29]

Third, US influence over the oil policy of the most important state – Saudi Arabia – has increased. According to oil expert Peter Odell, there are currently 'high prospects for the international expansion of the American oil corporations' and there is 'a particular opportunity which stands out above all others as a joint function of American foreign policy and the collaborative role of the major American oil companies'. This prospect is 'the emerging geopolitical reality of a long-term United States–Saudi Arabian compact in which the oil component is a central element'. This compact has been formed largely by Saudi reliance on US military power for protection more or less in return for oil pricing and production policies favourable to the US. Odell notes that 'the American–Saudi entente will effectively upstage OPEC [Organisation of Petroleum Exporting Countries], whose other members will become virtually powerless to influence prices as long as the United States and Saudi Arabia remain committed to current price levels'. Expansion of the oil industry will be put on hold and when development does go ahead, Odell notes that 'it will have to be in the context of the parameters established by the United States and Saudi Arabia for the evolution of the international oil market'. Odell concludes by noting:

> After three decades during which American companies' domination of international oil was undermined and, indeed, almost eliminated, the wheel of fortune now seems set to come full circle. The American hegemony within the industry is being reestablished. The essential involvement of Saudi Arabia in an alliance of strong political and commercial interests with respect to international oil could well prove as powerful set of forces as those which had previously established effective and long-lived systems in the world oil industry ... If so, then it could be well into the twenty-first century before the newly emerging structure comes under serious threat.[30]

The fourth major effect favourable to the United States is the consequent reduced ability of regional states and the international community to impose policies on Israel unless validated by the US. The Middle East 'peace process' has been conventionally viewed as ripe for progress in a post-Cold War world. But more reasonable is the view that, with the US now the undisputed controlling power and the Arab states having been in disarray throughout the 1991 Gulf crisis, the US and Israel are in a better position to secure their regional goals (discussed below) in the 'peace process', therefore it can proceed largely upon US–Israeli terms. Indeed, a key change in the post-Gulf War period has been the even greater disciplining of the Gulf states to accept the US order in the region as it affects Israel. The *Guardian*, for example, reports that 'Kuwait, which of all the Gulf countries used to pride itself on being the most active supporter of "Arab causes", has now taken the lead in staking out positions in Israel's favour.' The reason, the report notes, is 'because of Kuwait's growing reliance on non-Arab protection'.[31] Kuwait's mass expulsion of Palestinians following the war was perhaps another aspect of the new stance.

There are, however, also downsides to the current order in the Middle East from the perspective of Western planners. The barriers to Western control over the region are described in the propaganda system as 'threats', often to 'security interests'. Iran is such a threat principally since it does not accept the current 'security' order in the Gulf, defined by the West and its Gulf allies. The post-Gulf War period has increased Iran's relative power by undermining that of Iraq, Iran's chief rival. Much of Western policy towards Iraq, of course, has been informed by concerns about Iran – the policy during the 1991 war was to leave intact part of Iraq's military both to retain a counterweight to Iran as well as to allow the crushing of Kurdish separatism in Iraq, from which Iran might also benefit.

'Islamic fundamentalists' are also a threat, to be understood as Islamic forces that are not supportive of Western policies, in contrast to 'moderate' or 'conservative' forces, which are (even though the latter may be just as 'fundamentalist'). 'Islamic fundamentalism' is the latest in a long line of postwar 'threats' to Western interests in the Middle East. The first was Arab nationalism, represented above all by Egyptian leader Gamal Abdel Nasser from the 1950s; the second was the 'oil sheikhs' following the 1973 oil price rises. Saddam Hussein, previously a 'moderate', became the 'new Hitler' in the 1990s, but 'Islamic fundamentalism' is the current principle generic 'threat'. Dan Smith, a scholar with the Transnational Institute, has noted correctly that problems such as the proliferation of long-range missiles, chemical warfare capability and, perhaps eventually, nuclear weapons 'are real threats not to Europe and its people, for they provide no capacity to invade, conquer or even merely bully Europe, but to Western efforts to control Middle Eastern politics'.[32] The 'threats' are easily changeable but the purpose and utility of them are consistent.

There is also a considerable downside to the current order from the perspective of virtually the whole of the rest of the world, and especially the people of the region itself. In a study of the Arab world after Desert Storm, Muhammad Faour writes that 'the Arab world is now perhaps a more dangerous place than it was before the war'. The Iraqi threat is gone 'but in its aftermath the remaining vestiges of regional cooperation seem to have been stripped away, leaving a region more dependent on external assistance and more inclined towards internal belligerence'. Peace is threatened by the resurrection of old disputes between states, while most Arab governments 'seem reluctant to offer their people more than token gestures of democracy'.[33] It was little surprise, therefore, that while Western elites celebrated in the euphoria of the post-Gulf War world, there was little cause for celebration in the Arab world itself, one of whose territories had been 'liberated'. While the Gulf commands vast material resources, with, as noted above, huge amounts invested in the Western banking system, the average adult literacy rate in the Arab states (52 per cent) is below that of sub-Saharan Africa, even though its real gross domestic product (GDP) per capita is over three times as great reflecting gross inequalities.[34]

## The Middle East system and the five pillars of policy

Western policy in the Middle East amounts to a system that, I believe, has been best summarised by Noam Chomsky. Chomsky first notes that Western control over the Middle East was delegated to what British imperial officials described in the early part of the twentieth century as an 'an Arab facade' of weak and pliable rulers, with 'absorption' of the colonies 'veiled by constitutional fictions as a protectorate, a sphere of influence, a buffer state, and so on'. Chomsky then continues by noting that:

> The Facade would consist of family dictatorships that do what they are told, and ensure the flow of profits to the United States, its British client and their energy corporations. They are to be protected by regional enforcers, preferably non-Arab (Turkey, Israel, Iran

> under the Shah, Pakistan). British and US muscle stand in reserve, with military bases from the Azores through North Africa to the Indian Ocean and the Pacific. The system has operated with reasonable efficiency over a considerable period, and has new prospects today.[35]

The system is conclusively demonstrated in the planning documents and in the historical record, in my view and rests upon five pillars of policy.

## Sustaining pliant regimes

Former British Prime Minister Arthur Balfour once said that what Britain needed in the Middle East was 'supreme economic and political control, to be exercised ... in friendly and unostentatious cooperation with the Arabs, but nevertheless, in the last resort to be exercised'.[36] Thus, according to historian Jan Morris, the 'puppet regimes' Britain supported to effect this policy were 'essentially law and order governments', where Britain would bolster 'the Conservative forces of Islam' to stave off the 'dangers of radicalism'.[37] The first pillar of Western policy towards the Middle East lay in creating – nowadays, sustaining – such pliant regimes which will do the West's bidding, notably the Gulf oil states.

Harold Macmillan noted the need for this in a diary entry of 1961, with regard to Aden (now Yemen), then a British 'protectorate' threatening to break free from British tutelage. Macmillan wrote that 'the real problem is how to use the influence and power of the Sultans to help us keep the colony and its essential defence facilities ... We agreed to ... give as much power as we can to the Sultans who are on our side.'[38] His Foreign Minister Selwyn Lloyd similarly noted the British need in the areas under its control – Kuwait, Bahrain and the other Gulf sheikhdoms – to 'create politically viable entities buttressed by a comparatively scanty military presence on our part'. This would enable Britain to 'retain our influence and capacity to intervene in an emergency'.[39] This policy had been described by the Foreign Office in 1945 thus:

> It should be obvious to anybody that what we are aiming at in the Middle East is the creation of a number of respectable independent states which will rely on the Western powers for advice and help in coping with their very difficult and intricate technical problems.[40]

The full reassertion of control by the al-Sabah regime in Kuwait following the Gulf War is the most recent example of this fundamental

Western policy, which has not changed since Britain's imperial heyday.

### Aiding repression

The complement to creating and sustaining these pro-Western regimes has been to aid their maintenance of control over their own populations, or 'internal security', as the customary formulation has it. The US National Security Council correctly noted in 1958 that:

> Our economic and cultural interests in the area have led not unnaturally to close US relations with elements in the Arab world whose primary interest lies in the maintenance of relations with the West and the status quo in their countries.[41]

Harold Macmillan similarly noted in 1955: 'We need to promote internal political stability and in particular to influence individuals so that public opinion does not become so hostile to our oil companies that their commercial operation [sic] becomes impossible.'[42]

The need for 'internal security' was expressed in a joint Foreign Office, Treasury and Ministry of Defence secret memorandum of 1956, which noted that the supply of oil to Britain and Western Europe depends on the 'friendly cooperation of the producing and transit countries'. This meant not only ensuring 'defence against an external threat' but also 'providing economic and technical assistance' to their economies and 'countering hostile influence and propaganda within the countries themselves'. The memorandum noted that 'it is increasingly a political rather than a military problem' and that 'the Middle East is now the most critical theatre politically'. Britain 'should develop non-military methods of maintaining and extending our influence, including technical assistance and information services'.[43] Added to this, there was 'an immediate need to expand and improve local police forces and intelligence, thereby reducing the need for military intervention'. Thus British planners – then as now – saw 'great advantages in offering training facilities in this country to the military and police forces of the appropriate [sic] Middle East states':[44] military training, publicly justified for reasons of external security (the 'Soviet threat') but with the real reason – aiding domestic control – well understood and documented. Responsibility for such control was in the hands of favoured clients, with the supervising powers offering what support they could, but not needing to do the dirty work in the region themselves. (As when MI5 official Maurice Oldfield, in interrogation of suspected Jewish terrorists in the British 'mandate' of Palestine in the 1940s, used to speak 'cheerfully about beating them up and pushing people's heads under buckets of water'.[45])

The fact that the West was supporting repressive regimes is fully recognised in the documents. Macmillan stated in his diary that it was 'rather sad that circumstances compel us to support reactionary and really rather outmoded regimes because we know that the new forces, even if they begin with moderate opinions, always seem to drift into violent revolutionary and strongly anti-Western positions'.[46] The issue was starkly understood by Stafford Cripps, who, after becoming Chancellor in the Attlee government, asked: 'Why do we support reactionary, selfish and corrupt governments in the Middle East instead of leaders who have the interest of their people at heart?'[47]

Of the highly repressive Iraqi regime of the 1940s, where Britain supported the monarchy's authoritarian domestic policies, one Foreign Office official noted: 'British policy will be held responsible for the present reactionary trend of the Iraqi government.'[48] Indeed, in Iraq it was 'extremely improbable' that the army was 'of the slightest value' in fighting a major enemy: rather, Britain believed it 'essential' that the army 'should be able to maintain internal security in the country'.[49] US planners were also fully aware of the fact that 'among increasing numbers of Arabs, there is also a conviction that we are backing the corrupt governments now in power, without regard to the welfare of the masses'.[50]

It was also recognised that this policy ran the risk of resulting in the loss of Western control. The long-term outlook for the Western-supported regimes was 'bleak', a US intelligence report of 1961 noted. Arab nationalism held out the prospect of 'independence and neutralism, social and economic reform and varying degrees of Arab unity'.[51] Foreign Secretary Bevin understood that 'we could not afford to be represented as defending the pashas while the communists obtained the support of the common people'.[52] It was also believed that the feudal authority that Britain was supporting in parts of the region was, principally due to rising Arab nationalism, the 'losing horse'. 'We cannot hope to maintain our position in the Middle East by the methods of the last century', one official noted.[53]

## Backing regional policemen

The third pillar of Western policy – closely related to the previous two – has been the creation and sustenance of regional policemen: powers who, for their own interests, will support the regional order preferred by the Western states. Chomsky has again been at the forefront of exposing this particular part of the system. Former US

Defense Secretary Melvin Laird explained that: 'America will no longer play policeman to the world. Instead we will expect other nations to provide more cops on the beat in their own neighbourhood.'[54] US Senator and oil expert Henry Jackson noted in 1973 that Israel and Iran under the Shah were 'reliable friends of the United States' who, along with Saudi Arabia, 'have served to inhibit and contain those irresponsible and radical elements in certain Arab states ... who, were they free to do so, would pose a grave threat indeed to our principal sources of petroleum in the Persian Gulf'.[55]

The role of Saudi Arabia has included pressure on the smaller Gulf states to block political reform, especially in Kuwait (and notably since the war against Iraq), support in the earlier postwar period for other Gulf states facing rebellion (such as Oman) and direct funding of US foreign policy (for example, the Contras in Nicaragua). In the 1950s, Eisenhower sought 'to explore the possibilities of building up King Saud as a counterweight to Nasser' and had hoped that Saud 'might eventually rival Nasser as an Arab leader'.[56]

Iraq performed a similar role until its invasion of Kuwait. In the 1980s, the West and the Gulf states embarked upon a strategy to build up Iraq under Saddam to counter Iran. A declassified National Security directive signed by President Bush in October 1989 considered it a priority to provide money and technology to Iraq because the regime was seen as the 'West's policeman in the region'.[57] The US, along with Saudi Arabia, also provided encouragement for Iraq to attack Iran in 1980, known as 'the Iraqi solution' in countering Iran, and which began the eight-year-long war. The US shared intelligence information with Iraq during the war, gathered from Airborne Warning and Control System (AWACS) aircraft supplied by the US to Saudi Arabia.[58] Saddam also managed to perform another task of traditional concern (for reasons of regional 'stability') to the West – crushing Kurdish aspirations in northern Iraq.

Iran became regional policeman following the Shah's assumption to power. 'Since 1953', the US National Security Council noted in 1958, 'Iran has been regarded in the area as the symbol of US influence' and its 'strategic location between the USSR and the Persian Gulf' as well as 'its great oil reserves' made it 'critically important to the United States'.[59] A quarter of a century later, President Carter's National Security Adviser similarly reflected 'on the central importance of Iran to the safeguarding of the American ... interest in the oil region of the Persian Gulf'.[60] Throughout this period, not only did the Shah perform valuable services for Western oil companies operating in the country, he also ensured Iranian support for Western foreign policy objectives in the region. Iranian troops were despatched to Oman in 1973, for example, in order to help the British military quell the rebellion against the rule of the Sultan.[61] In so doing, Britain permitted the Shah's army the use of a British Royal Air Force (RAF) base in Oman (a policy which the Minister of Defence denied in Parliament).[62]

The Iranian regime became one of the world's most repressive, with widespread torture and with opposition brutally suppressed. For Kissinger, the Shah was 'that rarest of leaders, an unconditional ally, and one whose understanding of the world situation enhanced our own'.[63] As the Shah's troops killed hundreds of demonstrators against the regime during the 1978/9 revolution, President Carter stated that 'Iran under the great leadership of the Shah is an island of stability in one of the more troubled areas of the world. This is a great tribute to you, Your Majesty, and to your leadership, and to the respect, admiration and love which your people give to you.'[64] Carter also told the Shah's son in a statement that 'our friendship and alliance with Iran is one of our important bases on which our entire foreign policy depends'. The Shah's 'progressive administration is very valuable, I think, to the entire Western world', Carter also noted.[65] Indeed, for the human rights President, 'there is no leader with whom I have a deeper sense of personal gratitude and personal friendship'.[66]

Relations between Teheran and London were also amiable under the Shah. Former MI6 officer Anthony Verrier notes that MI6 and former employees of the Anglo-Iranian Oil Corporation (later British Petroleum) 'saw themselves as the Shah's men'. Verrier also states that from 1953 until the Shah's fall in 1978, 'the one member of any diplomatic mission in Teheran who had a regular audience with the Shah and virtually automatic access to him was the SIS [Secret Intelligence Service, or MI6] Station Officer'.[67] It appears that the British desire to curry favour with the Iranian authorities outlasted the Shah. While the Foreign Office was vetoing political action which might hinder economic relations with Iran, Britain turned away six US Embassy staff who had managed to escape being taken hostage during the revolution and who had sought sanctuary at the British Embassy.[68]

British SAS personnel 'on loan' to the Iranian military trained the Shah's Special Forces for operations against Kurdish guerrillas in the north of the country. When the Iranian secret police – SAVAK, the main body responsible for repression and torture – was established in 1957, some of its officers were trained in Britain.[69] But the US role was more important. According to Jesse Leaf, the CIA's chief Iran analyst from 1963 to 1972, 'we set them [SAVAK] up, we organised them, we taught them everything we knew'. This involved 'extreme interrogation techniques ... including torture'. Some methods were 'based on German torture techniques from World War II', while the 'torture rooms were toured and it was all paid for by the USA'. The CIA was joined by Israel's intelligence service, Mossad, in organising the new security service.[70]

US documents show that planners never had any illusions about the nature of the regime it was supporting. 'The Shah has consolidated all power under his personal authority and suppressed all real opposition', in a context of 'near-feudal economic and social conditions', one memorandum from 1958 read.[71] There was 'basic and widespread dissatisfaction with his regime'[72] and it was recognised as 'unlikely that he will effect such a fundamental reform program as would satisfy rising popular demand'.[73] The United States was thus 'closely identified' with the 'largely personal regime of the Shah', the NSC noted. 'Principal support for the Shah', it continued, 'comes from large landowners and their conservative business associates, the top ranks of the government bureaucracy, and senior military officers.' Increasing numbers of people 'find Iran's antiquated and feudal structure and the privileges of the ruling classes anachronistic in a modern world'. However, 'the absence of any constructive, pro-Western alternative' to the Shah's regime makes 'US support of the regime the best hope of furthering US interests in Iran'.[74]

The 'threat' to the Shah's regime was clearly internal, though US leaders publicly stated that US policy was based on the need to protect Iran from Soviet invasion or infiltration. In secret, the National Intelligence Estimate for 1959 noted that 'we do not believe the Soviet Union will invade Iran', although it might try and subvert the regime 'by clandestine means'. However, 'we believe it unlikely that Soviet efforts will have a major effect on the internal stability of the Shah's regime in the near future'.[75] 'The communists by themselves pose no direct threat to the regime, and are unlikely to do so in the foreseeable future', the President's Special Assistant for National Security Affairs was told in 1961.[76]

Thus Western military support for the Shah was intended mainly to ensure the continuation of his regime, and therefore reinforced the repression. The US supplied huge quantities of weapons to Iran as did Britain, including 800 Chieftain tanks. 'The Army exists in part ... as a tool of personal power for the ruler', one US memorandum read.[77] Also, a US official noted in 1962 that the military role of the Iranian armed forces was 'essentially defensive and for maintenance

[sic] of internal security'. The US has 'planned a military equipment program to modernise Iranian forces'. Further, 'the US believes that currently the threat to Iranian security comes as much if not more from internal rather than external sources'.[78] Thus US military planning of, for example, 1961, contained 'contingency plans for supporting Iran against internal strife or attack from other Middle Eastern countries'.[79]

US documents intriguingly indicate possible coup plots against the Shah. For example, the State Department noted in 1961 that 'several key conservative generals have in the past approached the United States and the United Kingdom for help in plots to overthrow the Shah with some civilian help'.[80] What became of these is not elucidated in the files that I have seen but it is clear that they never got too far, perhaps not surprisingly in the light of Anglo-American support for the trusted client and policeman.

Israel has been the other main regional policeman. Its function has been coherently explained by Israeli General Shlomo Gazit, a former Military Intelligence Commander and analyst who noted in 1992 that:

> Israel's main task has not changed at all, and remains of crucial importance. The geographical location of Israel at the centre of the Arab–Muslim Middle East predestines Israel to be a devoted guardian of stability in all the countries surrounding it. Its [role] is to protect the existing regimes, to prevent or halt the processes of radicalisation and to block the expansion of fundamentalist religious zealotry.

Thus Israel performs, in Gazit's view, a vital service for 'the industrially advanced states, all of which are keenly concerned with guaranteeing the stability in the Middle East [sic]'.[81]

There are several ways in which Israeli power might be seen as acting in this way in the post-Gulf War period. First, Israel has the capability for conducting air strikes against potential nuclear weapons sites in the region, especially in Iran (similar to its bombing of an Iraqi nuclear plant in 1981, an act strongly supported by the United States). Second, Israel's military power continues to serve as a direct counter to the Arab states and Iran. Third, Israeli power gives it greater bargaining leverage in the Middle East 'peace process', enabling the US–Israeli agenda to be pursued more easily.

Israel's role was outlined in 1979 by President Reagan, who noted that the 'fall of Iran' has 'increased Israel's value as perhaps the only remaining strategic asset in the region on which the United States can rely'.[82] President Bush noted in 1992 that in the past Israel has 'demonstrated strategic reliability', and the US was therefore committed to its 'long standing position' of maintaining Israel's 'qualitative military edge'.[83] According to Professor Moshe Ma'oz, an analyst with access to the Israeli security services, Israel's military power, much of which derives from the US, is designed 'to provide Israel with superiority over all neighbouring Arab states together'. In his view, the US, once Israel has withdrawn from the Syrian Golan Heights, will keep supplying arms to Israel 'so that it may retain its strategic superiority over the entire Middle East even in peacetime'.[84]

Israel's role is long standing. Anthony Verrier notes that the Balfour Declaration, calling for a homeland for the Jewish people, was 'a device for providing Britain with a secure strategic outpost in an Arab world', although it 'was habitually insecure and never wholly loyal to British interests'.[85] By 1947, the British Chief of Air Staff noted that 'Palestine was of special importance' to British interests in the Middle East since 'it was necessary to hold Palestine as a screen for the defence of Egypt'. Also, in peacetime, 'we must be able to use Palestine as a base for the mobile reserve of troops which must be kept ready to meet any emergency throughout the Middle East'.[86]

By 1950 – with Britain having withdrawn from its Palestine 'mandate' and with Israel an independent state, having captured Palestine in the first Arab–Israeli war of 1948 – US documents show that both the Marshal of the Royal Air Force (Lord Tedder) and the Chairman of the US Joint Chiefs of Staff (Omar Bradley) 'believed that the Israeli army would be the most effective force south of Turkey which could be utilised for delaying action', presumably against the Soviet Union.[87] By 1958, the US National Security Council concluded that the 'logical corollary' of opposition to radical Arab nationalism 'would be to support Israel as the only strong pro-Western power left in the Middle East'.[88] During the 'crisis' in the Middle East of 1958, when Britain landed troops in Jordan and the United States did likewise in Lebanon, President Eisenhower on several occasions considered the merits of 'unleashing' Israel (along with Turkey) against Egypt. The Chairman of the US Joint Chiefs of Staff, General Nathan Twining, proposed that Israel should seize the West Bank of Jordan as part of a regional offensive that would include British intervention in Iraq and Turkish intervention in Syria.[89] In all, it has been little wonder that the building under British auspices of a national home in the region for Jews was regarded by Arabs as a 'permanent imperialist bridgehead'.[90]

## Direct Western intervention

The fourth pillar of policy has often been utilised in the postwar era. The Western use of force remains the ultimate guarantor of control when regional efforts are viewed as either detrimental to the system or incapable of achieving the desired ends. This remains relevant in the 1990s when the Western field of manoeuvre in the Middle East is no longer constrained by the threat of Soviet intervention.

The Gulf War was history repeating itself, a modern-day slaughter out of the colonial textbook. The overall number of enemy deaths – running into the tens of thousands – in relation to the 243 'allied' deaths, is evidence of this, a comparable kill rate to that of the battle of Omdurman in 1882, when 10,000 Sudanese were killed for the loss of 28 Britons, for example.[91] The Basra Road turkey-shoot of retreating and trapped Iraqis by the US Air Force resembled the British slaughter of Tibetans in 1904. Jan Morris notes on the latter slaughter that 'at point blank range from either side the massed British riflemen opened fire upon the Tibetan mass, while the maxims sent a stream of fire into the melee'. 'There was no need to aim precisely', Morris comments, since 'the target was unmissable and could not escape'.[92]

The war also provided another imperial-style function: the testing of new weaponry in combat. The Tomahawk cruise missile was used by US forces for the first time in combat and other weapon prototypes – such as the JSTARS radar surveillance plane and the 'Magic Lantern' helicopter-borne laser – were also tested.[93] Imperial historian V. G. Kiernan notes that colonial theatres witnessed improvements in the weaponry of the Great Powers especially 'when there was scarcely any fighting in Europe'. Dumdum bullets, for example, were tried out in India while the British-invented rocket shell 'came in fact to be earmarked chiefly for colonial fighting', Kiernan notes. The rules of warfare that applied to conflict between European states did not apply to war with colonised areas. 'Colonists in North America and their promoters in England maintained that no restrictions were binding in warfare against enemies like Red Indians.' British Army General Sir Harry Smith, a leading figure in the wars in South Africa of the mid-nineteenth century, inveighed against 'canting ultra philanthropists' in England who criticised the treatment of blacks in the wars, noting that 'war against savages cannot be carried out according to acknowledged rules but to common sense'.[94]

The return to colonial history is evident in the form that war against Iraq takes. Cruise missiles launched from afar and with no danger of loss of life for the user – such as the attacks on Baghdad from US aircraft carriers in the Gulf – are the contemporary version of the nineteenth-century use of superior arms. The use of air power to destroy enemies is also an area in which the United States – especially in the war in Southeast Asia – and Britain – in earlier times in the Middle East – profess much technical expertise and experience. The Royal Air Force was engaged in bombing British possessions as part of 'colonial policing' virtually from the beginning of its existence. Air Marshal Sir Hugh Trenchard, known as the 'father of the RAF', was a strong proponent of the use of air power for such purposes in the years following the First World War.[95] The Middle East – then as now – was the primary object of British attentions and the region has 'long been the proving ground for the theory and practice of air control', J. E. Peterson comments.[96]

'We insisted on reserving the right to bomb niggers', Prime Minister David Lloyd George noted after Britain refused to renounce the use of bombing at the 1932 Disarmament Conference, arguing strongly for 'the use of such machines as are necessary for police purposes in outlying places'.[97] Winston Churchill had also recognised the use of similarly barbaric methods for controlling the Middle East. When Secretary of State at the War Office in 1919, he was approached by the RAF Middle East command for permission to use chemical weapons 'against recalcitrant Arabs as experiment'. Churchill agreed, noting:

> I do not understand this squeamishness about the use of gas ... I am strongly in favour of using poisoned [sic] gas against uncivilised tribes ... It is not necessary to use only the most deadly gasses; gasses can be used which cause great inconvenience and would spread a lively terror and yet would leave no serious permanent effects on most of those affected.[98]

Air power remained 'a principal British tool for providing both internal and external security until final withdrawal [from the Gulf] in 1971', Peterson comments in his study of Arabia.[99] To bring countries under control, 'all the RAF required', academic Jacob Abadi comments, 'was safe bases from which to operate ... This was the reason for Britain's insistence upon keeping the airfields of the Middle East until forced to evacuate them.' In the 1950s, Britain retained the use of airfields in Jordan, Iraq and Egypt and 'there was a constant search for alternative airfields in the Middle East throughout the entire postwar era'.[100]

The first British use of air power in colonial policing occurred along the North–West frontier and in Afghanistan in 1918–20. This policy was the direct descendant of nineteenth-century punitive Army expeditions, by which enemy tribes were frequently subdued: 'fun for the officers and good experience for the troops', Jan Morris notes.[101] It was in reference to British actions in the Afghan campaigns at the end of the nineteenth century that Churchill noted that 'there is no doubt that we are a very cruel people'. In these earlier wars all prisoners were killed (on both sides), many villages were burnt to the ground and, according to Morris, 'nobody who resisted the Raj could expect mercy'.[102]

The policy of air bombing was pursued with striking success in Somaliland in 1920 when the forces of one enemy tribe were routed in three weeks by a single bomber squadron.[103] These experimental actions were watched by military and police experts all over Africa and Asia 'with the most profound interest', V. G. Kiernan notes;[104] similar to the 1991 war against Iraq, also the subject of much analysis for lessons learned by academic and military circles.

Turning to Iraq, 'Saddam Hussein was not the first to use chemical weapons against the Iraqi population', Oxford academic David Omissi notes. In 1920 the British Army used gas shells – 'with excellent moral effect' – to subdue the tribes which had risen in rebellion against British military rule. Nine thousand Arab lives were lost as part of an almost continuous ten-year-long bombing campaign against Kurdish rebels. Churchill consistently urged the RAF to use mustard gas during these raids, though gas bombs were not used for technical rather than humanitarian reasons. Omissi notes that 'some Iraqi villages were destroyed merely because their inhabitants had not paid their taxes', and that 'during one raid in Iraq, British pilots machine-gunned women and children as they fled from their homes'. Arthur 'Bomber' Harris was one of those in the RAF who learned his trade – soon to be applied to German cities – against Kurdish villages in Iraq, once noting:

> They now know what real bombing means, in casualties and damage; they know now that within 45 minutes a full size village can be practically wiped out and a third of its inhabitants killed or injured by four or five machines which offer them no real target, no opportunity for glory as warriors, no effective means of escape.[105]

Harris also once suggested, again with regard to Iraq, that the RAF drop 'a bomb in every village that speaks out of turn'.[106] In a rare condemnation by a British Army officer, Lieutenant-Colonel Sir Arnold Wilson noted in a speech in 1932 the 'pertinacity with which ... the RAF has been bombing the Kurdish population for the last ten years'. 'Devastated villages, slaughtered cattle, maimed women and children bear witness to the spread, in the words of the special correspondent to *The Times*, of a uniform pattern of civilisation.'[107]

Other peoples of the Middle East were the object of 'police bombing', such as the Nuer people of Southern Sudan and tribesmen in Transjordan. In 1930 Britain sold planes, accompanied by British pilots and maintenance crew, to Saudi King Ibn Saud, for use against the rebellious Ikhwan, and a base was established for them on the shores of the Gulf:[108] an early example of the use of arms supplies to promote close relations with favoured clients, helping them with 'internal security'. Aden, Yemen and Oman were further objects of British control from the air, beginning in 1919 and lasting, in Aden, until the early 1960s.

The Colonial Office stated in 1947 that 'the practice of punitive air action against recalcitrant tribes is, in the case of the Aden protectorate, well established and understood by those against whom it is likely to be used'. Its view was that 'in suitable circumstances punitive air action as hitherto carried out remains the method of maintaining order most effective and least costly in human life'.[109]

Direct Western intervention in the Middle East – whether overt or covert – has been a regular feature of postwar history. Military interventions have occurred in, among others, Egypt (by Britain, 1956), Jordan (by Britain, 1958) Lebanon (by the US, 1958), Kuwait (by Britain, 1961), Oman (1950s, 1960s and 1970s, by Britain), Aden/South Yemen (by Britain, 1950s and 1960s), Lebanon (Western powers, 1980s), the Gulf (Western powers, 1980s), Iraq/Kuwait (Western and other powers, 1991). Coup plots and covert actions have included those in Iran (by the US and Britain, 1953 and, regarding the Kurds, in the mid-1970s), North Yemen (by Britain, 1960s) and Afghanistan (by the US, 1980s). In Syria, the CIA approached Chief of Staff General Husni Zaim in 1948 to discuss the 'possibility [of an] army supported dictatorship', something which occurred when Zaim overthrew the government a few months later (himself soon to be overthrown). In 1956, President Eisenhower approved an operation, organised jointly with the British government, to overthrow the pro-Nasser regime in Damascus.[110] The intrigues taking place at this time have been summarised by William Blum, in his revealing study of CIA actions: 'Iraq plotting with the British to topple governments in both Syria and Nasser's Egypt; the British pressuring the Americans to join the conspiracy; and the CIA compromising – leave Nasser alone, at least for the time being, and we'll do something about Syria.'[111]

With regard to Egypt, with anti-British riots taking place throughout 1951–52, Britain was planning a coup to restore order and install a military government appointed by the then Egyptian leader King Farouk. The Egyptian armed forces were regarded as dependable since they were British-trained. At the same time, British plans under the codename 'Rodeo' were devised for the occupation of two major Egyptian cities.[112] Farouk was, however, soon overthrown, in a coup backed by the CIA (an example of the US working to undermine the British position in the area).[113] MI6 later tried on several occasions to remove Egyptian leader Gamal Abdel Nasser both before and after Britain's invasion of Egypt in 1956. According to former MI6 officer Anthony Verrier, SIS disobeyed Eden's order to assassinate Nasser and 'an elaborate assassination plan was made, carefully arranged to fail. Nasser never did get the razor designed to explode when used.'[114]

The Gulf has been another traditional area for British coup-plotting: three Gulf emirates (Sharjah, Abu Dhabi and Oman) underwent such coups between 1965 and 1970, with British help. Former Labour Foreign Secretary Michael Stewart recalled in his memoirs that 'on two occasions while I was in office British residents had to arrange for the deposition of unpopular rulers ... On both occasions, it was done without bloodshed and the results were beneficial; but Britain could not carry out this responsibility indefinitely.'[115] A more recent coup occurred in Qatar in June 1995, when Sheikh Hamad Al-Thani ousted his father. Al-Thani had been appointed Crown Prince and Defence Minister in 1977 soon after his graduation from the British military academy, Sandhurst. The press reported that the United States 'quickly recognised the new government after receiving assurances that it would work cooperatively with its neighbours and the rest of the international community' (that is, that it would be the same as the previous regime and support the US).[116] By contrast, an attempted coup in Sharjah (one of the United Arab Emirates (UAE)) in 1987 by Sheikh Abdul-Aziz against his younger brother met with failure. The prospective leader had been trained at the Mons Officer Cadet school in Britain and had served with the British-controlled Trucial Oman Scouts before Oman's independence.[117]

According to William Blum, five Middle Eastern leaders have been targeted for assassination by the US: Egyptian President Nasser (1957); Iraqi President Abdul Kassem (1958); Ayatollah Khomeini (1982); Muammar Qadafi (1981–87); and Saddam Hussein (1990–91).[118] An example of the United States' direct sponsorship of terrorism is the 1985 car-bombing in Beirut which aimed to kill Hezbollah leader Sheikh Fadlallah, killing 80 people. According to US journalist Bob Woodward, the bombing was arranged by the CIA and its Saudi clients with the assistance of Lebanese intelligence and a British specialist.[119] The Mujaheddin guerrillas, recipients of CIA funding during the war against the Soviet occupation of Afghanistan, were also the recipients of largesse from MI6. According to Stephen Dorril, an expert on the British 'security services', 'for nearly a decade, MI6 helped the CIA fight a covert war against Kabul'. 'Although it worked in close cooperation with the CIA', Dorril notes, MI6 'pursued an independent strategy by promoting ex-King Zahir Shah'. Afghan Mujaheddin were trained, sometimes by the British private company Keeny Meeny Services (KMS), in Saudi Arabia and Oman, 'where there were secret CIA and MI6 bases'. 'During 1986', Dorril continues, 'as a favour to the CIA, MI6 ran a covert operation to supply the guerrilla commander Abdul Haq, of the fundamentalist Hezbe Islami, with British Blowpipe missiles'.[120]

### The nuclear threat

There is evidence that the use of nuclear weapons has been threatened by the Western states on nine occasions in the postwar Middle East:

Table 5.1: Western nuclear threats in the Middle East

| Situation | Year |
|---|---|
| Iran | 1946 |
| Suez crisis | 1956 |
| Iraq | 1958 |
| Jordan | 1958 |
| Turkey | 1963 |
| Jordan/Syria | 1970 |
| Arab–Israeli war | 1973 |
| Iran | 1980 |
| Iraq | 1991 |

Sources: Barry Blechman and Stephen Kaplan, *Force Without War: US Armed Forces as a Political Instrument*, Brookings Institution, Washington D.C., 1978, p. 48; Michio Kaku and Daniel Axelrod, *To Win a Nuclear War: The Pentagon's Secret War Plans*, Zed Books, London, 1987, p. 5; Paul Rogers, 'A note on the British deployment of nuclear weapons in crises', *Lobster*, No. 28, December 1994.

The first of these incidents occurred when the United States sought to remove Soviet troops from northern Iran in the aftermath of the Second World War. President Truman delivered an ultimatum to Soviet Foreign Minister Andrei Gromyko to the effect that the troops should be removed within 48 hours or the US would drop the atom bomb. 'We're going to drop it on you', Truman reportedly said to Gromyko. The US Secretary of State, James Byrnes, also declared that 'now we'll give it to them with both barrels'.[121]

Richard Nixon recalled how the US used the nuclear threat against the Soviet Union during the Suez crisis of 1956. 'In 1956 we considered using the bomb in Suez', Nixon noted, 'and we did use it diplomatically.' When the Soviet Union threatened to intervene unilaterally to support Egypt against the British and French invasion, Nixon recalled that President Eisenhower got the NATO commander to hold a press conference in which he 'said that if Khrushchev carried out his threat to use rockets against the British Isles, Moscow would be destroyed "as surely as night follows day". From that time on, the US has played the dominant role in the Mideast.'[122]

Two years later, in 1958, the US landed in Lebanon equipped with nuclear-capable howitzers and apparently prepared to use nuclear weapons against Iraq. In order to deter an Iraqi move into Kuwait or to help protect other friendly governments, President Eisenhower ordered the Chairman of the US Joint Chiefs of Staff to 'be prepared to employ, subject to [Eisenhower's] approval, *whatever* means might become necessary to prevent any unfriendly forces from moving into Kuwait'. Blechman and Kaplan, two US analysts who have conducted a detailed study of US nuclear threats, note that 'it seems clear that Eisenhower was referring to the possible use of nuclear weapons, an issue that was discussed several times during the crisis'.[123]

The US nuclear threat was further employed to support the regime of King Hussein of Jordan in 1970 – to prevent the Soviet Union's entrance into the war between the Jordanian government and the Palestine Liberation Organisation (PLO) – and in 1973 – to deter the Soviet Union from entering the Arab–Israeli war on Egypt's side.[124] Following the taking of the American hostages in Iran in 1979, a secret Pentagon study entitled 'Capabilities in the Persian Gulf' was leaked to the press, the headline of which read: 'Study says a Soviet move in Iran might require US atom arms'. The article stated that the study concluded that US forces could not stop 'a Soviet thrust into northern Iran and that the United States should therefore consider using "tactical" nuclear weapons in any conflict there'. A senior Pentagon official was also quoted as stating that 'nuclear armed cruise missiles launched from ships in the Indian Ocean' might possibly be employed. For the first six months of 1980, President Carter ordered a dozen conspicuous flights over the Arabian Sea by B-52 strategic bombers. According to Kaku and Axelrod (who have extensively analysed US nuclear war-fighting strategy), the Carter administration 'overreacted to the situation in the Persian Gulf, using the nuclear threat to compensate for its humiliation in Iran'.[125]

More recent evidence of Western deployment of nuclear weapons in a crisis concerns that by Britain during the Gulf crisis of 1990/1. According to Paul Rogers of the University of Bradford, various indications of the willingness to use nuclear weapons were given during the crisis. The clearest was that of a senior Army officer on his way with the 7th Armoured Brigade to the Gulf, who suggested that an Iraqi chemical attack on British forces would be met with a tactical nuclear response. Defence Minister Tom King had also spoken of 'very, very grave consequences indeed', saying that: 'I am not going to be specific, and I am not going to give any indication as to what form that might take.' (US Secretary of State James Baker had delivered a similar warning to Iraqi Foreign Minister Tariq Aziz, noting that a US response to Iraqi use of chemical weapons would be 'unrestrained'.[126]) Rogers notes that detailed planning was undertaken to make it possible for one British ship despatched to the region during the crisis to be equipped with tactical nuclear weapons, although there is no confirmation that they were actually deployed.[127]

These threats should be understood in the context that the Western states have consistently regarded nuclear arms as war-fighting weapons, not just simply means of deterrence;[128] though it is only the latter use which usually figures in the propaganda system. In a rare exception, one analyst notes in a study of nuclear policy drawing on official documentation that in planning associated with the Baghdad Pact in the mid-1950s, 'growing emphasis was placed on strategic and tactical nuclear weapons for deterrence and war-fighting purposes'.[129] Britain later declared to the Baghdad Pact bombers able to 'undertake both nuclear and conventional operations in general and limited war'.[130] US documents of 1962 on Iran also note that 'authorization by the President for the use of nuclear weapons will be given as required to achieve US objectives in the area'. If the United States were unable to turn back a Soviet invasion with conventional weapons, the US and its allies had the option of 'a limited nuclear action' or escalation to 'general nuclear war'.[131]

Currently, the Middle East is probably at the top of the list of objects of future nuclear threats and the possible use of nuclear weapons by the Western states in a crisis. In 1990, *Independent* defence correspondent Christopher Bellamy noted that the planned British nuclear weapons system – TASM (Tactical Air to Surface Missile) – 'would be suitable to cover future threats from the south – north Africa and the Middle East – as well as the east'.[132] TASM was scrapped but the Trident system – now adapted for tactical nuclear use[133] – could be expected to adopt the same coverage.

# 6

# The Gulf

The relationship between the Gulf states and the leading Western states has become closer in the post-Gulf War era and is one of the pillars of world order. By 1992, relations between the United States and the GCC states (comprising Saudi Arabia, Kuwait, Qatar, Bahrain, Oman and the UAE) had, according to a US official, 'reached a new plateau of cooperation across the board, especially on political, economic and military matters'.[1] This chapter considers this relationship and aims to shed some light on the historical and contemporary record. Here, the role of Britain is in many ways as important as that of the United States because of the traditionally close and friendly relations Britain has moulded with the Gulf states, helping to shape their outlook and place in international relations.

The reality of US and British policy in the region is a neglected area of study. There has been a plethora of academic studies on the West's relationship with the Gulf since the 1980s, especially since the 1979 Iranian revolution highlighted the threats to Western control over Middle Eastern oil. Virtually all these studies concentrate on Western 'security interests' in the region, many considering the forms of military intervention required to secure 'access' to oil in cases of regional strife, or the dangers posed to Western 'interests' by rising 'Islamic fundamentalism'. These studies are firmly entrenched within the required ideological framework and invariably obscure crucial aspects of the US and British role in the region: notably the overall need for control, the purpose and function of arms sales to the GCC states and the systematic contribution to domestic repression.

## Basic relations with the Gulf states

Britain's view of its relations with the Gulf states has been outlined by General Sir Michael Wilkes, Adjutant General and Middle East adviser to the Ministry of Defence, in an article entitled: '"What friends are for" – British defence policy in the Gulf'. Wilkes refers to 'our friends in the Gulf' and notes that these friendships 'have withstood the strains of world wars, the retreat from empire and changes of government on both sides'. The ships from Britain's 'permanent naval presence in the Gulf', Wilkes notes, 'demonstrate British interest in the region and maintain a presence in an area of great strategic importance to us as a nation'. Thus 'we take advantage of this presence to make regular port visits and to conduct joint exercises with our major allies and friendly navies in the Gulf region'. Holding joint exercises between the West and the Gulf states 'helps to build lasting friendships at the working level to supplement those between leaders'. Britain also gives 'high priority to students from Gulf states wishing to attend military training courses in Britain' and has also 'deployed teams of British Loan Service Officers to a number of countries in the Gulf, to assist with the development of modern command structures, tactical doctrine and training and logistics organisations'. These efforts, Wilkes notes, 'are also supported by the sale of selected equipments [sic] to friendly countries in the region'.[2]

British involvement in the Gulf goes further, and British advisers play important official and permanent roles in many Gulf states. In Dubai – one of the United Arab Emirates – a British brigadier advises the government and its defence minister on oil policies, commercial development and defence. In Oman, another former British intelligence officer advises the Sultan on the foreign press. This adviser's policies, the *Guardian* notes, 'have made Oman one of the most difficult countries for foreign newsmen to enter'. In Bahrain, a British adviser created the Special Branch and controls internal security.[3] Added to this are the exceedingly close contacts in the areas of military relations, arms supplies and oil which have developed between, on the one hand, the US and Britain and, on the other, Saudi Arabia and Kuwait especially in the aftermath of the 1991 Gulf War; these will be considered further below.

The relationship has changed little over the decades, as Wilkes correctly points out above. Prime Minister Harold Macmillan referred to 'our clients in the Gulf'[4] in his memoirs. The current situation was confirmed by the Kuwait Information Minister (which might be regarded, in the context of Kuwait, as an Orwellian term), who stated in 1994 that 'our security and stability are dependent on the United States and Britain and our interests lie in strengthening our ties with them'.[5]

Before independence for the Gulf states in 1971 (apart from Saudi Arabia which was already independent) Britain was the major power in the region, controlling the external (and largely internal) policies of the Gulf states in the form of 'protectorates' that dated back to the nineteenth century. The Chiefs of Staff noted in 1928 the importance of 'the maintenance of British supremacy in the Persian Gulf' and that this should be 'a cardinal feature of our policy'.[6] The

US position throughout the postwar period has essentially been to support this control. Thus the US Consulate General in Dharan, Saudi Arabia, noted in 1955 that 'our basic policy vis-a-vis British power in Persian Gulf area ... is position of supporting that power unless it is acting contrarily to our interest in the Persian Gulf [sic]'.[7] The US State Department noted in 1955: 'US shares with Britain desire to see retention UK influence in Persian Gulf area [sic]'.[8]

It has entered history that Britain 'withdrew' from the Gulf in 1971, after the Labour government, under domestic budgetary pressure, had announced plans for such a military withdrawal in 1968. But Britain has never withdrawn from the region. After 1971 Britain withdrew from its military bases in Bahrain and Sharjah but maintained its bases at Salala and Masirah in Oman until 1976. British officers continued to outnumber Omani officers in Oman's armed forces until the early 1980s and it was not until 1985 that Omanis began to replace British officers as commanders of the Omani Army, Navy and Air Force.[9] By this time, during the Iran–Iraq war, Britain's Armilla naval patrol had already been deployed in the Gulf. After 1971 British naval vessels continued to pay port visits to the their former bases and close military ties continued with its key allies. As noted above, British advisers also stayed behind in a number of states, ensuring continued British influence, including on military matters. Britain had no intention of withdrawing entirely from the region even if it could no longer maintain the 'supremacy' that was deemed so important in the earlier period.

After 1971 the role of regional enforcer fell to Iran under the Shah, a faithful ally whose internal repression was even worse than that of the Gulf states. When the Shah's regime was overthrown, the West saw Iraq under Saddam Hussein (and Saudi Arabia) as a chief asset in the region. Saddam's disobedience in invading Kuwait – a traditional Western preserve – permitted a renewed Western permanent presence in the region and a deepening of the client relationship with the West. The current era is thus a repetition of history, with the Western states finally having regained the firm foothold in the region they lost by degrees in both 1971 and 1979.

## Internal structures and the West

US academic Gregory Gause notes in his study of the Gulf states that:

> Political parties are formally illegal, and when they do exist are underground. Independent labour unions are also illegal. Professional syndicates and chambers of commerce are permitted,

> but are usually closely supervised by the state. Broadcast media – television and radio – are completely under state control. Print media are frequently controlled directly by the state or are in the hands of private concerns close to state authorities. Independent newspapers and other publications are subject to strict censorship. Even sports and cultural clubs tend to be brought within the state's ambit.

Gause notes that 'organised labour has, in effect, been destroyed as a political force in the Gulf monarchies as a result of the oil boom'. The unions that do exist are officially sponsored and controlled by the states.[10]

The 'state' is effectively the ruling family. Gause notes that in all six GCC states the Prime Minister is a member of the ruling family. In Oman and Saudi Arabia the head of state himself is Prime Minister; in Bahrain, Qatar and Kuwait either brothers, cousins or sons of the Emir serve as Prime Minister. Ruling families also supply a large number of the Ministers in each state: in 1992, 6 of 15 in Bahrain; 9 of 17 in Qatar; 5 of 30 in Oman (the lowest proportion, but where the Sultan is also the Defence, Foreign Affairs, Finance and Prime Minister); 4 out of 15 in Kuwait; 5 out of 21 in Saudi Arabia; and 9 of 24 in the UAE. Moreover, 'the ministries controlled by family members are usually among the most sensitive and powerful', Gause notes. At the end of 1992, family members held the interior portfolio in four out of six states; the defence portfolio in all six; and the foreign affairs portfolio in five.[11] Around half of the Gulf Cabinet Ministers have held their jobs for 20 years or more.[12]

Politics is a taboo subject in society, with both domestic and foreign policy simply the preserve of the ruling families. The income from oil is distributed in some sheikhdoms into the ruler's personal bank account, in others to thousands of princes who get paid a stipend from the Treasury.[13] Women hardly figure; in November 1994, it was reported that four Omani women were to take their seats in the 'parliament', becoming the first female legislators ever in the Gulf.[14]

The Western states effectively support the basic domestic structure of the Gulf states and play a key role in their domestic repression. This fact has always been recognised as central to Western planners, even if it has not permeated the numerous academic studies of the West–Gulf relationship. The US priority was outlined by the State Department in 1956, in a memorandum intended to be shared with the British Foreign Office: 'Our mutual position and our joint access to the resources of the area can most effectively be preserved by recognising the challenges to the West and *to traditional control in the area.*'[15] British planners believed that their 'prestige' and 'status' in the Middle East 'depended on its ability to support the sheikhdoms'.[16] Former MI6 officer Anthony Verrier also records that by the 1950s MI5 was 'active throughout the Gulf' and was 'concerned with "internal administration" – in a word, the prevention of subversion'.[17]

Support for the Gulf regimes was arguably made more important after 1971. In 1981, President Reagan pledged direct US support for Saudi internal stability by declaring that the US would not allow the regime to be toppled by the kind of upheaval that toppled the Shah.[18] Well known US plans to intervene militarily in Saudi Arabia in order to hold the oil fields are also based on both internal and external contingencies.[19] In 1980, a US State Department spokesman noted that the US was committed to protecting Saudi Arabia against 'all internal and external attempts to destabilise it'.[20]

It is also instructive to consider the origins of the principal US intervention force in the region – originally the Rapid Deployment Force (RDF), which later became CENTCOM (Central Command) and which, under General Norman Schwarzkopf, led the war against Iraq. The official rationale for the RDF was outlined by President Carter, in what became known as the 'Carter Doctrine': 'Any attempt by any outside force to gain control of the Persian Gulf region will be regarded as an assault on the vital interests of the United States of America and such an assault will be repelled by any means necessary, including military force.' Carter's doctrine was announced a month after the Soviet invasion of Afghanistan. Planning for the RDF, however, much predated the invasion; it was the domestic upheaval in Iran in 1978–79 which provided the real basis for the RDF. The announcement establishing the RDF was made in December 1979, two weeks before the Soviet invasion.[21]

Given the Gulf states' sensivitities to any external criticism, it is customary for Western leaders to provide cautious apologias for human rights abuses and repression in the Gulf states, while being careful not to assert explicitly their support for their domestic structures. The current Labour government's apparent support for Bahrain has been noted in Chapter 2. The then Foreign Secretary Douglas Hurd was asked in 1991 by a parliamentary committee about 'moves towards democracy' in the Gulf states and replied that 'each will find its own way' and 'each of them has its own way forward'.[22] These comments took place in a context where the Foreign Affairs Committee – an all-party group that is supposed to scrutinise British foreign policy – described the Gulf states as 'benevolent oligarchies'.[23] In fact, in the aftermath of the 1991 war, many of the Gulf states are moving even further away from democracy and are certainly far from benevolent.

As with the West's countering of democracy elsewhere in the South, the fear is that if either democratic and/or popular elements or more radical Islamist elements were to gain power they would be vigorously more opposed to the Western agenda in the Gulf and wider region than the current rulers. This fear is especially important regarding the Middle East, the region of greatest concern to the West and where more popular forces have traditionally been opposed to Western policies. Current Western policy is to encourage some degree of modest reform in the Gulf states' domestic political structures, for two main reasons: first, to help stave off the chances of more radical elements threatening internal 'stability'; second, for public relations purposes. Yet there is no reason to believe that overall policy is any different now than outlined by a US State Department official in 1958:

> Western efforts should be directed at stimulating modest political reforms to satisfy the demands of public opinion which have been generated by rapid economic progress ... [This] would facilitate the gradual development and modernisation of the Persian Gulf shaikhdoms [sic] *without imperiling internal stability or the fundamental authority of the ruling groups*.[24]

## Military relations and the utility of arms exports

The Middle East and, especially, the Gulf are top candidates for future military intervention. According to CIA Director Robert Gates, in 1992: 'If in the next few years it again becomes necessary for the United States to deploy combat power abroad, the strategically vital region encompassing the Middle East and Persian Gulf is at the top of the list of likely locales.'[25] To facilitate such intervention in the present era, the West has established bases or pre-positioning sites at various locations in the Middle East. In late 1994, for example, it was announced that Qatar and Kuwait had agreed to accept the pre-positioning of US military equipment on their territories: Qatar had accepted tanks and supplies for use by a brigade of over 2000 troops (or 4000, as later reported[26]); Kuwait had accepted a squadron of 24 attack jets, bringing the total number of US aircraft in the Gulf to about 130.[27] At the beginning of 1993, two years after the Gulf war,

60 US aircraft were still stationed in Saudi Arabia.[28] The press also noted that 'the US is now seeking to store enough armour on the ground in the Gulf region for three brigades representing about a division of 10,000 troops'.[29]

These pre-positioning agreements fulfil essentially the same function as outlined by the Foreign Office in 1947:

> Our strategic and security interests throughout the world will be best safeguarded by the establishment in suitable spots of 'police stations' fully equipped to deal with emergencies within a large radius. Kuwait is one such spot from which Iraq, South Persia, Saudi Arabia and the Persian Gulf could be controlled. It will be well worth while to go to considerable trouble and expense to establish and man a 'police station' there.[30]

The view that Kuwait could help 'control' the rest of the region is especially pertinent in the light of the 1991 war and the establishment in that country of Western equipment. Similarly, the Foreign Office noted, also in 1947, that the British base in Jordan provided Britain with an 'efficient military force which would be at our disposal in case of trouble'.[31]

These agreements complement the defence pacts agreed by Western and Gulf states in the aftermath of the 1991 war. The US signed a ten-year defence cooperation agreement with Kuwait in 1991, which 'allows for access to Kuwaiti military facilities and for the prepositioning of US defence equipment in Kuwait', US official Edward Djerejian noted.[32] The Kuwaiti Foreign Minister called it an 'agreement on military cooperation, use of facilities, logistical support, prepositioning of defence equipment and legal status of US forces in the State of Kuwait'.[33] Agreements containing similar US military access and pre-positioning rights were signed with Bahrain and Qatar, also in 1991. These pacts will enable the United States to hold military exercises with the Gulf states, train their forces as well as have access to naval bases and other military facilities.[34] With Oman, 'no new agreement is required', Djerejian states: the US has had a military facilities agreement with Oman since 1981, along with Britain, allowing for prepositioning of equipment.[35] Saudi Arabia reportedly rejected a US request for expanded basing facilities in the country and rebuffed offers of a formal military cooperation pact.[36]

Britain and France have signed similar agreements with Kuwait; Britain signed a memorandum of understanding on security cooperation with Kuwait in 1992; France signed a ten-year defence agreement with Kuwait later in the same year. France also signed a defence cooperation agreement with the UAE in January 1995.[37]

US organisation Human Rights Watch notes that the agreement on holding exercises with Kuwait 'amounts to a semi-permanent presence in the light of their frequency, duration and the large number of troops involved'.[38] US policy has been explained by the Assistant Secretary of State John Kelly: 'We do not intend to maintain a permanent ground combat force in the area, but we will continue to maintain an enhanced naval presence in the Gulf and will have a rotational air presence in the region.'[39] Kelly notes that 'enhanced presence' means 'more ships' and 'intermittent carrier battle groups there'; there would be frequent US Navy port calls and Marine amphibious troops would be 'afloat permanently' in the Gulf. In his remarks in 1991, he also noted that the US was 'discussing having a forward element of the command somewhere in the Gulf'.[40] In July 1995 the Clinton administration upgraded further the US presence in the region and announced the formation of a new, permanent US naval fleet to patrol the Gulf, including two submarines, 15 ships, an aircraft carrier with 70 warplanes and 10,000 sailors and marines.[41] The latter force was presented as part of the policy of containing Iran; the previous pacts as part of a policy of containing Iraq. The enemies change, but the fundamental alliance with the Gulf client states remains.

In the 1990s the web of military relations between the Western states and their Gulf allies is impressive. US military advisers are in Bahrain, Kuwait, Oman, Saudi Arabia and the UAE and military officials from all those countries except Oman are being trained in the United States. Britain has advisers in Bahrain, Kuwait, Oman, Qatar, Saudi Arabia and the UAE and military officials from all those countries are being trained in Britain. France has military advisers in Bahrain, Kuwait, Qatar, Saudi Arabia and the UAE with military officials from all those countries being trained in France.[42] The US is a major supplier of arms to Bahrain, Kuwait, Oman, Saudi Arabia and the UAE; Britain is a major supplier to Kuwait, Oman and Saudi Arabia; France is a major supplier to the UAE, Kuwait, Oman and Qatar.[43]

Arms exports have clear advantages for Western planners which are not exclusive to the Gulf. First, they help to cement close political relations between the Western states and the ruling families and enhance Western influence. Arms exports often bring with them technicians and military personnel. US Gulf analyst Charles Kupchan notes that the US technical teams – involving several thousand US personnel – which accompanied arms sales to the Gulf throughout the postwar period 'served as a psychological tie between the United States and the recipient state, if not an explicit means through which Washington could exercise influence over military operations in the host country'.[44] The sale of AWACS aircraft to Saudi Arabia in the 1980s brought hundreds of American advisers and technicians, meaning that 'the United States was virtually assured a military presence in Saudi Arabia for decades', Kupchan notes.[45] Britain's massive Yamamah project with Saudi Arabia (see below) provides around 5000 British Aerospace staff in the country.

This benefit of arms sales has also been explained by General Norman Schwarzkopf:

> Along with arms sales generally goes an advisory position, generally goes the spare parts position, generally goes an ability to influence how those arms are used ... I could make a good case that if you wanted to control the use of those arms, one of the best ways to do it us by providing the arms and then controlling the spare parts. We did that with Iran.[46]

Military training also helps to cement relations with future rulers. The State Department noted in 1961 that 'the United States has enjoyed through its Military Training Mission unusually close contacts with leaders of the Saudi military'. 'These contracts', it continued, 'are of great potential value as the regime in Saudi Arabia must surely change and new leadership is most likely to come from this element.'[47]

Arms sales are often simply bribes to keep friendly despots sweet. When Britain was the controlling power in the Gulf, it used to provide subsidies to compliant sheikhs to ensure their cooperation, this income in turn enhancing the Sheikhs' (and thus British) power over their territories. Arms provide a similar function today.

A second function – closely linked to the first – provided by arms sales to the Gulf is Western influence over oil production and pricing policy. This was especially clear by the late 1970s with regard to US arms sales to Saudi Arabia, which by then had clearly emerged as the most influential single actor in the world's oil industry. The provision of arms hoped to convince Riyadh to maintain production levels ensuring sufficient supplies at prices favourable to the United States. In the three years following the 1973 oil price rises, US arms exports to Saudi Arabia increased nearly fourfold in value as a quid pro quo for Saudi control of production levels. One member of the US Senate Foreign Relations Committee noted that the link between arms and oil was 'beyond question'.[48] Even more direct has been, apparently, the link between US military bases and oil. One US official noted in 1944 that the construction of a US airbase in Saudi Arabia, ostensibly for military purposes, was 'so that we, particularly our navy, would have access to some of King Ibn Saud's oil'.[49]

A third function of arms exports is that they facilitate the pre-positioning of equipment in a country, acting as part of the 'police station' policy for intervention outlined above.[50] In many cases in the Gulf the size of weapons imports is far beyond what is feasible to actually use and some states have embarked upon a 'policy of overbuying' to 'establish the infrastructure to support reinforcing powers'[51] – the pre-positioning and overbuilding of equipment is effectively available for use by the West in an emergency. This policy was outlined by US Defense Secretary Caspar Weinberger, referring to the sales of F-15 fighters and AWACS to Saudi Arabia in the early 1980s. The deal would:

> increase the effectiveness of our own military capabilities if we were ever called upon to deploy US forces to that area. The extensive logistics base and support infrastructure that will be a necessary part of this equipment package will be fully compatible with the defence needs of this whole vital area.[52]

A fourth function – of utmost importance – is the use of arms for control of the domestic population (discussed in the previous chapter and also below). US Senator Hubert Humphrey once noted that: 'Do you know what the head of the Iranian army told one of our people? He said the army was in good shape, thanks to US aid – it was now capable of coping with the civilian population.'[53] The US National Security Council similarly noted in 1961 that US military aid was important 'as a means of maintaining internal security' and recommended that this policy continue to enable Iran 'to maintain and properly deploy armed forces which will be capable of maintaining internal security'.[54] Overall, a US government memorandum noted in 1947: 'it is current American policy to confine arms sales to countries of the Middle East to reasonable quantities required for the maintenance of internal security'.[55]

This priority remains of clear relevance today and the armed forces of the Gulf states are equally if not more focused on internal security than external security. Traditionally – and with the exception of the Iraqi invasion of Kuwait – the main 'threats' to these states have more often been internal: such as in the wars in Oman in the 1960s and 1970s, the use of armed force in an internal struggle in the UAE in 1987, and Iranian revolutionary propaganda trying to encourage domesic interest in the 1980s. The powerful Saudi National Guard (see also below) is largely a guarantee against internal upheaval, while the forces of Kuwait, Bahrain and Qatar are so small compared to their potential enemies that, as evidenced in the Iraqi invasion of Kuwait, they are unlikely to be able to realistically defend themselves against an external threat anyway.[56] Recent arms transfers from British companies to the Gulf have included the installation of a torture chamber for the Special Branch of the Dubai police and the sending of gallows for use in Abu Dhabi.[57] In 1996, British arms manufacturers were reportedly bidding to sell up to £3 billion worth of armoured vehicles to Saudi Arabia's National Guard, the main internal security force, and were supplying armoured personnel carriers to the regime in Qatar.[58]

Given these advantages from the export of arms – not to mention the profits for arms manufacturers – it is hardly surprising to see a flourishing weapons trade in the region, described by a US official as a policy of 'bolstering the defensive capabilities of our friends in the Gulf region'.[59] President Bush's 'arms control proposal' in May 1991 outlining plans for the control of weapons in the Middle East was taken seriously by the world's media (similar to the solemn professions to restrict arms exports following the Falklands War, in which Argentinian forces used weapons supplied by Britain – then forgotten when the charade had outlived its political purpose). Bush's proposal was immediately followed by increased sales. A deal for £2.1 billion worth of arms (to Bahrain and the UAE) was announced by the US Defense Secretary Richard Cheney five days after the proposal. Cheney also noted that US plans for arms control in the Middle East 'did not mean that Washington was not going to supply more arms'.[60]

Other Western arms suppliers followed, as the Gulf states embarked upon major rearmament programmes in the aftermath of the Gulf War, Kuwait alone proposing to spend over $10 billion on arms by the end of the century.[61] Britain reportedly had the largest presence at 'the Gulf's largest arms bazaar' in Abu Dhabi in March 1995, attended by the British Defence Procurement Minister and the US Defense Secretary.[62] British suppliers have become so dependent on arms sales to the region that the loss to France of a large tank deal with the UAE was 'very, very bad news indeed', Labour's Defence spokesman noted. The Liberal Democrat spokesman noted that it was a 'big blow' to British manufacturing.[63]

I turn now to consideration of Anglo-American relations with individual countries of the Gulf.

## Saudi Arabia

Saudi Arabia, perhaps the most repressive and illiberal of all the Gulf states, has been the biggest Western prize in the region in terms of oil and long-standing Western policy has been to support the Saudi regimes against both internal and external threats. Moreover, Saudi Arabia in its current form owes its very existence to Western policy, since the latter helped to create it.

The founder, first king and conqueror of Saudi Arabia was Ibn Saud, who, in the early part of the twentieth century, destroyed his enemies to expand his rule across the Arabian peninsula. Said Aburish, in his exposé of the corruption of the Saud ruling family over the generations, notes that Ibn Saud was 'a lecher and a bloodthirsty autocrat', 'one of the most corrupt people of all time', 'whose savagery wreaked havoc across Arabia', terrorising and mercilessly slaughtering his enemies. Ibn Saud's political emergence occurred in 1902 when he reclaimed Riyadh, spiking the heads of his enemies and displaying them at the gates of the city, his followers burning 1200 people to death. It was Ibn Saud's conquest of what is now Saudi Arabia in the years from just before the First World War until the mid-1920s that mainly marked out the nature of his rule. In this conquest 400,000 people were killed since Saud's forces did not take prisoners, and over a million inhabitants of the conquered territories fled to other countries. Numerous rebellions took place against the House of Saud, each of them put down in 'mass killings of mostly innocent victims, including women and children', Aburish notes. By the time the country had been subdued and the territory divided into districts under the control of Saud's relatives and in-laws – a situation which largely prevails today – the regime carried out 40,000 public executions and 350,000 amputations (the latter amounting to 7 per cent of the population).

Britain played the key role in backing Ibn Saud and his conquests, supplying arms and advisers and a subsidy amounting to two-thirds of the country's annual income – until the discovery of oil in the 1930s. The British government had sent Harry St John Philby to assist Ibn Saud in 1917, and he remained with him until the latter's death in 1953. Philby's role, when not at Ibn Saud's side, was, according to Aburish, 'to consult with the Foreign Office over ways to consolidate the rule and extend the influence of' Saud. Ibn Saud's expansions across Arabia were 'British-sponsored conquests', Aburish notes, and 'the simple, undeniable fact behind Ibn Saud's rise to power was Britain's interest in finding someone to deputise for it on the eve of the First World War, when it was trying to wrest control of the Arabian Peninsula from Turkey's hands, and later, when the other Arab leaders were not as forthcoming'.[64]

The RAF and troops from the British-controlled army in Iraq helped Ibn Saud put down a rebellion against his regime in 1929–30: Britain was thus instrumental in 'saving' the Saudi regime, one senior British military officer commented.[65] (The direct British military role in aiding the Saudi regime was also evident in 1969, when British expatriates piloted Saudi aircraft in the confrontation with South Yemen along their border.[66]) In his study of the Gulf states, Hassan Hamdan al-Alkim correctly notes that Britain's support for Ibn Saud, and especially its role in putting down the rebellion, 'were highly appreciated by Ibn Saud and paved the way for the development of relations between the Saudi kingdom and the West that became the core of Saudi foreign policy'.[67] In his memoir, Churchill noted of Ibn Saud that 'my admiration for him was deep, because of his unfailing loyalty to us'. By the end of the Second World War, the Foreign Office could note that 'Ibn Saud is far and away our most influential friend among the Arabs.' Indeed, another memorandum from 1945 read: 'Ibn Saud's influence in the Middle East is very great, and it has been used consistently for a number of years in support of our policy.'[68] 'Without the West', Aburish simply notes, 'there would be no House of Saud.'[69]

US and British support for the Saudi regimes has continued ever since. Former Secretary of State Warren Christopher told Saudi leaders in 1992 that the US commitment to the security of Saudi Arabia 'like that of every president since Franklin Roosevelt, is firm and constant'.[70] Christopher was not exaggerating. Here is a selection from the declassified documents and historical record of expressions of support for the Saudi regimes:

> The relationship between the two countries [the US and Saudi Arabia] ... is unique among all our international relationships. There is no country in this section of the world in which we have this particular type of relationship ... It arises from the genuine personal friendships between our respective peoples.[71] (George McGhee, Assistant Secretary of State for Near Eastern Affairs) (1950)

> Your Majesty has justifiably established a reputation for being a loyal friend ... I pray God that He may have Your Majesty in His safekeeping and that you may be preserved many years for the welfare and happiness of your country.[72] (President Eisenhower, letter to King Ibn Saud) (1953)

> [The US should aim at] ... building up King Saud as a major figure in the Middle Eastern area. [73] (President Eisenhower) (1956)

> When asked by officials of other Arab states what they should do to improve their relations with the United States, [Saudi government representative] Sheikh Yusuf might simply tell them to behave as Saudi Arabia did.[74] (State Department official) (1957)

> Saudi Arabia remains the cornerstone for attaining US foreign objectives in the Arabian peninsula.[75] (Pentagon official) (1979)

> [Saudi Arabia is] ... the only government in the Arabian peninsula both friendly to the United States and capable of playing a regional security role. [76] (Richard Murphy, Assistant Secretary of State for Near Eastern and South Asian Affairs) (1985)

> [Saudi Arabia is] ... a very steady friend.[77] (Warren Christopher, US Secretary of State) (1994)

For Britain, the Foreign Office view is that Saudi Arabia is 'easily Britain's most important partner in the Middle East, whether politically, commercially or militarily'. By the mid-1980s, it noted that Saudi Arabia 'has been for some time the largest market for British exports outside Western Europe and North America'.[78] In 1996, meanwhile, the Foreign Office Minister noted that 'Saudi Arabia is not just a trading partner but a country whose foreign policy has shared similar objectives to our own', playing 'a crucial role in the promotion of moderate and sensible policies' as 'a bastion of stability' in the region.[79]

Admiration has been mutual. For example, the *Guardian* notes that 'Mrs Thatcher had established a close relationship with King Fahd: friends of the Saudi royal family say that his admiration for her verged on infatuation.'[80] In 1993, King Fahd stated that relations with Britain were 'wonderful'.[81] 'You're a member of the family now', a US State Department official quoted King Fahd as having told the US Ambassador in 1994.[82] This admiration is long standing. Ibn Saud, for example, used to refer to 'our American brothers' and other Saudi officials to the 'true friendship' which existed between Saudi Arabia and the United States.[83]

A recent expression of the special relationship between the West and Saudi Arabia was enunciated by Prince Khaled bin Sultan, Joint Forces Commander in the war against Iraq in 1991. In a speech at Chatham House in 1995, Khaled noted that 'Saudi Arabia's relationship with the West – and especially with Britain and the United States – is our single most important strategic asset.' 'We shall always be grateful to our friends for coming to our aid' during the crisis – 'Britain, of course, prominent among them', Khaled noted. The Gulf War 'cemented our ties with our Western friends' and 'there are few places in the world where Western interests overlap so intimately with those of the local states and people'. Khaled continued by stating that the 'large Al-Yamamah programme is just one expression of our close ties with the United Kingdom' and military ties with the West generally reflect 'a strong community of interest'.[84]

It is instructive to take a closer look at the nature of Saudi society. The US National Intelligence Estimate of 1960 noted 'the country's archaic social and political structure',[85] while the State Department understood in 1955 that 'the Saudis lived a feudal existence that was in many ways almost medieval in nature'.[86] Similar views are no doubt being expressed in secret memoranda now – though these are shielded from the public so as not to upset our Saudi clients.

Muhammad Faour has summarised the current situation in a recent study:

> The political system does not provide for elections, political parties, labour unions, strikes or demonstrations, freedom of expression or public observance of religion other than Islam. The judiciary, which is Islamic, is independent, but trials are closed. All printed matter is censored. Radio and television are tightly controlled public agencies. Non-Saudi, as well as Saudi, women have very restricted freedom and are the principal target of harassment by the religious police.[87]

The US human rights organisation Middle East Watch notes that Saudi Arabia:

> has no legal regime to protect human rights against arbitrary arrest, lengthy pre-trial detention or physical abuse. It has no bill of rights or comparable legal guarantees. And it has declined to sign most international human rights agreements, including the International Covenant for Civil and Political Rights and the Torture Convention. Indeed, Saudi Arabia was one of only a handful of countries that did not vote for the Universal Declaration of Human Rights, adopted by the UN General Assembly on December 10, 1948.[88]

Domestic repression increased in Saudi Arabia following the Gulf War. Middle East Watch notes that legal laws enacted in March 1992 mean that 'Saudi citizens today have fewer civil and political rights than they had in 1926'. There are indications that these laws 'are not the beginning of a gradual process of democratisation' but are the 'maximum concessions' the ruling family is willing to grant in response to internal and external pressures.[89] Such 'reforms' 'codify royal authoritarianism', Middle East Watch commented.[90] In August 1993, King Fahd announced the composition of a consultative council, consisting of 60 members, all appointed by the King. 'This council's powers', the *Guardian* comments, echoing Middle East Watch above, 'are even more limited than those of the one which the founder of the Kingdom, King Abdul Aziz [that is, Ibn Saud], set up in 1926.'[91] For the British Ambassador in Saudi Arabia, however, 'it's an important step'.[92] Meanwhile, the reshuffle in the 'government' of August 1995 entailed no changes to the control over the key ministries exercised by the Saud family.[93]

Human Rights Watch notes that:

> In 1994 Saudi Arabia witnessed the largest roundup in recent history of opposition activists and a new low in the dismal human rights record of the Kingdom. Arbitrary arrest, detention without trial and ill-treatment of prisoners remained the norm throughout the year, especially for those accused of political offences ... The ban on free speech, assembly and association was strictly enforced; violators were jailed, deported, banned from travel or dismissed from their government positions. Restrictions on the employment and movement of women were strictly observed, and harassment of non-Muslims and discrimination against the Shia continued unabated.[94]

The 'most significant development in 1994', Human Rights Watch continues, was the government's 'crackdown on peaceful dissent by Islamic groups' – something that the British government had done its bit to support, noted below. Torture and beheadings continued, while 'the royal family's concentration of power and the absence of a free press or parliament left the royal family immune to criticism and free to take advantage of their position'. This involved reports of 'murder and beatings of ordinary citizens and foreign residents'.[95]

Said Aburish notes in his study that 'I cannot unearth a single public statement by a Western leader about the country's abominable human rights record.'[96] When the human rights abuses and repression in the country receive media attention, the systematic connection with Anglo-American policy and its share of the responsibility for sustaining such a monstrous regime is never entertained.

The fact that there is no real difference between national and family wealth entails a significant rake-off of national wealth for personal use. Aburish has described how the system works:

> The greater part of the budget, $3–5 billion, is paid to King Fahd from the oil income before it is recorded as national income. The Oil Minister subtracts money from the country's oil income and transfers it to the King's personal account and declares the rest as national income. Fahd allocates the money he receives between the various members of his family in an improvised manner. The amount of money transferred to Fahd's personal account depends on him; he tells the Oil Minister how much he needs and the minister obeys him.[97]

Thus Britain's and the United States' main friend in the region is one of the richest men in history, with a personal wealth estimated at $28 billion.[98]

The huge wealth in the country has enabled social services to be funded, yet the image of a luxury life for all Saudis is a cultivated myth. The adult literacy rate, for example, is just 64 per cent, lower than Papua New Guinea. According to the UNDP, over 1 million people out of the total population of 16 million are without access to safe water, while nearly 3 million live without access to sanitation.[99] Only 77 per cent of children are enrolled in primary school, a number lower than in many poor countries.[100]

The effective Western support for Saudi domestic repression has been constant. In 1994, the US Secretary of State for Near Eastern Affairs, Robert Pelletreau, told Congress that 'the US believes that the government of Saudi Arabia continues to enjoy the support of the overwhelming majority of Saudi citizens' – without providing any supporting evidence; not surprisingly, since there would have been none.[101] This echoed the view of President Eisenhower in 1957, who noted that King Saud is 'a good king ... who has the welfare of his people primarily in mind'.[102]

In 1946, a US government memorandum noted that 'the United States has every interest in assisting the Government of Saudi Arabia in maintaining peace and order in the country'.[103] US Secretary of State John Dulles noted in 1957 that US interest in Saudi Arabia 'centres on the defense of the Dhahran air base and the Saudis ability to resist Communist aggression and to maintain internal security'.[104] The overall commitment to Saudi 'security' was enunciated by

President Truman in 1950, in a letter to King Saud: 'No threat to your Kingdom could occur which would not be a matter of immediate concern to the United States.'[105]

Military relations offer the same prospect of 'assisting the Government' in 'maintaining peace and order'. The US explained to Saudi Arabian officials in 1957, for example, that 'the United States recognised the need of Saudi Arabia for some additional military equipment in order to be better able to defend the Dhahran airfield and maintain internal order'.[106] Military training serves the same purpose (always publicly justified in terms of defence against an external threat). Britain helped train the Saudi White Army in 1947 and in 1963.[107] The White Army became the Saudi Arabian National Guard (SANG) – different than the regular army – which currently plays a primarily internal security role with a presence in every Saudi city.[108] US training of the SANG continues today; over 200 US government advisers and 1500 contract staff were employed in a contract worth $800 million in 1993.[109] Leading Middle East analyst Thomas McNaugher notes that the programme has sought to train the SANG to defend the oil fields. 'Yet', he adds, 'SANG units are not structured to meet the main external threats to the fields' and 'their more likely role remains internal security'.[110] Britain also currently has a military team, headed by a Brigadier, training the SANG.[111]

Previously, a United States Air Force (USAF) fighter squadron had been temporarily stationed along the Yemen border during the outbreak of the Yemeni civil war. The US also operated AWACS surveillance planes out of Riyadh during the border war between the two Yemens in 1979 and they returned during the Iranian hostage crisis.[112] Currently, US operators can read the Saudi AWACS system even when not operating directly with them, and have the data transferred by satellite either to the Pentagon or to its military base in Diego Garcia in the Indian Ocean.[113]

To support the Saud family's control over the country, CIA agents have been seconded and the regime has been provided with an electronic monitoring system to record telephone calls. As the US presence in the country grew in the 1950s, CIA activity consequently increased and senior agents advised the regime 'on everything from the use of fly killers to hiring the public relations firm Hill & Knowlton', Aburish notes.[114] The CIA presence continues in the 1990s, with recent visits paid by the former CIA Station Chief in Riyadh along with a team of security specialists.[115]

British interest in maintaining the regime has been explained by Peter de la Billiere, Commander of the British Forces during the Gulf war, who noted that, following the war:

> As we, the British, had backed the system of sheikhly rule ever since our own withdrawal from the Gulf in the early 1970s, and seen it prosper, we were keen that it should continue. Saudi Arabia was an old and proven friend of ours and had deployed its immense oil wealth in a benign and thoughtful way, with the result that standards of living had become very high. It was thus very much in our own interest that the country and its regime should remain stable after the war.[116]

Britain has been more than forthcoming in aiding Saudi domestic policy. *The Times* noted in October 1994, for example, that Foreign Secretary Douglas Hurd 'said yesterday that the basic system of government in the Kingdom was stable and commanded the support of the great majority of Saudis'. This statement occurred after 'exile sources reported a fresh wave of arrests in Saudi Arabia, including those of poets and university teachers'. It also occurred while a British business delegation was preparing to visit Saudi Arabia.[117]

Whitehall's priorities and intrigues were revealed in the case of Mohamed al-Masari, Saudi Arabia's leading dissident. After being forced to flee Saudi Arabia and having settled in London, Masari had organised a campaign against the Saudi regime with the intention of overthrowing it. The British government, making no secret of the fact that Masari's activities were threatening good relations and arms deals with Riyadh, and following intense Saudi pressure, ordered his deportation in January 1996 (though the High Court later found this decision unlawful and he was allowed to remain). The *Independent* noted that 'Britain's ambassador in Riyadh, David Gore-Booth, is believed to have argued for a tough line against Mr Masari and in favour of unflinching British support for the House of Saud'.[118] The Home Office Minister explained that Masari's activities in Britain 'were not illegal as such. However, what he was doing was to act against British interest.'[119]

A confidential memo obtained by the *Guardian* showed that some of Britain's biggest arms companies connived with Whitehall to try and stifle Masari and placate the Saudis. Britain passed on intelligence on Iraq to Saudi Arabia following a debriefing of Saddam Hussein's son-in-law, who had recently defected from Iraq. In a memo, Chief Executive of Vickers, Sir Colin Chandler, recorded a 'general feeling' in intelligence and business circles that 'direct Saudi intervention' against Masari 'could be difficult' since he was the son of a leading cleric. The affair clearly demonstrated the close links between the government and British arms manufacturers. Chandler had previously been seconded from British Aerospace to the Ministry of Defence for five years as head of the Defence Export Services Organisation, the main body responsible for promoting arms sales. It also emerged that Andrew Green, who had just been appointed Ambassador to Saudi Arabia and was Under-Secretary of State for Middle East Policy, had been a non-executive director of Vickers, a major arms exporter, for the past two years.[120]

Asylum applications were also made by other defectors. Mohammed Khilewi, who served with the Saudi mission to the United Nations, for example, sought asylum at the same time as claiming that he was in possession of around 14,000 documents showing 'a history, pattern and practice of terrorism and violations of human rights which would terribly embarrass my country and might cause the current regime to seek personal retribution against me'.[121] What became of Khilewi, and others such as Ahmed Zakrany, an official at a Saudi consulate in the US who applied for asylum in Britain,[122] was not reported in the press, to my knowledge.

The Yamamah ('dove') programme is Britain's largest economic stake in Saudi Arabia. This, to cite Aburish again, is 'not an arms deal in the conventional sense, rather a whole armaments programme which calls for the UK to meet the needs of Saudi Arabia in the areas of creating a modern air force and building an aerial defence system'.[123] The first part of the project was signed in 1985 and was worth around $10 billion: it included the purchase of 72 Tornado aircraft, Hawk trainer jets, improvements in Saudi airbases and the supply of spare parts and maintenance personnel. There are currently around 5000 British Aerospace staff working in Saudi Arabia in support of the project.[124] Yamamah II, signed in 1988, was even bigger, the initial part of which involved the export of 50 Tornado combat aircraft, 50 helicopters, 60 Hawk trainers, 4 minesweepers and the building of an airbase. This order was part of a 20-year programme.[125] A deal between Major and Fahd was signed in 1993 providing for the sale of 48 Tornados worth $5 billion.[126] In 1994, Saudi Arabia announced it would buy around 20 Hawk aircraft worth £500 million to train the pilots who will fly the 48 Tornados ordered in the 1993 deal (this brought the total number of Hawk aircraft sold by British Aerospace around the world to 700).[127] Private British firms also provided Saudi Arabia with 8000 electro-shock batons under Yamamah II, presumably for use by the Saudi police.[128]

The Yamamah project involves most of British military industry, though British Aerospace runs the commercial aspects of the deal on behalf of the government. The sheer size of the deals means that the commissions (essentially, bribes) paid are likely to be enormous. Direct commissions worth around $300 million were reportedly paid in the early stages of the project alone. An investigation by the government spending watchdog, the National Audit Office, into possible rake-offs has never been published, though the Conservative government claimed that nothing illegal was found. The Conservative government also refused to submit copies to the Public Accounts Committee, which also scrutinises government spending.[129]

The Western powers have been less successful in enticing the Saudis to sign the kind of prepositioning and base agreements they have signed with some of the other Gulf states. There are currently around 30,000 US citizens in the American compound at the Saudi military base in Dhahran[130] but the US has not had a formal military base in Saudi Arabia since its facilities at Dhahran – constructed in 1946 – were closed down in 1962. In the aftermath of the Gulf War the United States initially sought a prepositioning agreement with Riyadh that would allow for a stockpile of armour sufficient to equip 150,000 US soldiers. This was, however, scaled back, due to Saudi rejection, on the grounds that such an overt presence could heighten Islamic sensitivities in the country. Saudi Arabia also rejected a US plan to base a 'forward headquarters element' of the US Central Command on shore in the Gulf.[131] The following year the US press reported that while the US was seeking a formal security cooperation pact with Saudi Arabia, the Saudis, still worried about anti-American sentiment in the country, 'wanted to put any new security arrangements on a handshake or unspoken understandings'. At the same time, however, the US was planning to store around 400 aircraft in the region, most believed to be destined for Saudi Arabia.[132]

## Kuwait

Relations between the US and Britain and the second most important GCC state have recently flourished in terms of arms deals, diplomatic relations and military links, and with a permanent British military mission in the country helping to train and rebuild the Kuwaiti army.[133] The Queen met Kuwait's Emir, Sheikh Jaber al-Sabah, in October 1991 and again in May 1995 basically, it can be presumed, as a high-level arms seller, the first visit taking place at a time of gross human rights abuses by government forces, briefly considered below. (This is a traditional role for the royal family: Prince Charles visited the UAE in November 1996, for example, as a huge arms deal with Britain was being prepared.[134])

Both the CIA and MI6 have a long history of close relations with the regime. A CIA unit was working with the Kuwaiti government up until the invasion in 1990 and whose task it was, according to leading Egyptian commentator Mohamed Heikal, 'to foresee and avert any threat to the Sabah family'.[135] In the 1960s, according to one analyst of Iraq, the CIA had run clandestine radio stations in Kuwait which broadcasted the names and addresses of Iraqi democrats and alleged communists for the Iraqi regime 'to capture and murder'.[136] MI6, meanwhile, opened a station in Kuwait in 1961, according to former MI6 officer Anthony Verrier. One of MI6's tasks, Verrier notes, was to convince the Kuwaiti Emir that his country's future protection would require 'the occasional presence of British troops'. The Emir 'had to be persuaded if possible, or coerced if necessary, into signing a piece of paper which would enable British troops, "by invitation", to defend Kuwait in circumstances left vague enough to justify intervention and the exercise of a deterrent strategy'.[137]

This strategy appears to provide the background to the British military intervention in Kuwait in 1961, which was justified by the British government by reference to an alleged Iraqi threat to the country. The declassified planning record, however, strongly suggests that British planners fabricated such a threat to convince the emir that he needed continued British military protection and to serve as a pretext for intervention.[138] Verrier himself comments that Iraq 'was not considered a serious threat to Kuwait' and quotes from official sources to the effect that the British government 'did not contemplate aggression by Iraq very seriously'.[139] The record suggests that British planners were very keen to intervene militarily in Kuwait in 1961, fearful that Kuwait's formal independence would encourage it to pursue independent policies. British planners also considered military intervention in 1958, when Foreign Secretary Selwyn Lloyd considered 'immediate British occupation' of Kuwait. 'The advantage of this action', Lloyd noted, 'would be that we would get our hands firmly on the Kuwait oil.' Military action was at this point decided against and he suggested that a better policy would be to help create 'a kind of Kuwaiti Switzerland where the British do not exercise physical control', but without losing actual control. This, Noam Chomsky, describes, was 'what Saddam Hussein planned after invading Kuwait, top US government officials feared'.[140]

The US planning record also shows apparent joint US and British contemplation of an occupation of Kuwait in 1959. One memorandum notes 'a US–UK "study" of two years ago which envisaged roughly 90 per cent UK participation and 10 per cent US participation' in such an intervention.[141]

US planners were worried in 1961 that to 'the rest of the world' (that is, everyone except Britain) and especially to the Arabs, 'Kuwait is, after all, only a British colony'; also noting – after Kuwait had gained its independence – Kuwait's 'posture' as an independent Arab state. Nevertheless, in the aftermath of the British intervention in 1961, US planners stated that in future operations they 'should be prepared to consider British requests for logistical support' and 'we have developed in planning talks in London some understanding as to the possibilities for limited US assistance in these circumstances'.[142]

The long history of Western military planning to secure Kuwaiti oil – of which the 1991 war was a continuation – is matched by the more recent efforts to assist the Kuwaiti ruling family in organising domestic society appropriately. Middle East Watch (MEW) describes the Kuwait government's strategy following the defeat of Iraq as 'a government-inspired quest to root out those who collaborated with the Iraqi occupiers and to restructure Kuwait society in a fashion deemed more politically acceptable'. This involved widespread summary executions and deaths in detention, most of which were 'committed by official security forces or by irregular armed groups working closely with official forces'. MEW also noted that 'the [Bush] administration has acted far more as a defender of the Kuwaiti government ... than as a government intent on living up to the human rights principles which formed part of the rallying cry for war with Iraq'. MEW also noted that testimony received 'puts US officers in places of detention in Kuwait where torture has taken place', although 'this is not to say that Americans are participating in torture'.[143] One press article also reported that US special forces 'cooperated with Kuwait special forces in "sweeps" through Palestinian districts of Kuwait City'.[144]

After talks with the Kuwaiti Emir in May 1991 – while the Kuwaiti security forces were indulging in these atrocities – British Foreign Secretary Hurd noted that:

> The emir said that Kuwait would not tolerate abuses of human rights. He made the point, and it seems to be fair, that in the immediate aftermath of liberation, after all they had endured, it was not entirely surprising that there should be a period of suspicion, anger and retaliation. But that is now over, he told me.[145]

By 1995, the Palestinian population had been reduced from 400,000 before the invasion to 20,000, as a result of Kuwaiti mass expulsions.[146] The attitude was summed up by the Kuwaiti Ambassador to the United States, who declared: 'if you in the US are so concerned about human rights and leaving hundreds of thousands of Palestinians in Kuwait, we'll be more than happy to airlift them to you free of charge, and you can give them American citizenship'.[147]

As in Saudi Arabia, political repression has increased in recent years, again free from any serious Western pressure for change. Kuwaiti promises during the occupation to deepen democracy in the country resulted in elections in 1992 in which 50 out of 279 candidates were freely elected – the most liberal system in the Gulf. The electorate, however, consists of male citizens over the age of 21 whose ancestors lived in Kuwait prior to 1920 – in all, just 8 per cent of all citizens have the right to vote in this democratic showcase for the rest of the Gulf.[148] In 1995, however, the Conservative government spokesperson informed the House of Commons of the 'excellent relationship' between Britain and Kuwait and 'our friendship ... founded on close co-operation in many fields, particularly in defence'. He continued by noting that:

> Every country has the right to develop its political structure in accordance with its culture, heritage and traditions. The ruling family, government and people have an impressive record. We are encouraged by the democratically elected National Assembly in Kuwait since the election in 1992.[149]

In 1993, Human Rights Watch noted that 'the year was marked by intensified persecution of those minority communities whose loyalty to the government was in doubt' while 'the Kuwaiti government accelerated its long-term strategy of restructuring its population in a fashion that violated human rights, through arbitrary arrests and summary deportations'. None of those implicated in the killing and torture of hundreds of people following the war were brought to justice and there were no plans to conduct any further investigations. 'Mass unidentified graves of people buried after the war – apparent victims of Kuwait forces – remained to be exhumed.'[150]

In 1994, with the government policy to pressure undesirables to leave the country continuing, the authorities reiterated their ban on political parties and reinforced a moratorium on the formation of new private associations. This followed the closing down of all human rights groups as part of a ban on unlicensed organisations in 1993. Groups that attempted to defy the ban by holding public meetings were threatened with the use of force.[151]

## Oman

Oman has traditionally acted as another Western outpost in the region. Its highly repressive regimes have been directly aided by Britain, which helped to put down internal rebellions from the 1950s to the 1970s and engineered a coup in the country in 1970, while British officers commanded the Sultan's armed forces until the mid-1980s. The regime which lasted until the coup in 1970 was especially vile, conducting gross repression of the population.[152] This regime received full backing from Britain; Prime Minister Harold Macmillan, for example, believed that 'the Sultan is a true friend to the West and is doing his best for his people'.[153] Sultan Qaboos, another Sandhurst graduate who also served in a British infantry battalion, took over in 1970 and remains in power today.[154] Soon after he was installed, the SAS despatched a team providing his bodyguard.[155] The British Ambassador to Oman declared in 1985:

> The relationship between Oman and Britain is broad, deep and rooted in history. Furthermore – and this is rare in contacts between nations – it is remarkably free from friction: the two peoples, since they first encountered each other, have almost always been friends.

A similar view was expressed by then Defence Secretary Michael Heseltine, who also noted that there were 'no issues of any kind to be resolved' between the two countries, Oman's virtually complete suppression of any even remotely democratic tendencies apparently unworthy even of discussion. *Financial Times* reporter Bridget Bloom, whose article contained an uncritical analysis of the two quotes above, added thoughtfully: 'a relationship which involves so few stresses and such obvious advantage provides a welcome respite from the cruder and more normal experience of international relations'.[156]

Relations with Britain have been especially deep in the military sphere. As well as retaining command of the Omani Army, Air Force and Navy until the mid-1980s, around 2000 seconded British military and civilian personnel were employed in the Omani armed forces by 1986.[157] By the early 1990s, there remained several hundred British personnel training the Omani armed forces.[158] Its military equipment, meanwhile, was and remains bought largely from Britain, including Chieftain tanks, Scorpion armoured vehicles, Blowpipe missiles, and Tornado, Hawk and Jaguar aircraft. Britain also has access to an airbase in the country, prepositions supplies there (along with the United States) and conducts regular port visits and exercises with the Omani armed forces.

Links with Western 'security' services remain close, as far as can be ascertained. The British private 'security' firm KMS – which provides military training for its clients – has trained Oman's Special Forces and, according to Stephen Dorril, 'is said to virtually run the [Omani] internal security services, which have strong links with MI6'. Dorril also notes that all KMS's important contracts are cleared by the British government.[159] The CIA is also thought to have a large presence in the country. In 1985, for example, it was reported that a former CIA officer was acting as one of the closest advisers to the Sultan, and was one of 20 US, British and Arab advisers. Their role was to be 'involved in writing Omani laws', 'providing security for the nation's ruler and lobbying for Oman in the United States'. A former Treasury Secretary in the Eisenhower administration, Robert Anderson, who became an economic adviser to the Sultan, disclosed that his role was 'to consult on ways to improve their economy' and get Oman 'out from under the dominance of the British'.[160]

## Bahrain

British officials controlled Bahraini policy before independence and the British 'withdrawal' from the Gulf in 1971. Mass opposition to the regime was clearly expressed in the riots of 1956 and 1965, both successfully put down by the authorities. When British troops pulled out of South Yemen in 1967, Bahrain became the centre of Britain's Middle East Command; at the same time international capital moved in force into Bahrain, eventually turning it into one of the world's major financial centres.

Following Bahraini independence the police force remained commanded by British officers.[161] The State Investigation Service, responsible for internal security, is headed by a Briton, Ian Henderson, and currently employs up to 12 British ex-policemen. Henderson was recruited in 1966 and had previously served as assistant commissioner of police in pre-independence Kenya, 'where he became famous for hunting down Mau Mau leaders', the *Guardian* notes. 'In Bahrain, he created the Special Branch and is said to have played a key role in framing internment laws which allow the security forces to detain suspects for three years.' Those detained are routinely tortured. According to Islamic opposition leader Sheikh Ali Salman, referring to such detentions: 'the torture is carried out by Bahrainis, but it is supervised by British officials', claiming that interrogators read from questions written in English. Salman also claimed that his deportation in January 1995 was supervised by a Briton.[162] According to a Bahraini opposition group, Henderson was thus singled out for denunciation at funerals of people killed in the unrest.[163]

An appointed Consultative Council held its first session in 1993. US analyst Gregory Gause notes that 'the Bahraini Council's powers are limited to review of legislation sent to it by the Council of Ministers and to oversight of government activity through questioning of ministers'. British priorities with regard to this system and popular opposition to it were shown in late 1994 and early 1995, when demonstrations and unrest lasting several months took place, and which called for the restoration of the 1973 constitution that had been dissolved in 1975. In response, the Bahraini authorities arrested thousands of people in incidents in which some people were killed and dozens injured. Amnesty International noted people had been arrested under 'a law so vague that the mildest criticism of the government' was sufficient for a lengthy detention.[164] The security forces also beat and ill-treated women and systematically used torture to extract confessions from detainees. According to Amnesty International, Saudi Arabian riot police were also brought in to help its neighbour and live ammunition was used by Bahraini forces to disperse demonstrators.[165]

The independent Bahrain Human Rights Organisation (BHRO) noted that in a security operation mounted in one village in April 1995, 'security forces opened fire at any person [who] attempted to emerge from the houses of the village'. Security forces 'continued breaking into houses, looting, terrorising and arbitrarily arresting hundreds of citizens'. The BHRO states that 'human rights violations in the current events are far more than arbitrary detention and accidental killings'; they look more like 'massacres' 'in order to quell numerous peaceful demonstrations'.[166]

The Conservative British government played a supportive role to the Bahraini authorities in the diplomatic field. During the unrest Foreign Secretary Douglas Hurd delivered a speech in London criticising Arab dissidents in Britain for 'indulging in malevolent propaganda campaigns against our good friends in the region'. He also stated: 'Our thoughts are with the government of Bahrain in the difficulties they face. As old friends they should know they have our full support as they work to ensure a stable and prosperous future for all the people of Bahrain.'[167] He also stated that the British government had 'no evidence' of Bahraini police using unnecessary force in making their arrests.[168] This statement happened to coincide with talks between the British Defence Minister and the Bahraini government on military cooperation in the Gulf and joint military exercises in the Gulf between the RAF, the USAF and the Bahraini military.[169]

Foreign Office Minister Baroness Chalker similarly noted in a House of Lords debate in June 1995 that 'Bahrain has been a good and close friend to the United Kingdom' and 'in recent years Bahrain has made considerable progress on human rights'. Similar to Hurd, she also used the standard line of noting that some 'foreign dissidents' in Britain 'encourage terrorism' ('terrorism' in this useful example being taken to mean anyone opposing British policy).[170] From the evidence (see Chapter 2) Labour is continuing this policy of fundamental support for the Bahraini regime.

# Part IV

# The United Nations

# 7

# The US, Britain and the UN in History

In recent years, the role of the United Nations in international affairs has received much attention. This has come partly from those who have placed a lot of faith in the UN's ability to become a greater force for good in the world after the end of the Cold War. It has also come from those who, from the opposite perspective, especially from rightwing members of the US Congress, see such a UN role as a distinctive threat to the pursuit of national policy. The concept of 'humanitarian intervention' in particular has become a regular part of the lexicon of international affairs. This chapter and Chapter 8 assess the past and current policy towards the UN, mainly the Security Council, of the United States and Britain, two states which have shaped the institution and which remain key to its functioning and non-functioning in the current era. It is argued here that these policies have been sorely misinterpreted but need to be understood to assess the UN's future.

## 2 + 2 = 5

Two notions have in recent years risen to the status of religious truths in the discussions of the United Nations. The first is that the Soviet veto was responsible for the non-functioning of the United Nations in the postwar period. The second – linked to the first – is that it was the Cold War that made it impossible for solutions to be found in the UN to regional security questions.

Consider first the question of the veto. As Table 7.1 shows that, from the establishment of the UN until the collapse of the Soviet Union in 1991, the USSR cast 114 vetoes, China 3, the United States 69, Britain 30 and France 18. The three Western powers therefore cast an equal number of vetoes to the two communist states over the whole period. However, in the last quarter of a century before the collapse of the Soviet Union (1965–90), a rather different picture emerges: the United States cast over five times as many vetoes as the Soviet Union, and the three Western states as a whole over seven times as many as the two communist states.

Table 7.1: Vetoes of draft resolutions of the Security Council

| | 1945–90 | 1965–90 |
|---|---|---|
| US | 68 | 69 |
| USSR | 114 | 13 |
| Britain | 30 | 27 |
| France | 18 | 14 |
| China | 3 | 2 |

Source: FCO, *Table of Vetoed Draft Resolutions in the United Nations Security Council 1946–1993*, Foreign Policy Document No. 249, FCO, London, January 1994.

These Western vetoes effectively scuppered all UN attempts to deal with three major issues. First, the US has delivered more than 27 (at the last count) vetoes in support of Israeli positions at the UN, thus vetoing the possibility of collective international action over the Israeli-occupied territories and its invasions of Lebanon. Second, all three Western powers ensured that the white-ruled governments of Rhodesia and South Africa were protected from international action, in both their domestic policies and, in the case of governments in Pretoria, their acts of aggression in Angola, Namibia and other frontline states. Third, the US ensured that its war against Nicaragua in the 1980s proceeded free from international interference, by delivering seven Security Council vetoes in 1982–86. Other cases of obstruction of the UN are documented in part below.

Of particular interest is the fact that the last veto cast by the Soviet Union was in 1984 – over the next six years, the US proceeded to deliver no less than 32 vetoes; Britain, 10. It might be thought, therefore, that these vetoes would be firmly in the minds of commentators analysing the recent history of the United Nations, in the dozens of articles appearing on the subject at the end of the Cold War in 1989–91.

This is not the case, however. An analysis of press and academic commentary on the UN in these years yields virtually no mention of the fact that the Western states cast any vetoes in the Security Council at all, let alone that they, and not the Soviet Union, were primarily responsible for its non-functioning. The story that the West scuppered UN action throughout the postwar period is the wrong one, and is therefore hardly entertained in the propaganda system, despite being hard not to notice.

The *Independent*, for example, noted in an editorial in June 1993, that the UN Security Council 'suffered badly from the harsh climate of the Cold War, when it was paralysed by walkouts, abstentions and vetoes by China and the Soviet Union'.[1] The inclusion of China here appears simply gratuitous, since it cast just three vetoes throughout the period. Elsewhere, *Independent* editors note that 'the United Nations was virtually captive to the organisation of so-called "Non-Aligned Nations", whipped in to toe the Soviet line by the Cubans'. The editorial continues by noting that 'during the Reagan administration', the US 'lost almost all patience with an organisation that seemed little more than a front for America's enemies'.[2] Translated, during the Reagan administration, US policy was so completely opposed to international opinion that it was forced to cast dozens of vetoes – concerning Israel, South Africa and Nicaragua, among others – to ensure that its policies were not subject to international interference.

The second crucial notion is that it was the Cold War which made it impossible to reach solutions in the UN to regional security issues. For this to hold true, the Cold War needs to be understood as the primary or major facet of the conflicts in, for example, Southern Africa, the Middle East and Central America. This is plainly not the case. As I tried to show elsewhere,[3] the underlying basis of Western foreign policies in the postwar period was not the Cold War – although the Cold War was certainly a reality and helps to explain policy in some areas, it provided in many other areas a convenient ideological background or pretext for interventions and policies conducted for other purposes. The US war against Nicaragua, for example, cannot be understood as mainly part of the Cold War, but rather as a war conducted against independent nationalism in the wider Central America region.[4] Western policies towards Israel and South Africa were only marginally motivated by Cold War considerations, on any reasonable interpretation.

This reality tends to be expressed only in obscure circles for Western audiences. Thus Indian academic Rajaram Panda correctly writes in the Delhi journal *India Quarterly* that:

> In its 46 years of existence the UN has been used more often than not as a tool for Western – shall we say US – foreign policy goals. UN ineffectiveness over the years cannot be blamed entirely on Cold War divisions. An overwhelming majority of the UN Security Council resolutions were vetoed by the US and Britain. Most had

little or nothing to do with the Cold War, but were supporting anti-colonial struggles in the Third World.[5]

However, it was indeed the end of the Cold War, *Guardian* editors argue, that 'brought an end to the paralysis that overtook the organisation [that is, the UN] when the communist bloc allied with the new African and Asian members to attack the West, Israel and South Africa'.[6] *Independent* editors concur with this basic argument, noting that 'in crisis after crisis, superpower rivalry and the use of the veto prevented action'.[7] *The Times* notes:

> The original UN commitment was to support collective security in the shared interest of a world under the rule of law. This was later submerged beneath the Cold War. But there is now no hostile Soviet Union to inhibit the Western democracies from putting principle into practice.[8]

Here, then, Western states are excused by the Cold War from pursuing principled foreign policies in the postwar period.

This view is repeated in academia with next to no exceptions. The highly reputed International Institute for Strategic Studies (IISS), for example, comments in its annual review of world affairs that it was 'Cold War antagonisms that hobbled' the UN 'for the whole of its existence'.[9] Leading academic Paul Wilkinson has also commented on 'the UN Security Council, so long paralysed by the Cold War into helplessness'.[10] Numerous other examples could be cited.

It was not so much the Cold War as basic Western priorities that largely prevented the UN's proper functioning throughout the postwar period. This situation changed in the 1990s as Russia – now much dependent on Western financial aid – learnt to 'behave', and the Third World was further disciplined into accepting Anglo-American policies, thus no longer necessitating the use of the Western veto.

## 'An instrument of Anglo-American foreign policy'

From the beginning of the postwar period until the present day, a primary aim of the leading Western states – and especially the United States and Britain – has been to render the United Nations an instrument of their foreign policies: serviceable as such when required; discarded when not. This simple truism is clearly revealed in the

British and US planning documents of the early postwar years. A British Foreign Office memorandum of 1952, for example, called for strengthening the UN 'as an instrument of Anglo-American foreign policy'.[11]

British planners believed the UN offered particular advantages in helping to maintain empire. The Foreign Office noted in 1945:

> It seems natural that the Great Powers should each be primarily responsible for organising effective arrangements in the different parts of the world which are of particular interest to each of them. The San Francisco charter [establishing the UN] provides for 'regional arrangements' and, under the present order of things, it will fall to Great Britain to organise those in the Middle East.[12]

Secret US State Department despatches confirmed the British view:

> There is undoubtedly a tendency among certain circles in Great Britain to enter into a series of compromises with the Russians in the hope that the Soviet Union may be satisfied by obtaining the control of certain territory now belonging to third powers and of achieving strategic defensive positions at the expense of other members of the United Nations. If the British government should actually embark upon such a policy, it would appear that the United Nations Organisation would either disappear as a force in world affairs or would tend to become merely an instrument for the use of the Great Powers in carving up the world into respective spheres of influence.[13]

This State Department prophesy occurred with no little help from the authors of this despatch. It is also prophetic in view of the use of the UN by the Great Powers in the 1990s – as a legitimising instrument to control their 'respective spheres of influence', a theme to which I return below.

These documents reveal another permanent feature of the Western stance towards the UN: that the latter acts as an international cover for the pursuit of national foreign policy. An April 1950 Foreign Office memorandum on the UN stated that the organisation 'provides a way of presenting to the peoples of Asia and the Middle East schemes which, if presented outside the United Nations, might be suspect as an attempt to impose Western supervision'.[14] In January 1951, the Foreign Office noted that:

> Neglecting the views of many friendly governments the United States government are trying to impose on the United Nations a policy which is the direct result of past American failures in the Far East and which does not at all spring from the needs of the United Nations or of other member states.

The US thus had an 'urgent need' of the UN 'as an umbrella to cover them in their Far Eastern policy'.[15]

The British Ambassador to the UN declared in 1952 that the US administration 'had always argued' that US foreign policy must be based on the UN 'because they could not otherwise justify the predominant role which the United States must now play in international affairs and carry American public opinion with them in support of it'.[16] In the British view the US government always needed 'some assurance of United Nations cover for certain aspects of their foreign policy'.[17]

However, Britain's Ambassador to the UN commented in 1953 that the UN could sometimes act 'to our disadvantage'. 'Recent events in Iran', he noted, 'have not been such as to encourage one to put much faith in United Nations solutions when our own interests are at stake.'[18] The Ambassador was referring to the Iranian government's nationalisation of British oil operations in the country, and the referral of the case to the UN. Before the year was out, Britain had organised with the CIA a plot to overthrow the government, thus assuring a 'more reasonable government', as Foreign Secretary Anthony Eden put it.[19]

Democracy in the UN also posed a threat. In June 1950 the Foreign Office noted that:

> The possibility, under the system of 'one state, one vote', for small nations to exert undue influence may endanger the ability of the United Kingdom and Commonwealth to preserve their essential interests from United Nations interference.[20]

A decade later Prime Minister Harold Macmillan voiced a similar view by noting that one problem of the Cold War was that 'it puts a tremendous blackmailing weapon into the hands of quite unimportant countries in the Afro-Asian camps'.[21]

Similar British concerns about democracy are revealed in attitudes towards the Commonwealth. 'These small countries inhabited by primitive peoples', a 1953 memorandum read, 'are not at present mentally equipped' to be 'adult nations'. If they were to become 'full members of the Club' they would 'rapidly destroy the Commonwealth and the whole influence for good which it exercises in the world'. 'Even the presence of the representatives of the Asiatic Dominions has completely destroyed the atmosphere of confidence which previously existed' in high-level meetings.[22] Britain's Commonwealth Secretary wrote that it would 'uncomfortable' to have newly independent territories as full Commonwealth members, so the 'wiser course' would be to admit them to 'a status of nominal equality' whilst seeking 'from the start to ensure that ... they will remain within our sphere of influence'. Countries which 'are never likely to achieve full independence' from Britain, however, and therefore who 'cannot aspire to the status of full Commonwealth membership', included Cyprus, Gambia, Mauritius and the Seychelles. For these countries Colonial rule would be 'appropriate for many years to come – even though we may find it necessary to abandon the term "colonial", in deference to latter-day susceptibilities and misrepresentation in the United Nations'. The overall reason for the British policy was to 'maintain our influence as a world power' by remaining as 'primus inter pares in a group of independent Commonwealth countries'.[23]

One long-standing British fear was international interference in the government of its colonies: 'at this stage more than any other in the history of the Colonial Empire ignorant or prejudiced outside interference would do uncalculable harm', the Colonial Office noted in 1950, referring to the United Nations. It also feared that colonial powers would have to become 'accountable to the United Nations', something which necessarily had to be avoided.[24] The acceptance of the right of the UN to 'interfere in the affairs of the Colonial Empire' would have 'serious and dangerous consequences' for achieving the objectives of colonial policy, the Colonial Office pointed out. An especially interesting analysis of this fear ran thus:

> The introduction of accountability to the United Nations would inevitably, in the eyes of the colonial peoples, devalue the Crown as the symbol of ultimate authority to which allegiance is owing and from which protection flows, and thereby undermine the present and potential contribution of the Commonwealth to world stability. It would encourage disgruntled elements in the colonies to appeal to the United Nations over the heads of His Majesty's Government, and if the colonial peoples were encouraged to look all the time to an external Court of Appeal in the shape of the United Nations it would be incomparably more difficult to encourage in them loyalty to their own local governments, a proper sense of responsibility and, in multi-racial communities,

> that sense of local cohesion which is a necessary prerequisite to ultimate nationhood.

British planners were opposed to colonial issues even being a 'legitimate subject for debate in the United Nations'.[25]

Britain was anxious 'to prevent the UN weakening our hold on our colonies',[26] not only in the early postwar years but throughout 'decolonisation'. General Assembly Resolution 1514(xv) of December 1960, for example, requested 'immediate steps' to be taken 'to transfer all powers to the peoples of those [colonial] territories without any condition or reservations'. Britain abstained from voting on the resolution and never officially accepted the declaration. It also refused for years to allow delegations from the committee established to monitor implementation of the resolution to inspect its territories.[27] General Assembly Resolution 2709(xx) of December 1970, meanwhile, reiterated the call for the implementation of the 1960 resolution. A month later Britain resigned in protest from the committee that had drafted the resolution.[28]

An overriding fear of the utmost importance in understanding Western policy towards the UN is offered in a Foreign Office memorandum from March 1952. This argued that various countries were assailing the British position in the UN and noted:

> The general rise of the under-privileged against the privilege[d]. This is directed as much against the U.S. as ourselves, c.f. the demands for funds for undeveloped territories.[29]

The real significance of the UN, then, is as a forum for the 'under-privileged' to challenge the 'privileged'. The UN has therefore to be controlled, and its proceedings blocked if they fail to favour the policies of the powerful.

US and British planners were fully conscious of the fact that their policies undermined the prospects for a UN able to play a significant role in the world. The US recognised, for example, that a unilateral programme of US 'assistance' to countries outside the Soviet orbit 'will certainly prevent achievement of the general overall understanding and peace settlement required for' achieving a UN capable of playing an effective role in the maintenance of international security.[30] A State Department memorandum of February 1948 criticised what it viewed as the current US foreign policy of concentrating on 'the universalistic principle of the UN'. The memorandum outlined the problem thus:

> The universalistic approach looks to the solution of international problems by providing a universalistic pattern of rules and procedures which would be applicable to all countries, or at least all countries prepared to join, in an identical way ... It favours legalistic and mechanical solutions, applicable to all countries alike. It has already been embodied in the United Nations, in the proposed ITO charter, in UNESCO [United Nations Educational Scientific and Cultural Orgsanisation]... and in similar efforts at universal world collaboration in given spheres of foreign policy.

Rather, the memorandum suggested rejection of this approach, arguing that 'a truly stable world order can proceed, within our lifetime, only from the older, mellower and more advanced nations of the world'.[31]

## Themes of policy

The basic US and British policy priorities outlined in the early postwar documents have largely continued into the present. US and British policy towards the United Nations might best be considered under five themes of policy: protecting rogue regimes, supporting interstate aggression, expediting their own aggression, preventing international agreements, and exercising control.

### Protecting rogue regimes

One prominent aspect of Western policy at the United Nations has been support for rogue regimes, most notably South Africa and Israel. These states have been described by Anthony Parsons, Britain's Permanent Representative at the UN in 1979–82, as 'regional proteges – Israel in the case of the United States, South Africa in the case of the three Western Permanent Members'.[32]

I have documented the level of British and US support for apartheid South Africa at the United Nations elsewhere,[33] especially in the early postwar period when Britain and the US were especially keen to see apartheid off the UN agenda and helped to prevent international action against the regimes in Pretoria. Britain's Commonwealth Secretary noted in 1950, for example, that in UN discussion of the treatment of Indians in South Africa the British government had maintained a policy of 'strict neutrality and had avoided being drawn into the merits of the dispute'. He added that 'we should abstain from voting on any resolution which was strongly condemnatory of South

Africa'.[34] British policy towards South Africa overall remained as outlined by the Commonwealth Secretary in 1951: 'to give the Union what help and guidance we decently can at the United Nations'.[35]

As the postwar period progressed British policy was especially useful to South Africa on a number of fronts. With regard to South Africa's occupation of Namibia, Britain defied UN Security Council resolutions (as well as rulings by the International Court of Justice [ICJ]) declaring the occupation illegal. British governments – Labour and Conservative alike – violated international law and the ICJ judgment and effectively upheld the occupation by permitting British business to operate in the territory.[36]

Britain also played its traditional role of chief UN sanctions-buster. Having been a key supplier of arms to South Africa in the 1950s (many of which were used for internal repression) Britain reluctantly agreed to the UN arms embargo in the early 1960s, but permitted the continuation of deliveries throughout the 1960s until the new government of 1970 announced the official resumption of arms sales.[37] In the 1960s, the Labour government continued to issue export licences for spare parts and ammunition for the British-supplied aircraft used by the South African Air Force and for 'practice shells' used by naval vessels. It also permitted the sale of a military radar complex worth $70–80 million. It has been estimated that, during the 1960s, Britain exported $199 million worth of military equipment to South Africa, with as much as half of these sales occurring after the arms ban had been put in place.[38]

By the end of the 1980s five British companies and five transnational oil corporations were involved in oil shipments to South Africa – the lifeline of the regime – in violation of the UN ban. Britain also provided export licences for Plessey and Marconi radar systems which have military functions, thus effectively evading the ban on arms sales made mandatory in 1977. It also promoted the sale of security and military services and computers, and allowed the importation of thousands of tonnes of steel products, in violation of the ban on iron and steel imports. Evading the voluntary ban on new direct investment, meanwhile, the Department of Trade encouraged British companies to set up subsidiaries in South Africa, whilst Shell, Lonrho and Consolidated Gold Fields, amongst others, made new investments from 1986–89.[39]

This traditional sanctions-busting role of the West has continued in the 1990s, notably with US arms supplies to the Croatian and Bosnian governments, in breach of the UN arms embargo. Secret files reported by the *Guardian* show that in November 1994 the Croatian

Defence Minister wrote to the then US Deputy Defense Secretary, John Deutsch, asking for direct US aid to Croatia's military. Deutsch explained that the embargo prevented such direct involvement but, according to the *Guardian*, said that 'it could be organised through a private consultancy'.[40]

From 1980–88, the Western states vetoed twelve separate UN Security Council resolutions condemning apartheid South Africa – the US vetoing all twelve, Britain eleven and France four. Six of these concerned South Africa's occupation of Namibia, and four concerned South African aggression in neighbouring states. South Africa was protected from full international pariah status after its brutal invasion of Angola when the US vetoed (with Britain abstaining) a resolution in August 1981. Both states cast vetoes in May 1986 after Pretoria's attacks on Botswana, Zambia and Zimbabwe. The following month Britain and the US vetoed a resolution condemning South Africa for further attacks on Angola.

The second major case of Western protection of a rogue regime concerns US policy towards Israel. Since 1973, the US has delivered 27 vetoes of Security Council resolutions concerning Israel, most of them concerning its brutality in the Occupied Territories and in the repeated attacks on Lebanon.[41] The pattern has been that all major acts of Israeli aggression or terrorism have been supported by the US and protected by Washington from full international opprobrium, vetoing any UN ability to enforce civilised standards of behaviour on Israel. The Israeli bombing of PLO headquarters in Tunis in 1986 was unusual in that the US merely abstained on a resolution condemning Israel for this violation of international law. Israel has itself demonstrated little but contempt for the UN. According to Amnesty International, the Israeli army deliberately attacked a UN compound in April 1996, killing over 100 civilians. It has also reported that the UN peacekeeping force in Lebanon has come under 'close fire' from Israeli forces on 270 occasions.[42]

Probably the most penetrating analysis of the US–Israeli relationship, especially in respect of the UN, is that by Noam Chomsky, who has uncovered from the ideological memory hole the reality of the US–Israeli rejectionism on the Palestine question. Chomsky notes that:

> The first major Arab peace initiative ... was in February 1971, when President Sadat accepted UN mediator Gunnar Jarring's proposal for a full peace treaty on the international borders ... This proposal, which conformed closely to the official US stand, was

> recognised by Israel to be a genuine peace offer, but rejected. Israel was backed by the US, which preferred 'stalemate', as later explained by Henry Kissinger.[43]

The Israeli government recognised that the proposal offered the prospect of Egypt entering into a full peace agreement with Israel in return for the latter's withdrawal from the Sinai and the Gaza Strip. Yet Israel rejected it because the government decided it was not prepared to withdraw to the pre-1967 borders, thus terminating the initiative.[44] Chomsky continues by noting that:

> Another major Arab initiative was in January 1976, when Syria, Jordan and Egypt backed a UN Security Council resolution calling for a two-state settlement on the international borders with 'appropriate arrangements ... to guarantee ... the sovereignty, territorial integrity and political independence of all states in the area and their right to live in peace within secure and recognised boundaries'. This is the crucial wording of UN 242 ... The Security Council resolution was openly backed by the PLO which actually 'prepared' it according to Chaim Herzog, then Israel's UN ambassador. Israel refused to attend the UN session. The Labour government announced that it would not negotiate with any Palestinians on any political issue and would not negotiate with the PLO under any circumstances.[45]

Thus there was indeed a basis for a political settlement to the Arab–Israeli question some time before the peace deals of the 1990s, but these were blocked by the US and Israel.

In the 'peace process' of the 1990s the US achieved a long-standing aim, debarring the UN from any but a ceremonial role, in order to impose US preferences. Indian academic Rajaram Panda notes that 'given the high profile of the United Nations during the Gulf crisis, it seems strange that its lack of involvement in the Madrid Middle East peace conference was barely noticed', also noting that 'the United States acquiesced in Israel's insistence that the UN should have only observer status'.[46]

Recent US positioning at the UN has continued to protect Israel. In 1993, the US opposed a resolution referring to East Jerusalem as occupied territory and which endorsed 'the need to provide protection and security for the Palestinian people'. In March of that year a resolution passed only after the Security Council had accepted a US demand for a paragraph-by-paragraph vote. Alone on the Security Council, the US abstained on passages regarding international protection and Jerusalem.[47] In June 1995, the US vetoed a resolution calling on the Israeli government to rescind a recent case of illegal seizure of land in Jerusalem.

## Supporting interstate aggression

Western support for, or condoning of, interstate aggression has been a regular feature of postwar international relations – examples include the Turkish invasion of Cyprus in 1974, the Moroccan invasion of the Western Sahara in 1975, the Somali invasion of Ethiopia in 1977 and the Iraqi invasion of Iran in 1980. An especially clear example of how the Western powers manoeuvred in the United Nations to prevent action against an act of aggression of which they approved is that of the Indonesian invasion of East Timor in December 1975. This was a particularly brutal campaign, involving mass executions and destruction on a colossal scale, resulting in over 200,000 deaths, and with repression in the territory continuing until today, indeed with continuing effective Western support.

From 1975–82 there were two Security Council Resolutions and eight General Assembly Resolutions condemning the invasion and urging Indonesian withdrawal. Britain and the United States abstained on, or voted against, all the General Assembly Resolutions and voted in favour of the two in the Security Council. The latter, however, were weakly worded and watered down and, as Carmel Budiardjo of the Indonesian Human Rights Campaign, TAPOL, points out, 'led to no effective action to compel Indonesia to withdraw its troops from East Timor'.[48] The first Security Council Resolution merely stated that it '*calls upon* the government of Indonesia to withdraw without delay all its forces from the Territory' – a 'rather wishy-washy compromise resolution', according to Thomas Franck, a professor of law at New York University, testifying before Congress.[49] With regard to the second Security Council vote in April 1976, the US was reportedly 'seeking to water down' the resolution by making it 'less offensive to Indonesia'. The Western members of the Security Council reportedly 'regarded a call for an immediate, unconditional withdrawal as impractical and unlikely to be acceptable to Indonesia'.[50]

The success of US policy in steering the UN away from effective action on the invasion is confirmed by Daniel Moynihan, the then US Ambassador to the UN, who noted in a cable in January 1976 that he had made 'considerable progress ... towards a basic foreign policy goal, that of breaking up the massive bloc of nations, mostly new nations, which for so long has been arrayed against us in international forums and in diplomatic encounters generally'. Examples of this were US policy towards the Moroccan invasion of the Western Sahara and the Indonesian invasion of East Timor. On the latter, Moynihan notes in his memoirs that 'the Department of State desired that the United Nations prove utterly ineffective in whatever measures it undertook. This task was given to me, and I carried it forward with no inconsiderable success.'[51]

An Australian press report a month after the invasion quoted a State Department official as saying that:

> In terms of the bilateral relations between the US and Indonesia, we are more or less condoning the incursion into East Timor ... The United States wants to keep its relationship with Indonesia close and friendly. We regard Indonesia as a friendly, non-aligned nation – a nation we do a lot of business with.[52]

The British position had been similar; its Ambassador to Indonesia cabled to the Foreign Office five months before the invasion that the situation demanded 'greater sympathy towards Indonesia' if the latter decided to 'to take strong action' in East Timor. Furthermore, 'it is in Britain's interest that Indonesia should absorb the territory as soon and as unobtrusively as possible'. If 'there is a row in the United Nations, ... we should keep our heads down and avoid taking sides' against Indonesia.[53]

The British government's position has been consistent ever since. For example, a 1993 resolution of the UN Commission on Human Rights expressed 'deep concern' over continuing human rights abuses in East Timor and urged the dispatch of UN rapporteurs to the territory. In discussion on the draft resolution, the Indonesian government claimed there was no need for any investigations and congratulated itself on the steps it had recently taken to improve human rights in East Timor. TAPOL noted that 'Britain, and later Germany, terrified of losing their lucrative arms deals with Indonesia, played a disgraceful role trying to bully the EC [which had sponsored the resolution] into accepting Indonesia's self-congratulatory statement. Showing itself as a state without morals, the United Kingdom was guided only by politics and economics.'[54] A similar situation prevailed at the Human Rights Commission the following year. TAPOL notes that with 'countries like the UK unwilling even to consider pushing for a resolution should talks to reach consensus break down, it was obvious that little would be achieved'.[55]

Other acts of interstate aggression in the 1990s have been allowed to pass without any UN action being taken, notably the Israeli invasion of Lebanon in 1996 and repeated Turkish incursions into northern Iraq. Both of these have been supported by the US and Britain; had similar acts been perpetrated by official enemies a quite different UN response would surely have been forthcoming.

## Expediting their own aggression

A third category of Western policy at the United Nations has been the particularly important one of ensuring either that the UN is prevented from acting on, or facilitates, Western states' own acts of aggression.

This has especially been the case with regard to US interventions in Latin America, for example the CIA-organised invasion of Guatemala in 1954 to overthrow the government of Jacobo Arbenz. A Guatemalan government request for the Security Council to consider its complaints about the external aggression taking place was rejected partly due to abstentions by Britain and France. This prompted President Eisenhower and Secretary of State Dulles to express satisfaction with Britain's 'willingness to cooperate in regard to the UN aspect' of US policy. With the UN barred from taking action, the US-backed invasion could proceed free from restriction, overthrowing the democratically elected government, and paving the way for a succession of brutal, military regimes.[56]

The UN was also kept out of the next major US military intervention in Latin America – in the Dominican Republic in 1965. Juan Bosch had been elected President in the country's first free elections in 1962 and had enacted a number of reforms under a broadly nationalist-capitalist programme, including land reform, attacks on corruption and the provision of greater public services. Overthrown nine months later in a military coup, the succeeding regime was itself toppled in 1965 by a constitutionalist coup aimed at restoring Bosch to power. The US intervened with 23,000 troops to prevent this outcome under the pretext of protecting American lives, fought and defeated the constitutionalists and helped install a new regime. Britain supported the pretext for the invasion. The Foreign Secretary in the Labour government parroted the US contention of 'sending forces necessary for the protection of its own nationals' and declared: 'I think it has long been recognised that where swift action is necessary to save lives, a nation is entitled to take it.'[57] The US ensured that UN involvement was 'marginal' and sought to 'exclude any UN role' in the crisis after it had been brought before the Security Council by the Soviet Union.[58]

UN involvement was also prevented in the three major acts of US aggression in the 1980s: in Grenada, Nicaragua and Panama. On the invasion of Grenada in 1983, condemned by virtually the entire world,

President Reagan noted that 'one hundred nations in the UN have not agreed with us on just about everything that's come before them where we're involved, and it didn't upset my breakfast at all'.[59] Britain was the only European state not to condemn the invasion and was joined in abstaining in the Security Council by Zaire and Togo.[60]

Regarding Nicaragua, the US vetoed seven Security Council resolutions between 1982 and 1986, as noted above. On all seven votes, the junior partner declared its de facto support for the US by abstaining. Thus Britain could not bring itself to condemn the mining of Nicaraguan ports by the United States or support the ruling of the ICJ, which found the US aggression against Nicaragua to be illegal and called on the US to comply with international law. Britain abstained when the ICJ matter was brought before the General Assembly in 1989. It also abstained on a 1982 resolution which 'reminds all members states of their obligation to respect the principles of the [UN] charter', at a time when US military exercises with Honduras were raising the fear that this was a dress rehearsal for a US invasion of Nicaragua. Britain was joined in abstaining solely by President Mobutu's Zaire.[61]

The 1989 US invasion of Panama (or 'unilateral relief effort', as one commentator has described it![62]) elicited a similar response. Not only the US, but also Britain and France, vetoed a draft resolution condemning the invasion and calling for a withdrawal of US troops. The US also vetoed – with Britain the sole abstainer – a resolution condemning the ransacking by US troops of the residence of Nicaragua's ambassador to Panama. The resolution noted that these actions were a violation of diplomatic immunities recognised under international law.[63]

It is also instructive to turn briefly to earlier examples in this category, this time cases of British obstruction of the UN at times of British aggression. The invasion of Egypt in October 1956 produced Britain's first two Security Council vetoes, delivered on the same day to prevent the imposition of a ceasefire. The Council then passed the issue to the General Assembly, where, two days later, a ceasefire resolution was approved by 64 to 5 (opposed by Britain, France, Australia, New Zealand and Israel). Overall, Britain decided not to rely on the UN to help solve its dispute with Egypt since, as the Foreign Office Minister later explained, 'neither the Security Council nor the General Assembly could give us what we wanted'.[64] In a study of the UN, Geoff Simons comments that in the months leading up to the invasion of Egypt, Prime Minister Eden 'was prepared to have the crisis discussed in the Security Council but only as a prelude to independent British action'. Thus when Britain took the case to the Security Council this was only in order to 'clear the decks for action', Foreign Secretary Selwyn Lloyd noted. Simons comments that 'the UN Secretary-General Dag Hammarskjold did his best to ensure the success of the talks, but there was a substantial British interest in their failure, and fail they did', thus paving the way for military aggression.[65]

The previous year, files show a British fear relating to the territory of the Buraimi oasis, which was disputed between Saudi Arabia, on the one hand, and Britain and Oman on the other. A US State Department memo notes that 'we fear that reference to UN' in proposing a solution to the dispute 'may bring about just type of neutral intervention by UN which UK fears [sic]'.[66] (Similar US concerns prevailed over Vietnam a decade later. As US aggression mounted in 1965, Clark Clifford, Special Adviser to the President, noted that 'I don't think it advisable to go to the UN ... A resolution in the UN with all the dramatic debate it would produce is bad for us.'[67])

Another example is the British military intervention in Jordan in 1958 (which was intended to coincide with the US intervention in Lebanon) and which, as I have shown elsewhere,[68] came as the result of a probable fabrication by British planners of a coup threat to the country. The intervention was intended to bolster pro-Western forces in the region. Anthony Eden recalled in his memoirs:

> The governments of the Lebanon and Jordan, knowing themselves threatened by [Egyptian president] Nasser's subversive tactics in their own countries, asked for help from the West. The United Nations observers on the spot denied that there was subversive activity by Nasser in either country. The Secretary-General, Mr Hammarskjold, supported his observers. Ignoring this myopic tendency, the United States landed forces in the Lebanon and the United Kingdom flew troops into Jordan, without prior reference to the United Nations. This action was necessary if the right to live [sic] of these two small countries was to be preserved; it was unquestionably against the terms of the Charter as interpreted at the time of our intervention at Port Said [Suez]. Since the United Nations observers were already on the spot and proclaiming that the motives for Anglo-American intervention did not exist, it was rather more heinous.[69]

Merely to glance at the UN charter is to confirm how juxtaposed to its principles are the foreign policies of the leading Western states:

> ... armed force shall not be used, save in the common interest ... (preamble)

> ... the suppression of acts of aggression or other breaches of the peace, and to bring about by peaceful means, and in conformity with the principles of justice and international law, adjustment or settlement of international disputes ... (Article 1)

> All members shall refrain in their international relations from the threat or use of force against the territorial integrity or political independence of any state ... (Article 2).[70]

### Preventing international agreements

On issues such as arms control, terrorism and global security, the Western states on the Security Council, and especially the United States, have been, and remain, the rogue states in international affairs, as the voting record clearly reveals. For the 1990s, this is analysed in the following chapter (first section). In the earlier period, to give just some examples: the 1987 session of the General Assembly voted 154 to 1 (US) opposing the build-up of weapons in outer space; 135 to 1 (US) against developing new weapons of mass destruction; 143 to 2 (US, France) on a comprehensive nuclear test ban; and 137 to 3 (US, Britain, France) for a halt to all nuclear explosions.[71] In 1984 the United States cast the sole 'no' vote on six separate General Assembly resolutions, which called for a comprehensive test ban, a nuclear weapons freeze, cessation of the nuclear arms race, a chemical weapons ban and the prevention of the militarisation of outer space.[72]

The 1987 General Assembly session also produced a resolution condemning international terrorism and stating that:

> Nothing in the present resolution could in any way prejudice the right to self-determination, freedom and independence, as derived from the Charter of the United Nations, of peoples forcibly deprived of that right ... particularly peoples under colonial and racist regimes and foreign occupation or other forms of colonial domination, nor ... the right of these peoples to struggle to this end and to seek and receive support [in accordance with the Charter].[73]

This resolution passed 153 to 2 (US; Israel).

**Exercising control**

The Western states' ability to exercise full control over the UN was previously constrained mainly by the presence of the USSR on the Security Council and the fact that virtually the entire world opposed their policies on major issues ranging from Middle Eastern politics to Southern Africa to international security. This meant that Western states' policy at the UN previously centred on preventing action being taken against them by the rest of the world. The sheer power and resources available to the United States enabled it to occasionally shore up its position at the UN. William Fulbright, long-serving Chairman of the Senate Foreign Relations Committee, has noted that 'because we had lots of money ... we could send aid all around the world to gain the support and allegiance of various countries ... That is, in part, how we got so many votes on our side in the United Nations.'[74] In fact, given the precise failure of the US to secure votes on many important issues in recent years, one can only wonder how much more isolated the US would have been without such bribery.

It was towards the end of the 1980s that the Western states could truly begin exercising the degree of control over the organisation they had intended in the early postwar period, due to the collapse of the Soviet Union and the disciplining of the Third World through, for example, debt burdens and structural adjustment. The 1991 war against Iraq is a supreme example of this control, where the UN acted as little more than ratifier of US policy. The US did, however, have to offer financial and other rewards to other countries to enlist support for its policies, though not, of course, to Britain, which willingly acted as the United States' lieutenant.

Anglo-American power and diplomacy remains a crucial element in the functioning of the Security Council. Establishment commentator John Dickie notes that:

> One aspect of British expertise which came to be highly regarded in the last two years of the Reagan–Thatcher era was Tea Party Diplomacy at the United Nations. It enabled the Americans to get action taken at the Security Council which otherwise might have been blocked as a superpower's bid to bulldoze the rest of the Council. Britain's status as being friendly with, but being seen as not unwilling to disagree with, the United States provided the Americans with a means of securing results without appearing to be directly involved.[75]

Anglo-American power in the UN is also currently clearly to be seen in policy towards Libya. Here, the two states have succeeded in having sanctions imposed – a long-standing desire for which, following the collapse of the USSR, only a pretext was lacking – by claiming that Libyan officials had masterminded the Lockerbie aircraft bombing. The US and Britain have also been able to withstand pressure from other UN members to retain the sanctions against Iraq. A 1996 report by researchers from Harvard University and the London School of Economics noted that 'Iraq is a clear example of the Security Council allowing humanitarian rights to be violated through the imposition of sanctions right across the board'. It reported that more than 500,000 children may have died in the last six years as a result of sanctions, and stated that the policy was 'tantamount to shooting down a plane full of innocent people because there are hijackers aboard'.[76]

The intended function of the UN to act as an 'instrument of Anglo-American foreign policy' outlined in the secret documents of 1952, remains relevant to the contemporary world, with severe effects.

# 8

# Current Policy, Intervention and the Case of Rwanda

## Current realities

A reasonable starting point for gauging the recent US and British stance towards the United Nations is voting at the General Assembly. 1991 is an especially significant year since by then the Cold War was clearly over and the US and its Western and Middle Eastern allies had just fought a war in the Gulf in the name of a New World Order and the UN. In the General Assembly session that year, the US and Britain were the only states to vote against a resolution calling upon administering powers of colonies to 'take all necessary steps to enable the people of the territories concerned to exercise fully as soon as possible their right to self-determination and independence'. In all, 137 nations supported the resolution, with 22 abstentions (virtually all European states). On the same day the same two states voted against a resolution which:

> considers it important for the United Nations to continue to play an active role in the process of decolonisation and to intensify its efforts to ensure the widest possible dissemination of information on decolonisation, with a view to further mobilising international public opinion in support of complete decolonisation by the year 2000.

This resolution passed with 142 in favour, and 16 abstentions.

The US and Britain also maintained their support for apartheid South Africa in the General Assembly, being the only two states to vote against (121 in favour, 34 abstentions) a resolution on military collaboration with the South African government. Joined by Swaziland, they were also the only states to vote against (127 in favour, 28 abstentions) a resolution calling for the maintenance of the oil embargo against Pretoria.

The same two states were also the only ones to vote against a resolution calling for a 'comprehensive nuclear test ban at an early date' – carried by 110 states, with 35 abstentions. The United States was joined by France in opposing a resolution calling for 'a treaty to achieve the prohibition of all nuclear test explosions by all states in all environments for all time'. Britain was one of four states to abstain (along with Israel, China and Micronesia); 147 states voted in favour.

The US and Britain were also isolated on a resolution reaffirming 'the urgent need to reach an early agreement on effective international arrangements to assure non-nuclear weapon states against the use or threat of use of nuclear weapons'; 150 countries voted in favour, with no abstentions. The two countries were, meanwhile, joined by France and Japan in opposing a resolution calling for implementation of a declaration in favour of making the Indian Ocean a zone of peace; 127 states voted in favour, with 30 abstentions.

Finally, eleven states (all OECD countries, plus Israel) voted against a resolution condemning the use of mercenaries as a means of violating human rights and impeding the exercise of the right of peoples to self-determination, notably by the South African regime, and calling on states to extend humanitarian aid to victims of situations resulting from the use of mercenaries 'as well as from colonial or alien domination or foreign occupation'.[1] (This resolution, as with others here, was repeated the following year, resulting in a vote of 118 in favour with 10 against, including the US and Britain, with 36 abstentions.[2])

If we turn to 1992, we find similarly isolated positions on the part of the leading Western states on many crucial international security issues. The United States was the only country to oppose a resolution urging states to take further steps to promote the UN system of collective security and calling on states to respect the principles enshrined in the UN charter.[3] Washington was also the only state (144 voting in favour, with no abstentions) to oppose a resolution reaffirming the South Atlantic as a zone of peace and cooperation.[4] The UK was the only state to abstain on, and the US was the only state to vote against, a resolution calling for greater regional confidence building measures in Africa.[5]

At the risk of being repetitive, I turn to 1993. A particularly instructive analysis of voting patterns at the United Nations is that by the US Department of State.[6] It notes that no other country voted with the United States on as many occasions as Britain – in 36 General Assembly resolutions. Israel was another state which, with the UK, was, 'as in past years ... among the highest in voting coincidence with the United States' – 93.5 per cent of all General Assembly resolutions. The report also considers the particular votes at the General Assembly which 'directly affect important United

States interests and on which the United States lobbied extensively'. On one of these, concerning the US embargo against Cuba, the United States was one of only four countries to oppose a call for, as the State Department report notes, 'states to refrain from promulgating and applying laws and measures whose extra-territorial effects affect the sovereignty of other states'.[7]

On another of the resolutions on which US diplomats lobbied extensively, the US was one of only two states (the other being Israel) to oppose a resolution declaring Israel's occupation of the Golan Heights as 'illegal, null and void' and demanding Israeli withdrawal. The US was one of five states opposing a resolution calling for the peaceful settlement of the Palestine question and reaffirming the principles for achievement of a final settlement. It was also the only state to oppose a resolution calling for reductions in the external debt of Third World countries; 164 states voted in favour, with no abstentions.[8]

The State Department report for the 1996 session at the General Assembly notes that on the votes that were not adopted by consensus, 'the average overall General Assembly voting coincidence of all UN members with the United States ... was 49.4 per cent'. The states that voted most with the United States were, in descending order, Israel, Palau, Rwanda, Lithuania, Tajikistan and Britain. On the twelve 'important votes', in the view of the State Department, the US was in the minority on five: it was one of three states opposing (with 137 supporting) an end to its embargo of Cuba; one of four states opposing (with 56 supporting and 76 abstaining) an end to extra-territorial laws that impose sanctions on companies and nationals of other states; one of 22 states opposing (with 115 supporting) calls to begin moves towards a convention prohibiting the use of, and eliminating, nuclear weapons; and one of three states opposing (with 159 supporting) Palestinian self-determination. Five of the other votes were condemnations of human rights abuses in Iran, Iraq, the former Yugoslavia, Cuba and Sudan.[9]

Many newspapers have in recent years reported the opening of the General Assembly in September each year. None of them, to my knowledge, have ever reported systematically (and most not at all) on the actual voting which takes place. Readers will thus be unaware of the isolation of the US and Britain on many important international issues and the extent of opposition in the international community to many of their policies. Western leaders can therefore make professions of support for the UN on the proper occasions, which are considered with appropriate solemnity by media and academic commentators rather than being the object of ridicule.

The current state of affairs at the UN has been described by Martin Khor of the Third World Network in Malaysia, writing in *Third World Resurgence*. He notes that the Security Council's deliberations are so secretive 'that the General Assembly is hardly even informed or briefed, let alone consulted or allowed to participate in issues' on the Council's agenda. Decisions are 'often made informally and behind closed doors, and no minutes of meetings are available'. The 'underlying discontent', Khor notes, is that the Security Council 'has become a body that is in appearance "international" (supposedly reflecting the will of UN member states) but in reality an instrument of a few major countries (especially the United States)'. These powers 'make use of the Council's multilateral image' to legitimise actions that reflect their 'narrow national foreign policy interests'. Thus 'actions that would otherwise have been criticised by a majority of countries are thus instead acclaimed by the major powers (or the mainstream international media) as being carried out on behalf of the "international community"'.[10]

Former adviser to the Secretary-General, Erskine Childers, notes that the Western powers have long used 'economic bribery and intimidation' to get their way at the World Bank and the IMF, and that 'this has now been extended to the United Nations':

> Whenever the [Western] powers are determined to get a given vote through either the Security Council (ie, the Gulf crisis and sanctions against Libya) or the General Assembly (ie, rescindment of the Zionism is racism resolution), governments are warned. If they do not 'behave' they will not get debt relief, World Bank capital projects, easier IMF 'adjustment conditionalities' or urgently-needed hard currency IMF credit to pay oil bills. Reduction or cut-off in bilateral aid is an additional threat.

Childers continues by noting that 'in effect, the [Western] powers have taken to employing a form of state terrorism at the UN – the threat being more death, malnutrition, disease or no education among millions of already poor people'. Thus most of the UN membership has over the past few years lost confidence in the Security Council since 'the Council is now regarded as a captive, where the North secures decisions by economic intimidation, abuses the peaceful-redress procedures inscribed in the charter and authorises a kind of vigilantism against countries of the North's own choosing'.[11]

Illustrative of the degree of control over the UN system is the accession of Russia on to the Security Council. The Western powers were especially keen on seeing Russia replace the Soviet Union as the holder of the permanent seat on the Security Council after the collapse of the Soviet Union. Britain particularly feared that a long drawn-out process would provoke wider discussion on the composition of the Council, and thus threaten its own place on it. 'The British needed the question of the permanent five sewn up quickly', one source close to the US State Department was reported as saying.[12] The *Daily Telegraph* noted that 'Mr Major believes it is important for world peace and continuity that Russia, as the most natural successor to the Soviet Union, assumes its responsibilities in the UN as quickly as possible.'[13] Britain thus hastily arranged a Security Council summit to push through the change, securing the accession of the West's ally on to the Council with the minimum fuss and scrutiny. According to Geoff Simons, in his study of the UN:

> The transfer of the permanent seat from the erstwhile Soviet Union to Russia, without a vote in the UN General Assembly, was in blatant violation of Article 108 of the UN charter. The current Russian permanent seat on the Security Council is therefore illegal.[14]

(Article 108 requires all amendments of the UN charter to be adopted by two thirds of the members of the General Assembly.[15])

Other illustrations are provided by the current UN 'peacebuilding' operations, notably in Cambodia, El Salvador, Angola and Mozambique. In all four cases movements or parties which perpetrated mass killings and repression have been welcomed into the international community in the 1990s as acceptable faces in UN-supervised processes of political 'reconciliation' and 'elections'. The Khmer Rouge in Cambodia, the ARENA party in El Salvador, UNITA in Angola and RENAMO in Mozambique have another thing in common apart from their gruesome past – they were once all US allies. With the wars in these countries over or diminishing, these US allies took their place alongside the factions that opposed them and the civilian populations who were terrorised and largely destroyed by them. According to Alejandro Bendana, of the Centre for International Studies in Managua, Nicaragua, writing on El Salvador:

> El Salvador provides another example of how what the United States could not accomplish by war, it seeks to attain by negotiations within a United Nations framework ... Under United Nations supervision and what was virtually a UN-imposed settlement hurriedly signed before the assumption to office by a new Secretary General more amenable to the new geopolitical realities, the FMLN signed the peace accords. In doing so, it enters into a political

> framework where it is at a distinct disadvantage having been outside of the civil arena for some time and still not having full assurances of security.[16]

One might add as an aside that any reasonably democratic international system might demand US compensation for the destruction wrought by the parties it previously funded and armed.

The degree of structural control over the United Nations in the 1990s exercised by the Western powers is – as well as being a prize of 'winning' the Cold War – largely a fulfilment of aims for the postwar world clearly laid down in US and British planning documents, and considered in the previous chapter.[17] In the Anglo-American division of labour the US provides the military and economic might and intimidation, as Childers notes, and Britain often the diplomatic expertise in the context of a uniquely wide set of alliance relationships and historical contacts. Overall, Britain plays a similar supporting role to the US at the United Nations as the former Soviet republics of Byelorussia and Ukraine – which were allowed to retain separate UN membership throughout the postwar era – did for the Soviet Union. A serious decline in the special relationship would enhance Britain's position as a mere European power and undermine the rationale for retaining a Security Council seat.

For the US, it follows that since the majority of the world's countries oppose the US stance on many of the major questions in international affairs, a key policy aim for Washington is to prevent the UN functioning in a democratic way. But even the UN is still viewed as a threat to US interests by the establishment. This is indeed a major reason why the US and other Western states have worked through the World Bank – which is even more closely controlled than the UN – in international economic policies and why the WTO was established outside of UN auspices. The basic requirement has also led to the complete demise of any chance that a global security system under the auspices of the United Nations would arise after the end of the Cold War. Simply, the US is militarily supreme and US military power – and that of its allies, recipients of military aid and arms exports – directly shapes the overall security order in many regions, notably in the Middle East and Latin America. Similar concerns apply in the economic sphere. However, even this systematic undermining of the prospect of improved global collaboration is still not complete enough for the hardline politicians on the US right, who, it is clear, barely support UN membership, let alone pursuing democratic internationalism.

## The difficulties of reform

Many recent proposals for a progressive reform of the UN have been systematically blocked by the world's superpower, with the backing of the junior partner in London. The first major proposal for enhancing global security after the end of the Cold War was the UN Secretary-General's report, *An Agenda for Peace*, published in June 1992. It is worth noting that the proposals contained in the document were very modest, calling for improved mechanisms for financing the UN, improving systems for early warning of conflicts and preventive diplomacy and for the establishment of permanent UN armed forces, for example, but within an international context which required no changes in the global security order that would seriously undermine Western power. Even in this highly conservative context, virtually all of the main proposals have been either ignored or specifically rejected.

Much recent debate on UN reform has centred around changes in the Security Council. This has already happened with the illegal accession of Russia, noted above, although this event hardly ever features in the vast academic literature on Security Council reform. It is certainly true that the power and composition of the Security Council is fundamentally undemocratic and testimony to the current state of world affairs that the organisation theoretically most capable of solving global problems is the one least capable of acting so unless the great powers want it to. As the 1994 report of the International Commission on Peace and Food notes, 'in no other constitution or organisation founded on democratic principles is it accepted that a few members [in the Security Council] may thus invalidate the decisions of the majority [in the General Assembly]'.[18]

Yet reform of the Security Council on anything like the terms now regularly proposed is a peripheral issue (thus a central one in the mainstream debate on the UN) to enhancing global security. One might wonder how the accession to the Council of Japan and Germany is supposed to add to the UN's global democratic credentials in any meaningful sense. It is also patently a weak argument to assert that the accession to the Council of larger Third World states like Nigeria (currently under a vile military government), Indonesia (guilty of mass slaughter and repression) or Brazil (a rich country with gross inequities and mass impoverishment) will improve the UN's accountability to Southern peoples to any but a marginal extent. US power may be so great when its real interests are at stake – as demonstrated during the war against Iraq – as to be able to secure control over the Security Council, no matter which countries are represented on it. Security Council reform is desirable, but it is an extremely limited step in tackling the central issues: one is how to ensure the role of *people* in decision making in global fora; the major one concerns the need to curb the overall power in world affairs of the United States and governments allied to it in both North and South.[19] This issue, however, far from being addressed, is not recognised as a serious concern in the mainstream.

The pressure on Britain to give up its Security Council seat has provoked support for its retention in various quarters of the establishment. The *Independent*, for example, under the heading 'an anachronism that works', declares that Britain and France have 'global foreign policies' 'thanks to their histories as imperial powers'. The paper's editors paraphrase and support 'John Major's comment' that 'he would not like anything done that would make the Security Council less effective' and also that of Douglas Hurd referring to Britain's 'wish to go on playing a worthy part in averting a slide into international disorder'. The current composition of the Council represents 'the best hope of the UN being an effective force for world peace'.[20] Elsewhere, *Independent* editors note that Britain and France 'have the diplomatic experience, the military skill and the political will to take their share in safeguarding the world's security'. The manner in which they do this, the paper continues, 'has led other nations, however grudgingly, to accept their permanent representation'.[21]

A major reform issue concerns funding of the UN's activities. The US refusal to pay all its UN costs has severely hampered the organisation. As Erskine Childers has pointed out, it is a violation of the UN charter itself to withhold any part of assessed contributions to the UN for political reasons or out of dislike for any aspect of UN administration.[22] The UN system certainly needs radical change but US policy is intent more on disciplining it to act in ways it would like rather then on securing the necessary more democratic structure and operations.

It is, however, in the military sphere where principally the US but also Britain have been most reluctant to agree to proposed reform. In 1992, for example, a proposal was made at the UN to establish an independent intelligence-gathering facility in order to improve the UN's early warning capabilities and 'aimed at turning the UN into an effective instrument of preventive diplomacy', in the words of the *Independent*. The proposal was made by the EC, Russia, the Nordic countries, Australia, Canada and New Zealand but, the paper reported, 'touched off a furious response from the United States, which appears to be resolutely opposed to any moves that would enhance the UN's ability to gather and analyse sensitive information in an independent fashion'.[23]

It is also instructive to consider the stance towards the establishment of permanent UN armed forces, intended to intervene quickly in a crisis when needed. There is little doubt, for example, that the failure to dispatch an adequate UN force to Rwanda in mid-1994 encouraged massacres of hundreds of thousands of people. The Clinton administration's view is that 'the US does not support a standing UN army, nor will we earmark specific US military units for participation in UN operations'.[24] It has, therefore, 'no intention' of transferring troops into a UN army.[25] Nearly 50 years separate these comments from a secret US planning document drawn up by the US Joint Chiefs of Staff in 1946. This notes that:

> Establishment of international armed forces on a permanent basis is contrary to present United States policy ... The United States and British delegates [to the UN] rejected the principle of permanent international forces ... When the United States ratified the [UN] charter, the United States objection to the principle of permanent international security forces became national policy ... Therefore, the representatives of the Joint Chiefs of Staff on the Military Staff Committee of the United Nations should initiate no discussion of the formation of permanent international armed forces and under no circumstances should they indicate approval of such a proposal.[26]

Under the Conservatives the Foreign Office noted that the proposal for permanent UN armed forces is 'not viable'.[27] The Labour government has pledged to earmark British troops to a UN force when required but has not supported a permanent UN force. The position is, as with the US, consistent with that at the beginning of the postwar world, when the Foreign Office also rejected proposals for an establishment of a UN force, in order not to compromise the unilateral pursuit of British objectives and strategic interests.[28]

David Howell, former Chairman of the House of Commons Foreign Affairs Committee, once noted: 'a simple, central truth about the UN' is that it is 'neither a replacement for strong and confident states ... nor a distraction from firm national purposes'. 'Strong and confident nation states and a strong and confident UN go together', he added, and 'each have their roles at different times in different situations.' 'True world leaders', Howell continued, 'will always know how to make the distinction' – which is certainly true, and which places the Saddams and Qadafis of the world in the same category, on this issue, as the Clintons and the Blairs.[29]

## The peculiarities of peacekeeping

Peacekeeping and 'humanitarian intervention' have been important issues in the 1990s and US policy in these areas has been clearly articulated by the Clinton administration. First, peacekeeping and 'humanitarian intervention' are considered peripheral to US policy generally. As former National Security Adviser Anthony Lake noted: 'Let us be clear: peacekeeping is not at the centre of our foreign or defence policy. Our armed forces' primary mission is not to conduct peace operations but to win wars.'[30] Former US Ambassador to the UN and then Secretary of State, Madeleine Albright, has been equally clear, noting that 'multilateral peacekeeping is a potentially valuable foreign policy tool' but it cannot guarantee US interests or substitute for 'vigorous regional alliances'. Thus the US will not rely on 'elusive notions of global collective security'.[31] For every $1 the US allocates to peacekeeping, Albright points out, it allocates $250–$300 dollars for US 'defence'.[32]

Second, the term 'multilateralism' is understood in a particular way and US policy is to control ('exercise leadership') the multilateral operations in which it is involved. According to Albright:

> Though sometimes we will act alone, our foreign policy will necessarily point toward multilateral engagement. But unless the United States also exercises leadership within collective bodies like the United Nations, there is a risk that multilateralism will not serve our national interest well – in fact, it may undermine our interests.[33]

Similarly, Albright notes:

> When large-scale or high-risk operations are contemplated and American involvement is necessary, we will be unlikely to accept UN leadership. Rather we will ordinarily rely on our own resources or those of a regional alliance – such as NATO – or an appropriate coalition – such as that assembled during Operation Desert Storm.

Thus 'the president will never relinquish command authority over US forces'.[34] As for the relationship between UN and US military commanders in operations, a draft US directive on peacekeeping policy 'directs American military commanders to disobey UN orders they judge illegal or militarily imprudent'.[35]

The third principle of US policy is that whilst the US will control the multilateral operations it engages in, it will veto and block those of which it disapproves: 'The United States is one of five countries with the power to veto any UN peacekeeping operation. I can assure you that we will use our influence – and if necessary our veto – to block operations that would harm our interests.'[36]

Fourth, peacekeeping is an instrument of US foreign policy and can provide a cover for the attainment of US interests and priorities which it would otherwise have to pursue unilaterally and consequently bear the sole risks and costs. The Clinton administration's policy on peacekeeping was elaborated in a report issued in May 1994 and which noted:

> UN and other multilateral peace operations will at times offer the best way to prevent, contain or resolve conflicts that could otherwise be more costly and deadly. In such cases, the United States benefits from having to bear only a share of the burden. We also benefit by being able to invoke the voice of the community of nations on behalf of a cause we support ... US participation may be one way to exercise US influence over an important UN mission, without unilaterally bearing the burden.[37]

Overall, according to Anthony Lake, 'peacekeeping can be an important and effective tool in our overall national security strategy' since on occasions 'the UN is an appropriate and valuable forum for gaining international participation and financing for objectives the United States supports'.[38] A 'peacekeeping' intervention can support US policy in another way. According to Madeleine Albright, 'it reduces the likelihood of unwelcome interventions by regional powers'.[39] Thus US enemies can be kept at bay by an intervention conducted instead by countries friendly to the US.

The British Defence Secretary under the Conservatives, Malcolm Rifkind, similarly explained the utility of the UN: 'If there was no UN, or if it were hamstrung, the burden would fall by default on the more powerful nations – and one in particular, the United States. An effective UN, adapting to the modern demands, helps to share that burden.'[40]

## The phenomenon of 'humanitarian intervention'

'Humanitarian intervention' has been understood as: 'the use of armed force by a state (or states) to protect citizens of the target state from large-scale human rights violations there;'[41] or, very similarly, as 'the threat or use of armed force by a state, a belligerent country, or an international organisation, with the object of human rights'.[42] In the 1990s, operations in Iraq, Haiti, Rwanda, Somalia, the former Yugoslavia, Liberia and others have been understood in this sense.

In the context of the historical record, it is perhaps testimony to the power of the propaganda system that the assertion that the US and Britain conduct interventions specifically for humanitarian ends can even be contemplated. This is especially the case in regard to the Third World, where humanitarian aims have not exactly been uppermost in planners' minds for last few centuries. It is argued here that US and British policy towards 'humanitarian intervention' is best understood by reference to three pretexts: the military, the interventionist and the public.

### The military pretext

The new 'demand' for peacekeeping is allowing Western states to justify continuing high military spending, with an emphasis on intervention capability in the South. The US intervention in Somalia in December 1992, authorised by an outgoing President Bush, seemed especially motivated by the concern to protect the military budget before the arrival of the new Clinton administration.[43] Lawrence Eagleburger, the then Acting US Secretary of State, noted in 1992 that 'what we are seeing in Somalia is that the US military may well have a new role'.[44] The British government noted in 1995 that 'we can expect to see growing calls on the United Kingdom to support conflict prevention, conflict resolution, peacekeeping and humanitarian aid missions'. Therefore, 'we will need the ability to respond, especially where our national interests are placed under serious threat'.[45]

The necessary reasoning has been outlined by a leading British academic in the international security field:

> Given the increase in the number of UN 'peacekeeping missions', many of which involve considerable danger, the post-Cold War world seems unlikely to be one where military force and violence have a completely negligible role ... The demand for capable, disciplined troops for peacekeeping and peacemaking missions seems likely to remain substantial.[46]

### The interventionist pretext

In this case, humanitarian intervention is largely a cover for actions undertaken for other purposes. Examples are the US intervention in Haiti in 1994 and French intervention in Rwanda in August 1994.

However, the big precedent for such military intervention in the South – even though not understood as an humanitarian intervention as such – is the 1991 war against Iraq.

It is worth noting that interventions have always been described as motivated by concerns other than their real ones. In March 1939, for example, Hitler issued a proclamation on the German occupation of Czechoslovakia on the pretext of assaults taking place on minorities and proclaimed the intention for Germany to disarm Czech troops threatening those people.[47] Colonial adventures were justified by reference to moral impulses (expansion into Africa was championed on the grounds of abolishing the slave trade) as were the majority of US and British interventions in the postwar period. But a recent British Foreign Office document notes that 'the overwhelming majority of contemporary legal opinion comes down against the existence of a right of humanitarian intervention'. Such a right, it notes, is not recognised by the UN Charter and serves as a pretext for 'other less laudable motives for intervening'.[48]

A British Army Staff College draft paper notes that:

> Colonial policing is a background which tends to be suitable for humanitarian intervention as aid missions involve the spreading of a [sic] humanitarian message, much as the colonialism of the 17th and 18th centuries was encouraged by the spreading of the message of Christianity.[49]

Along with the rise of humanitarian intervention has come the rehabilitation of colonialism and imperialism. Writing in the *World Policy Journal*, a liberal academic journal, David Rieff, for example, notes that 'there is little doubt' that 'the only hope for certain parts of Africa is the revival of a sort of G-7 colonialism – assuming, that is, that the rich countries have the inclination for such a move'. Rieff continues by noting that 'the only question is how to humanize these activities'.[50] For Barbara Amiel, meanwhile, feature writer at the *Sunday Times*, 'colonialism was a giant peacekeeping movement for India and Africa'.[51] In this context, former British Foreign Secretary Douglas Hurd notes that the UN should undertake an 'imperial role': 'when bits of Africa collapsed in chaos in the last century, colonial powers came in and there was the scramble for Africa. But that's not on; they're not going to do that again, and therefore it is only going to be the UN.'[52]

An especially enlightening analysis of the current ideology surrounding 'humanitarian intervention' is that by Frank Furedi, of the University of Kent. Furedi notes that 'intervention is not justified on militaristic grounds, as a glorious imperial mission'. Rather, 'it is rationalised on the plane of morality, as a [sic] humanitarian act'. According to Furedi, 'the Gulf War marked a turning point in the moral rehabilitation of imperialism'. 'The moral case for Western intervention is seldom questioned today' and 'military intervention is now seen as an acceptable method for regulating relations within and between states'. Thus Western-led humanitarian interventions 'can be depicted as acts of disinterested generosity by a reluctant Western power'.[53]

A key element of current 'humanitarian' intervention is its regionalisation, similar to 'spheres of influence'. Thus the US has led three main interventions in the 1990s, all of them in the two regions it traditionally controls and has attempted to exclude its allies from: the Middle East (Iraq/Kurdistan and, on the periphery of the region, Somalia) and Latin America (Haiti). France unilaterally intervened, under UN authorisation, in the outer edge of its sphere of interest in Francophone Africa, by the 1994 mission to Rwanda. Nigeria has claimed the mantle of regional superpower in West Africa by dominating the 'peacekeeping' missions in Liberia and Sierra Leone. Russia, meanwhile, has conducted often brutal military operations under the peacekeeping mantle in the former Soviet republics, policies which have attempted to reintegrate them into Russia's sphere of influence, with Western backing. Such a division of the world is essentially consistent both with the colonial era and with the current regionalisation of economic activity among the great blocs.

## The public pretext

Relatively low-key 'humanitarian intervention' serves the pretext of convincing the public of a commitment to humanitarian ends, to show that 'something is being done'. A good example is the three-month British deployment of troops to Rwanda in late 1994, which occurred at a time when Britain was obstructing UN attempts to find a political solution and enhance regional security (see next section). Another example is strategy in the former Yugoslavia, where the policy of providing humanitarian aid was the alternative to, rather than the counterpart of, the search for a just political solution to the conflict. British and other Western governments preferred the option of effective support for Serbian and Croatian aggression and territorial conquests, while emphasising that this was a 'civil war' they could do little about.

Policy often receives a different appreciation, however. For example, Philip Sabin, of Kings College, London, notes in the leading academic journal *International Affairs* that recent British interventions in Iraq, Cambodia and the former Yugoslavia have been 'governed by a convoluted mixture of historical prejudices, humanitarian impulses, international expectations and perceptions of "vital interest"'. Britain no longer has the 'narrow security aim of ensuring successful deterrence of a Warsaw Pact attack' but instead has 'a broader and more diffuse set of foreign policy objectives ranging from the maintenance of Britain's privileged position as a permanent member of the UN Security Council to the fulfilment of humanitarian impulses as in Bosnia and Iraq'.[54] In this reasoning, one set of essentially noble aims has thus been replaced by another. It is axiomatic that, within the propaganda system, no other less laudible motives can be contemplated.

According to Adam Roberts, distinguished professor of international relations at Oxford University and perhaps the leading British analyst of peacekeeping, 'the clearest clarion call for something approaching humanitarian warfare has come from ex-president Ronald Reagan'. It might be thought inconceivable that humanitarianism and Reagan could sit together in a single sentence, unless, that is, the basic framework of thinking is conditioned by the view that:

> Perhaps the United States has been particularly prominent in humanitarian missions because of its past self-image as a haven for the hungry, poor and persecuted throughout the world. If they cannot be admitted to the United States any more, they can at least be helped where they are.[55]

US benevolence is so great that, according to the Director of Studies at the IISS:

> Now that the need to counter Soviet power no longer exists, it will be possible and necessary for the United States, often through a reinvigorated United Nations, to return to the elaboration and promotion of first principles in international affairs. US promotion of the values of democracy, free market economics and international law will be less fettered by the Realpolitik requirement to put the containment of another superpower above all other strategic goals.[56]

Similarly, a US academic, writing in the same reputed British academic journal, warns of the danger of the US becoming involved in 'potentially endless acts of charity'[57] – truly a major concern!

## Genocide in Rwanda

In an article in April 1995 on the genocide in Rwanda, Francoise Bouchet-Saulnier, the director of legal affairs at the French aid agency, Médecins Sans Frontières (MSF), noted that 'the same countries who, in 1938, considered the massacre of Jews to be a German domestic problem, are now directing the UN'.[58] The comment was apt since, from the beginning of the genocide in Rwanda in April 1994 – the world's worst mass killing in recent years, which led to perhaps a million deaths – the leading Western states played a deliberately obstructive role in the UN, prevented punishment of the aggressors and undermined the prospects for enhancing human rights and security in the region. Indeed, their policies contributed to the slaughter.

The British role in the Rwanda tragedy was significant, though it has been almost completely ignored.[59] Although there were hundreds of press articles on the events in Rwanda after April 1994, readers would hardly have been made aware of the British government's stance nor its role in the UN Security Council (only a couple of reports noted a British role, albeit very briefly). That Britain was a major obstacle to international action over Rwanda should come as no surprise. In the last quarter of a century, Britain has been the biggest obstructor of UN action on crises in Africa, having cast more Security Council vetoes (23) than any other country.

After the killings began in April 1994, the Security Council took the decision to reduce the UN's troop presence (United Nations Assistance Mission in Rwanda – UNAMIR) from 2500 to 270 personnel. The United States took the lead role in this decision, which gave a clear signal to those perpetrating the crimes, which now escalated to mass killing.[60] The following month, with massacres reaching genocidal proportions, a UN resolution to dispatch 5500 troops to Rwanda was delayed by pressure from the US Ambassador at the UN and then blunted by US insistence on sending only an initial 150 observers and 800 troops.[61] A report on Rwanda for Oxfam by Guy Vassall-Adams notes that 'just as it had taken the lead in advocating UNAMIR's reduction, the USA took the lead in pressing for a plan that would confine UNAMIR to the borders of Rwanda'. The Secretary-General's plan had called for troops to be dispatched to the interior of the country in view of the fact that 'there was clear evidence that the majority of those [people] under threat were within Rwanda itself'.[62] A watered-down version of the plan acceptable to the United States ensured that the troops would have no mandate to use force to end the massacres.[63] 'What the US wants, the US gets', one UN insider was reported as saying.[64] Overall, the director of MSF noted, the US 'used its influence within the UN to ensure that no action was forced upon it'.[65]

The US also refused to provide the military airlift capability for the African states which were offering troops for the proposed deployment. This policy was also aided by Britain, which could itself have offered airlift capability but did not. Paul Rogers, of the University of Bradford, wrote in the *Observer* that 'the RAF has more than 60 Hercules C-130 transport aircraft. A quarter of these could transform the situation, saving thousands of lives.'[66] Vassall-Adams comments that 'having refused to send their own troops, Security Council members now failed even to deliver the means by which African troops could be sent'. The US responded by offering to loan 50 armoured vehicles; Britain offered 50 trucks.[67] Holly Burkhalter of the human rights organisation, Human Rights Watch, notes that Pentagon defence experts told her that the Defense Department possessed the capacity to jam the radio broadcasts the killers were using to encourage their campaign of slaughter and could have deployed this capacity 'at any point during the genocide', but did not.[68]

Britain, along with the other states on the Security Council, allowed Rwanda to retain its Security Council seat throughout the period when his government's forces were committing genocide. The Rwandan Ambassador 'has even been permitted to speak at length in debates and to vote on resolutions concerning Rwanda', Human Rights Watch pointed out.[69] This permitted the Rwandan Ambassador to deliver a speech blaming the victims – predominantly Tutsis – for the massacres.[70] Despite 200,000 deaths by then, Britain did not express an objection to the ambassador's remarks – in fact, Britain's UN Ambassador was at this time reportedly still dealing regularly with his Rwandan counterpart.[71] Rwanda's representative on the UN Human Rights Commission, meanwhile – in an emergency session on the situation in Rwanda – referred to 'a few problems here and there' in the country.[72]

The dilution of the May plan paved the way for Security Council authorisation for the French intervention in June, which lasted until August when the French force withdrew. The US statement to the Security Council supporting the French intervention noted 'the need for cooperative action by member states who are willing and able to supplement UN peace operations in particular situations'. It cited recent examples as the allied 'coalition' which waged war against Iraq and the intervention force in Somalia.[73] Britain also voted in favour of the resolution calling for the French intervention, thus acquiescing in the farcical display of an 'humanitarian intervention' by a country which was continuing arms supplies to the armed forces of a government engaged in genocide, which it (France) had previously trained and advised.[74]

The next phase of the tragedy involved the movement of hundreds of thousands of refugees (including the militia who organised and conducted the slaughter) from Rwanda into neighbouring countries, mainly Zaire. By November 1994, after these former government forces had regrouped and tightened their grip over the refugee camps and much of the humanitarian aid effort, the UN Secretary-General proposed the dispatch of a 5000-strong force to reassert UN control. This plan called for 'a United Nations peacekeeping operation, set up in accordance with normal procedures, to establish security progressively in the camps, area by area, over a period of time'. Thus 'the task of such a force would be to provide security for international relief workers, protection for the storage and delivery of humanitarian assistance and safe passage to the Rwandese border for those refugees who wish to return'.[75]

Two weeks before this plan was presented, Foreign Secretary Douglas Hurd had told the House of Commons that Britain 'will support any action that he [Boutros Boutros-Ghali] thinks is justified'.[76] A day before the Secretary-General's report was issued, Hurd told the House of Commons: 'I do not think that any of us, looking back, can be satisfied with the way in which the international community responded [to the crisis]. Action, not hand wringing, is now needed.'[77] (Hurd's call for 'action' was matched by noting that the British force despatched to Rwanda 'will be coming home this weekend'.) But Britain had no intention of supporting the UN Secretary-General's plan. Rather, as an alternative to it, Britain 'played a constructive role in the negotiation'[78] of a statement issued by the Security Council which called for 'further elucidation' of the plan due to the 'complex issues' raised in it, a stalling mechanism designed to block it.[79] The de facto rejection of the Secretary-General's plan was taken in the full knowledge that, in the words of Lynda Chalker, Minister for Overseas Development, 'increased refugee return depends on greater security in the camps outside Rwanda and efforts to rebuild the country's economic and social fabric'.[80]

During the 'refugee crisis' Britain began to take on a greater public role, eventually delivering over £60 million in emergency assistance. As in Bosnia, such aid was the alternative to, not a counterpart of, political action to help resolve the crisis. The British government – and thus the press – continued to portray this simply as a 'humanitarian' crisis, which absolved actors from having to deal with its political causes. MSF's Secretary-General, however, wrote in the press what all aid workers on the ground knew, that the refugees 'were terrorised into the exodus by their Hutu-led government'.[81] The massive quantities of humanitarian aid funnelled to the refugee camps in Zaire served to convince the world that the international community was doing something, a policy aided by the numerous NGOs who also got involved.

Consider the 600-strong force Britain sent on a three-month deployment to Rwanda in August 1994. This force was under a strict 'humanitarian' mandate only – mainly involving medical assistance – despite the fact that, on the day it arrived, the UN security force of 5500 authorised in May had not even reached 1000. A British military spokesman said that the 'principal task' of the British contingent was 'to provide a corridor down which refugees can be enticed to come into the interior'.[82] This principal task was not achieved, and no significant return of refugees occurred, but the British left anyway after three months, with a minister noting that 'that task is now complete'.[83] Presumably the real objective – which was to convince the world that Britain was doing something – was, however, achieved. 'The United Kingdom can be proud of what we have been doing in Rwanda', the Foreign Office minister informed the House of Commons in October.[84]

The policy of treating the tragedy as an 'humanitarian' one had enabled the regrouping, rearming and retraining in the refugee camps of the former Rwandan government forces and their militias. Former MSF Secretary-General, Alain Destexhe, noted in an article in February 1995 that 'in the last seven months international aid has allowed the militias to reorganise, stockpile food and recruit and train new members'.[85] A report by MSF in January 1995 exposed this policy by noting:

> The massive deployment of humanitarian aid around Goma [the largest refugee concentration] somehow disguised the culpable failure to come to the assistance of Tutsis in mortal danger. In Bosnia, humanitarian assistance elevated to the status of official policy ... has encouraged and fostered aggression. The humanitarian brotherhood is playing an increasingly amnesiac role.

This report coincided with one from the Red Cross, noting that humanitarian aid is too often 'becoming a substitute for efforts to find political solutions'.[86]

The British government was apparently aware of the effect of the policy of providing aid to the refugee camps. Douglas Hurd noted in a speech in February 1995 that: 'It would be tragic indeed if humanitarian aid to the camps helped to perpetuate the very problem it was designed to solve. We are starting to shift the focus towards reconstruction within Rwanda.'[87] Yet this shift in focus was occurring seven months after the refugee crisis erupted in July. It took the international community until January 1995 before Rwanda received pledges of aid, worth $587 million, for reconstruction.

Thus the consequence of rushing 'humanitarian' aid to the refugee camps by Britain and other donors, while at the same time scuppering plans to enhance security and a political solution to the crisis, may have made further war more likely. By early 1995, indeed, there were persistent reports of an imminent restart to the war and of a 'consolidated and well-planned insurgency campaign' by the former government militias and their allies in the Zairean refugee camps.[88]

This chronology of obstacles is matched by the principles by which the British government tried to frame the tragedy. First was the myth that the killings were primarily due to 'civil strife', as Chalker put it, or mindless tribal slaughters and age-old ethnic hatreds.[89] Hurd noted that Rwanda is 'a true "heart of darkness"'.[90] As noted above, the fiction of 'civil war' – implying equal blame on the factions – absolved outside powers from acting. The press reported these matters as required.[91] However, the massacres which began in April 1994 were planned months in advance and were an orchestrated campaign of slaughter.[92] Indeed, the UNAMIR commander sent a secret cable to UN headquarters three months before the massacres began, warning of such an extermination plan.[93] The first targets were political parties opposed to the hardline Hutus perpetrating the massacres, most of these victims being Hutus. After this, attention turned to intellectuals, priests, journalists, businessmen and then Tutsis.[94]

Also important was the question of genocide. In late April 1994 the Security Council adopted a declaration which rejected the use of the term 'genocide'. A July 1994 resolution spoke of 'possible acts of genocide' and all other Security Council documents used similarly restrained language.[95] The Western states feared official use of this term since to talk of genocide by name would have obligated them to 'prevent and punish' genocide under the terms of the Geneva Convention. However, in a speech to the UN in September, Douglas Hurd noted that 'in Rwanda, the UN's efforts failed to avert genocide'.[96] Unsurprisingly, this understanding was not matched by British government action under the Convention, or indeed by any perceptible change in policy.

Overall, the British policy towards the Rwandan holocaust is perhaps best symbolised by a Government Minister's response to a parliamentary question in the House of Commons asking what it intended to do to prevent future war crimes in Rwanda. 'War crimes will stop when human nature changes', came the reply.[97]

## Conclusion

It is fitting to end this study with consideration of Anglo-American policy in the Rwanda genocide, showing as it does a callous disregard for human life. If we looked at the world with honesty, we would see this is a leitmotif of these countries' foreign policies, clearly visible to all those who choose to look with anything like an independent eye. Unfortunately, however, this excludes the overwhelming majority of commentators in the media and academia who prefer, consciously or unconsciously, to adopt frameworks of analysis that accord with the ruling groups who control policy.

In the real world, and in a systematic way, the professed Anglo-American promotion of 'human rights' amounts to undermining human rights, promoting 'security' amounts to maintaining insecurity and promoting 'development' leads to poverty. The first task for those concerned with creating a better world – especially those people and organisations in the UK and US – is to take a more independent and critical look at their own governments' policies – which are significantly responsible for shaping world order – and help to expose the great deception that they are currently part of the solution to the world's horrors.

# Notes

## Introduction

1. *US Department of State Dispatch* (hereafter *Dispatch*), 20 February 1995, p. 111.
2. Charles Maynes, 'The limitations of force', in *The United States and the Use of Force in the Post-Cold War Era: A Report by the Aspen Strategy Group*, Aspen Institute, Maryland, 1995, p. 31.
3. *Statement on the Defence Estimates 1995*, Cmnd. 2800, HMSO, London, May 1995, p. 9.
4. Cited in Robert Tucker and David Hendrickson, *Imperial Temptation: The New World Order and America's Purpose*, Council on Foreign Relations, New York, 1992, p. 87.
5. Steven David, 'The necessity for American military intervention in the post-Cold War world', in Aspen Institute, *The United States and the Use of Force*, p. 68.
6. Cited in Walden Bello, *Dark Victory: The United States, Structural Adjustment and Global Poverty*, Pluto Press, London, 1994, p. 105.
7. Speech by Prof. Robert O'Neill, *Britain in the World: Conference Proceedings*, RIIA, London, 29 March 1995, p. 42.
8. Speech by the Prince of Wales, *Britain in the World*, p. 161.
9. Frank Furedi, *The New Ideology of Imperialism: Renewing the Moral Imperative*, Pluto Press, London, 1994, pp. 99–100.
10. Cited in John Pilger, *Distant Voices*, Vintage, London, 1992, p. 131.
11. Anthony Kemp, *The SAS Savage Wars of Peace*, Signet, London, 1994, p. 78.
12. Michael Cox, *US Foreign Policy After the Cold War: Superpower Without a Mission?*, Pinter/RIIA, London, 1995, p. 5.
13. *The Challenge to the South: The Report of the South Commission*, Oxford University Press, Oxford, 1990, p. 3.
14. John Ikenberry, 'The myth of post-Cold War chaos', *Foreign Affairs*, Vol. 75, No. 3, May/June 1996.
15. Ian Brownlie (ed.), *Basic Documents on Human Rights*, Clarendon, Oxford, 1971, p. 112.
16. Edward Herman, *Beyond Hypocrisy: Decoding the News in an Age of Propaganda*, South End Press, Boston, 1992, p. 109.

## Chapter One

1. See Mark Curtis, *The Ambiguities of Power: British Foreign Policy Since 1945*, Zed Books, London, 1995, p. 17.
2. See, for example, Gabriel Kolko, *The Politics of War: The World and United States Foreign Policy 1943–1945*, Random House, New York, 1968, p. 624.
3. Cited in Kolko, *Politics of War*, p. 251.
4. Curtis, *Ambiguities of Power*, p. 18.
5. Cited in Christopher Hitchens, *Blood, Class and Nostalgia: Anglo-American Ironies*, Vintage, London, 1990, p. 207.
6. Noam Chomsky, *Deterring Democracy*, Vintage, London, 1992, p. 336.
7. Gabriel Kolko, *Confronting the Third World: United States Foreign Policy 1945–80*, Pantheon, New York, 1988, pp. 4–5.
8. Kolko, *Confronting the Third World*, p. 291.
9. Curtis, *Ambiguities of Power*, p. 22.
10. Ibid., p. 21.
11. Policy Paper by the State Department's Bureau of Near Eastern, South Asian and African Affairs, 18 April 1950, *Foreign Relations of the United States* (hereafter *FRUS*), 1950, Vol. V, USGPO, Washington, D.C. , p. 1527.
12. Curtis, *Ambiguities of Power*, p. 19.
13. Policy Paper by the State Department's Bureau of Near Eastern, South Asian and African Affairs, 29 December 1950, *FRUS*, 1950, Vol. V, p. 1589.
14. National Security Council, Statement of US policy toward South, Central and East Africa, 19 January 1960, *FRUS*, 1958–60, Vol. XIV, pp. 79, 83.
15. Enclosure to report by the Joint Strategic Survey Committee, 29 April 1947, *FRUS*, 1947, Vol. I, p. 743.
16. Cited in Andrew, *For the President's Eyes Only: Secret Intelligence and the American Presidency from Washington to Bush*, HarperCollins, London, 1995, p. 28.
17. Kolko, *Confronting the Third World*, p. 35.
18. See *Ambiguities of Power*, pp. 165–74.
19. Ibid., pp. 157–74.
20. John Prados, *Presidents' Secret Wars: CIA and Pentagon Covert Operations From World War II through the Persian Gulf*, Elephant, Chicago, 1996, p. 447.
21. Stephen Dorril, *The Silent Conspiracy: Inside the Intelligence Services in the 1990s*, Mandarin, London, 1993, pp. 271–2.
22. See Hugh O'Shaughnessy, 'Preface', and James Ferguson, James Painter and Jenny Pearce, 'Under attack: Central America and the Caribbean', in Latin America Bureau, *The Thatcher Years: Britain and Latin America*, LAB, London, 1988, pp. 7–8, 41–3.

23. See Curtis, *Ambiguities of Power*, passim.
24. 'Some notes on British foreign policy', memorandum by Sir Roger Makins, 11 August 1951, *British Documents on the End of Empire* [hereafter *BDEE*], Ser. A, Vol. 2, Part II, p. 376.
25. Final report of the joint MDAP survey mission to Southeast Asia, 6 December 1950, *FRUS*, 1950, Vol. VI, p. 172.
26. Cited in Chomsky, *Deterring Democracy*, p. 49.
27. Cited in Noam Chomsky, *Powers and Prospects: Reflections on Human Nature and the Social Order*, Pluto Press, London, 1996, p. 109.
28. Dianna Melrose, *Nicaragua: The Threat of a Good Example?*, Oxfam, Oxford, 1985.
29. Prados, *Presidents' Secret Wars*, p. 176.
30. Cited in Andrew, *For the President's Eyes Only*, p. 282.
31. Noam Chomsky, *Year 501: The Conquest Continues*, Verso, London, 1993, p. 37.
32. Department of Agriculture memorandum, 17 April 1950, *FRUS*, 1950, Vol. VI, pp. 143–4.
33. Cited on Channel 4 news, Britain, 1 May 1995.
34. Curtis, *Ambiguities of Power*, p. 18.
35. Kolko, *Confronting the Third World*, p. 296.
36. Cited in Anthony Verrier, *Through the Looking Glass: British Foreign Policy in an Age of Illusions*, Jonathan Cape, London, 1983, p. 85.
37. Report by Sir William Strang, 17 March 1949, *BDEE*, Ser. A, Vol. 2, Part II, p. 338.
38. Richard Clarke, 'The world dollar crisis', June 1947, in Sir Alec Cairncross (ed.), *Anglo-American Economic Collaboration in War and Peace, 1942–1949, by Sir Richard Clarke*, Clarendon, Oxford, 1982, p. 172.
39. See Curtis, *Ambiguities of Power*, p. 12.
40. Ibid., p. 13.
41. Ibid., pp. 15–16.
42. Ibid., p. 14.
43. Ibid.
44. Cabinet memorandum by Bevin, 4 January 1948, *BDEE*, Ser. A, Vol. 2, Part II, p. 318.
45. Colonial Office memorandum by J. S. Bennett, 'International aspects of colonial policy', 30 April 1947, *BDEE*, Ser. A, Vol. 2, Part II, p. 417.
46. V. G. Kiernan, *European Empires from Conquest to Collapse, 1815–1960*, Fontana, London, 1982, p. 205.
47. Note of a meeting in the Foreign Office on colonial issues, 3 May 1950, *BDEE*, Ser. A, Vol. 2, Part II, p. 467.
48. Clement Attlee to Ernest Bevin, 5 January 1947, *BDEE*, Ser. A, Vol. 2, Part III, p. 224.
49. See Curtis, *Ambiguities of Power*, pp. 65–74.
50. Ibid., p. 71.

51. Ibid., p. 78.
52. Ibid., p. 21.
53. Ibid., p. 91.
54. Cabinet conclusions, 'Suez canal', *BDEE*, Ser. A, Vol. 3, Part I, pp. 166–8.
55. Curtis, *Ambiguities of Power*, pp. 96–7.
56. Cited in Andrew, *For the President's Eyes Only*, p. 236.
57. Curtis, *Ambiguities of Power*, pp. 98–100.
58. Ibid., pp. 102–5.
59. Ibid., pp. 105–8.
60. Ibid., pp. 149–52.
61. Jonathan Bloch and Patrick Fitzgerald, *British Intelligence and Covert Action: Africa, Middle East and Europe Since 1945*, Junction, London, 1983, p. 64.
62. Curtis, *Ambiguities of Power*, pp. 117–19.
63. Ibid., pp. 119–29.
64. Anthony Hartley, 'America and Britain: Is the relationship still special?', *Policy Study no. 137*, Centre for Policy Studies, London, 1994, p. 10.
65. Raymond Seitz, 'Britain and America: Towards strategic coincidence', *World Today*, Vol. 49, No. 5, May 1993, pp. 85–7.
66. Kolko, *Politics of War*, p. 280.
67. Cited in Hitchens, *Blood, Class and Nostalgia*, p. 135.
68. Ibid., p. 309.
69. Report by the Policy Planning Staff, 24 February 1948, *FRUS*, 1948, Vol. I, p. 520. Emphasis in the original.
70. State Department Policy statement, 'Great Britain', 11 June 1948, *FRUS*, 1948, Vol. III, pp. 1091, 1106.
71. Hitchens, *Blood, Class and Nostalgia*, p. 261.
72. Cited in Hartley, 'America and Britain: Is the relationship still special?', p. 9.
73. Churchill to Eisenhower, 12 April 1953, in Peter Boyle (ed.), *The Churchill–Eisenhower Correspondence*, University of North Carolina Press, Chapel Hill, 1990, p. 43.
74. Hitchens, *Blood, Class and Nostalgia*, p. 215.
75. J. Balfour to E. Bevin, 9 August 1945, *Documents on British Policy Overseas* (hereafter *DBPO*), R. Bullen and M. Pelly (eds), Ser. I, Vol. III, HMSO, London, 1986, p. 17.
76. Report by William Strang, 17 March 1949, *BDEE*, Ser. A, Vol. 2, Part II, p. 339.
77. Cited in Chomsky, *Deterring Democracy*, p. 91.
78. See Prados, *Presidents' Secret Wars*, pp. 40–3, 56–7.
79. Andrew, *For the President's Eyes Only*, pp. 467–8.
80. See Duncan Campbell, *The Unsinkable Aircraft Carrier: American Military Power in Britain*, Michael Joseph, London, 1984.
81. See Curtis, *Ambiguities of Power*, pp. 165–74.
82. Ibid., pp. 196–206.

83. Cited in Hitchens, *Blood, Class and Nostalgia*, p. 337.
84. Cited in Andrew, *For the President's Eyes Only*, p. 254.
85. See Curtis, *Ambiguities of Power*, pp. 217–18.
86. See Mark Curtis, 'Democratic genocide', *Ecologist*, Vol. 26, No. 5, September/October 1996.
87. Cited in Hitchens, *Blood, Class and Nostalgia*, pp. 18–19.
88. Ibid., p. 104.
89. Peter de la Billiere, *Storm Command: A Personal Account of the Gulf War*, HarperCollins, London, 1993, p. 299. Emphasis in the original.
90. Ian Black, 'Isolated allies sing mutual praises', *Guardian*, 6 September 1996.
91. *Public Papers of the Presidents of the United States: William J. Clinton, 1995, Book I*, USGPO, Washington D.C., 1996, pp. 449–54.

## Chapter Two

1. Robert Tucker and David Hendrickson, *Imperial Temptation: The New World Order and America's Purpose*, Council on Foreign Relations, New York, 1992, pp. 1–16, 205–9.
2. William Kristol and Robert Kagan, 'Towards a neo-Reaganite foreign policy', *Foreign Affairs*, Vol. 75, No. 4, July/August 1996, pp. 20, 26–8.
3. Michael Mandelbaum, 'Foreign policy as social work', *Foreign Affairs*, Vol. 75, No. 1, January/February 1996, pp. 16, 18, 28–9.
4. *Dispatch*, 27 September 1993, p. 659.
5. Ibid., 29 May 1995, p. 462.
6. Tony Smith, 'Democracy resurgent', in Nicholas Rizopoulos (ed.), *Sea Changes: American Foreign Policy in a World Transformed*, Council on Foreign Relations, New York, 1990, p. 156.
7. Kristol and Kagan, 'Towards a neo-Reaganite foreign policy', p. 32.
8. *Dispatch*, 14 November 1994, pp. 776–7.
9. Ibid., 22 November 1993, p. 797.
10. Ibid., 20 February 1995, p. 112.
11. Ibid., 22 November 1993, p. 798.
12. See Mark Curtis, *The Ambiguities of Power: British Foreign Policy Since 1945*, Zed Books, London, 1995, pp. 184–5.
13. Alvin Bernstein, 'Conflict and technology: The next generation', in G. Wilson (ed.), *British Security 2010: Proceedings of a Conference Held at Church House, Westminster*, November 1995, pp. 182–3.
14. Alexander Haig, 'The challenges to American leadership', in Greg Schmergel (ed.), *United States Foreign Policy in the 1990s*, Macmillan, London, 1991, p. 37.
15. Richard Haass, 'Paradigm lost', *Foreign Affairs*, Vol. 74, No. 1, January/February 1995, pp. 52, 56, 58.

16. Tucker and Hendrickson, *Imperial Temptation*, pp. 5, 8–9.
17. University of London, Centre for Defence Studies, *The Framework of United Kingdom Defence Policy: Key Speeches on Defence Policy by the Rt. Hon. Malcolm Rifkind*, CDS, London, 1995, pp. 50–1.
18. *Dispatch*, 26 September 1994, p. 638.
19. See *Hearing before the Select Committee on Intelligence*, US Senate, 22 February 1996, USGPO, Washington D.C., 1996, p. 8.
20. Cited in Tim Lang and Colin Hines, *The New Protectionism: Protecting the Future against Free Trade*, Earthscan, London, 1993, p. 26.
21. *Dispatch*, 25 October 1993, p. 751.
22. William Robinson, 'The new face of global domination', *Covert Action Quarterly*, No. 50, Fall 1994.
23. William Robinson, *Promoting Polyarchy: Globalisation, US Intervention and Hegemony*, Cambridge University Press, Cambridge, 1996, pp. 16, 35, 51, 319, 365.
24. Cited in Christopher Simpson, *National Security Directives of the Reagan and Bush Administrations*, Westview, Boulder, 1995, p. 517.
25. Ibid., p. 665.
26. Cited in Robinson, 'The new face of global domination', p. 46.
27. Strobe Talbott, 'Democracy and the national interest', *Foreign Affairs*, Vol. 75, No. 6, November/December 1996, pp. 49, 52.
28. US House of Representatives, *Hearing before the Committee on Foreign Affairs*, 2 February 1993, USGPO, Washington D.C. , 1993, p. 11.
29. *Dispatch*, 27 September 1993, pp. 658–63.
30. Isabel Hilton, 'A flawed martial plan', *Guardian*, 28 May 1997.
31. Cited in World Development Movement, *Biting the Bullet: Real Security in a New World*, WDM, London, undated, p. 9.
32. Cited in Jeremy Seabrook, 'Re-examining the lexicon of development', in *Third World Resurgence*, No. 61/62, p. 13.
33. *Hearing before the Select Committee on Intelligence*, US Senate, 22 February 1996, USGPO, Washington D.C., 1996, p. 237.
34. *The Framework of United Kingdom Defence Policy*, p. 57.
35. Ibid., p. 46.
36. *Defence Estimates 1995*, p. 23.
37. Steve Schofield, 'Militarism, the UK economy and conversion policies in the North', in Geoff Tansey et al. (eds), *A World Divided: Militarism and Development after the Cold War*, Earthscan, London, 1994, pp. 67–8.
38. Michael Cox, *US Foreign Policy After the Cold War: Superpower Without a Mission?*, Pinter/RIIA, London, 1995, p. 52.
39. *Arms Control*, No. 34, July 1994, p. 15.
40. Michael Portillo, 'Russia and international security: A UK perspective', *RUSI Journal*, February 1997; Ministry of Defence, *British Defence Doctrine*, Joint warfare publication 0–01, MoD,

London, 1996, pp. 5.5 and 5.6; *Framework of United Kingdom Defence Policy*, p. 176.

41. See *Hearing before the Select Committee on Intelligence*, US Senate, 22 February 1996, USGPO, Washington, D.C. , 1996, pp. 5, 8, 44.
42. *Dispatch*, 27 September 1993, p. 665.
43. Ibid., 19 September 1994, p. 623.
44. Ibid., 27 September 1993, p. 659.
45. Curt Gasteyger, 'Sources of future conflict: A global overview', in Wilson (ed.), *British Security 2010*, pp. 21–2.
46. George Joffe, 'The impact on security of demographic and environmental change', in Wilson (ed.), *British Security 2010*, p. 38.
47. Christopher Coker, 'The academic view of the role of Britain's forces in future conflict – further discussion', in Wilson (ed.), *British Security 2010*, pp. 253–4.
48. Stephen Dorril, *The Silent Conspiracy: Inside the Intelligence Services in the 1990s*, Mandarin, London, 1993, pp. 11, 35.
49. Cited in Tucker and Hendrickson, *Imperial Temptation*, p. 36.
50. Cox, *US Foreign Policy After the Cold War*, p. 44.
51. Steven David, 'The nesessity for American military intervention in the post-Cold War World', in *The United States and the Use of Force in the Post-Cold War Era: A Report by the Aspen Strategy Group*, Aspen Institute, Maryland, 1995, pp. 47–8.
52. Cited in Martin Walker, 'US army faces cut to Gulf war size', *Guardian*, 30 April 1997.
53. Richard Haass, 'Military intervention: A taxonomy of challenges and responses', in Aspen Institute, *The United States and the Use of Force*, pp. 2–8, 16.
54. Charles Maynes, 'The limitation of force', in Aspen Institute, *The United States and the Use of Force*, pp. 20–1, 24.
55. Anthony Lake, Speech at George Washington University, 6 March 1996, *Official Text*, 8 March 1996.
56. Andrew Kohut and Robert Toth, 'The people, the press, and the use of force', in Aspen Institute, *The United States and the Use of Force*, p. 133.
57. David, 'The necessity for American military intervention', p. 57.
58. Nestor Sanchez, 'Covert military operations and American foreign policy', in Schmergel (ed.), *United States Foreign Policy*, p. 211.
59. *Defence Estimates 1995*, p. 30.
60. 'The services' view of the role of British forces in future conflict – further discussion', in Wilson (ed.), *British Security 2010*, p. 298.
61. Sir Peter Inge, 'The roles and challenges of the British armed forces', *RUSI Journal*, February 1996, p. 4.
62. Black Robertson, 'Joint needs in 2010', in Wilson (ed.), *British Security 2010*, p. 279.
63. Centre for Defence Studies, *The Framework of United Kingdom Defence Policy*, p. 92.

64. Cited in Kiernan, *European Empires from Conquest to Collapse,* 1815–1960, Fontana, London, 1982, pp. 32–3.
65. Michael Binyon, 'Cook makes grand entrance for role on the world stage', *The Times,* 13 May 1997; Ian Black, 'Cook gives ethics priority', *Guardian,* 13 May 1997.
66. Labour Party, 'A fresh start for Britain: Labour's strategy for Britain in the modern world', undated [1996], p. 2.
67. Speech by Tony Blair, Manchester, 21 April 1997.
68. Ian Black and John Palmer, 'Portillo on short list for Bosnia mediator post', *Guardian,* 23 May 1997.
69. Ian Black, 'Major's former spokesman to be our man in US', *Guardian,* 25 July 1997.
70. David Fairhall, 'MPs urge minister to spell out impact of defence review', *Guardian,* 31 July 1997.
71. George Monbiot, 'No fudging – the House of Lords has to go', *Guardian,* 29 July 1997.
72. Lord Simon, *Hansard,* House of Lords, 22 July 1997, WA157.
73. *Hansard,* House of Commons, 28 October 1997, Col. 711.
74. Margaret Beckett, 'Towards full market access', *Financial Times,* 10 July 1997.
75. Labour Party, 'A fresh start', pp. 7–8, 22.
76. Cited in Larry Elliott, 'Short shrift for free trade mania', *Guardian,* 23 May 1997.
77. *Eliminating World Poverty: A Challenge for the 21st Century, White Paper on International Development,* Cmnd. 3789, HMSO, London, November 1997, p. 62.
78. Baroness Symons, *Hansard,* House of Lords, 10 November 1997, Cols 15, 14.
79. Labour Party, 'A fresh start', pp. 21–2.
80. Robin Cook, 'Human rights into a new century', Speech at the Foreign Office, 17 July 1997.
81. See *Hansard,* House of Lords, 25 June 1997, Cols 1571–3; Paul Foot, 'The injustices darkening our skies', *Guardian,* 14 July 1997.
82. See *Hansard,* House of Commons, 14 July 1997, Col. 43.
83. *Hansard,* House of Lords, 8 July 1997, Col. 614.
84. Ian Black, 'Nigeria "must be kept out"', *Guardian,* 26 July 1997.
85. Kathy Evans, 'British backing for Bahrain', *Guardian,* 25 July 1997.
86. *Hansard,* House of Commons, 15 October 1996, Col. 621.
87. Jonathan Steele, 'La bombe's eternal shadow – even without any "enemies"', *Guardian,* 23 August 1997.
88. 'Trident tested nuclear strategy', *Guardian,* 29 April 1997.
89. *Hansard,* House of Commons, 4 November 1997, Col. 111.
90. Ian Traynor, 'Britain battles to save Eurofighter', *Guardian,* 5 June 1997.
91. Lord Gilbert, *Hansard,* House of Commons, 14 July 1997, Col. 824.
92. David Fairhall, 'UK says yes to £14bn workhorse', *Guardian,* 1 August 1997.

93. Ian Black and Richard Norton-Taylor, 'Britain bans the use and sale of mines', *Guardian*, 22 May 1997.
94. *Hansard*, House of Lords, 1 July 1997, WA23.
95. *Hansard*, House of Lords, 29 July 1997, Cols WA20–22. Emphasis added.
96. Ian Black and Richard Norton-Taylor, 'Cook says Indonesia arms sales go ahead', *Guardian*, 29 July 1997.
97. David Fairhall, 'Trenchant answer to naval forebodings', *Guardian*, 17 May 1997,
98. Ian Black and Richard Norton-Taylor, 'Britain hints at arms sale limits', *Guardian*, 24 May 1997.
99. *Hansard*, House of Lords, 24 July 1997, Col. 1513.
100. Cited in Ben Jackson, 'Promoting real security: Implications for policy in the North', in Tansey et al. (eds), *A World Divided*, p. 90.
101. Cited in Simpson, *National Security Directives*, p. 32.
102. Special Ad-Hoc Committee of the State–War–Navy Coordinating Committee, 'Policies and principles for extension of US aid to foreign nations', April 1947, *FRUS*, 1947, Vol. III, pp. 216–18.
103. Appendix to Report of the Special 'Ad-hoc' Committee of the State–War–Navy Coordinating Committee, 21 April 1947, *FRUS*, 1947, Vol. III, p. 217; Report by the Policy Planning Council, undated [1961], *FRUS*, 1961–1963, Vol. IX, p. 189.
104. Enclosure to report by the Joint Strategic Survey Committee, 29 April 1947, *FRUS*, 1947, Vol. I, p. 744.
105. Cited in Paul Barber, *Partners in Repression: The Reality of British Aid to Indonesia*, TAPOL, Thornton Heath, Surrey, November 1995, p. 24.
106. *TAPOL Bulletin*, No. 121, February 1994, p. 6.
107. *Indonesia and East Timor: An Amnesty International Briefing*, September 1994, p. 1.
108. 'Two Faces of Indonesia', *International Herald Tribune*, 5 November 1994.
109. Human Rights Watch, *Human Rights Watch Report 1995*, HRW, New York, 1994, p. 160.
110. *Indonesia and East Timor: An Amnesty International Briefing*, September 1994, p. 4.
111. See Project on Demilitarisation and Democracy, *Financing Military Rule: The Clinton Administration, the World Bank and Indonesia*, Washington, D.C. , April 1994.
112. *Indonesia and East Timor: An Amnesty International Briefing*, September 1994, pp. 2, 5.
113. See memorandum by TAPOL to the Foreign Affairs Committee, in House of Commons, Foreign Affairs Committee, Session 1993–94, Third Report, *Public Expenditure: Pergau Hydro-Electric Project, Malaysia, the Aid and Trade Provision and Related Matters, Volume II*, HMSO, London, 13 July 1994, pp. 281–2.
114. Ibid., p. 282.

115. Report by the National Security Council, 1 July 1948, *FRUS*, 1948, Vol. I, p. 586.
116. Report by the Policy Planning Council, undated [1961], *FRUS*, 1961–1963, Vol. IX, p. 189.
117. Report by the Chiefs of Staff, 3 July 1956, *BDEE*, Ser. A, Vol. 3, Part I, p. 151.
118. MoD, *British Defence Doctrine*, p. 6.6.
119. *Hansard*, House of Commons, 19 February 1991, Col. 136.
120. Vicky Imerman, 'SOA – School of the Americas', *Covert Action Quarterly*, No. 46, Fall 1993, pp. 16–18; *Red Pepper*, June 1994, p. 16.
121. Speech by Sir Peter Inge, *Britain in the World: Conference Proceedings*, RIIA, London, 29 March 1995, p. 37.
122. *Hansard*, House of Lords, 21 July 1997, WA145–7.
123. *Hansard*, House of Lords, 31 July 1997, WA78–80.
124. Cited in Campaign Against the Arms Trade, *Death on Delivery: The Impact of the Arms Trade on the Third World*, CAAT, London, 1989, p. 76.
125. See Terry Barker, Paul Dunne and Ron Smith, 'Measuring the peace dividend in the United Kingdom', *Journal of Peace Research*, Vol. 28, No. 4, 1991.
126. Neil Cooper, 'British defence exports: Trends, policies and security implications', *Contemporary Security Policy*, Vol. 16, No. 2, August 1995, pp. 219–37.
127. 'Policy and the world', *The Times*, 7 April 1997.

## Chapter Three

1. Calculated from statistics in UNDP, *Human Development Report 1994*, Oxford University Press, New York, 1994, p. 63.
2. House of Lords, *Hansard*, 30 November 1995, Cols 695–6.
3. See, for example, Gabriel Kolko, *Confronting the Third World: United States Foreign Policy 1945–80*, Pantheon, New York, 1988, and *The Politics of War: The World and United States Foreign Policy 1943–1945*, Random House, New York, 1968.
4. 'Commonwealth membership', Cabinet memorandum by Lord Swinton, 11 October 1954, *BDEE*, Ser. A, Vol. 3, Part II, pp. 30, 36.
5. CRO paper on the probable development of the Commonwealth over the next ten or fifteen years, June 1956, *BDEE*, Ser. A, Vol. 3, Part I, p. 95.
6. Paper by Richard Clarke, 11 May 1945, in Sir Alec Cairncross (ed.), *Anglo-American Economic Collaboration in War and Peace, 1942–1949, by Sir Richard Clarke*, Clarendon, Oxford, 1982, pp. 109–11.
7. Jan Morris, *Pax Britannica: The Climax of an Empire*, Penguin, Harmondsworth, 1979, p. 109.

8. Lawrence James, *The Rise and Fall of the British Empire*, Abacus, London, 1994, p. 29.
9. National Advisory Council on International Monetary and Financial Problems, 'Investments in less developed areas', 12 December 1955, *FRUS*, 1955–1957, Vol. IX, p. 353.
10. Report by the Chairman of the Council on Foreign Economic Policy, September 1956, *FRUS*, 1955–1957, Vol. IX, pp. 23–5.
11. Memorandum by. G. Kennan to Secretary of State, 6 January 1950, *FRUS*, 1950, Vol. I, p. 134.
12. Memorandum by the Officer in Charge of Economic Affairs, Office of Philippine and Southeast Asian Affairs, 16 March 1950, *FRUS*, 1950, Vol. VI, p. 62.
13. See Noam Chomsky, *World Orders, Old and New*, Pluto Press, London, 1994, pp. 122–3.
14. Current Economic Developments, Issue No. 641, 16 January 1962, *FRUS*, 1961–1963, Vol. IX, p. 424.
15. Letter from W. Strang to T. Lloyd, 21 June 1952, *BDEE*, Ser. A, Vol. 3, Part I, pp. 13–19.
16. 'Mining policy', despatch by Oliver Lyttleton to governors, 13 May 1952, *BDEE*, Ser. A, Vol. 3, Part III, p. 163. Another official remarked in 1952 that 'if allowed to continue unchecked in its present influence in international politics, will lead to the disintegration of our position in the world'. Cited in Frank Furedi, *The New Ideology of Imperialism: Renewing the Moral Imperative*, Pluto Press, London, 1994, p. 67.
17. Letter from T. Lloyd to W. Strang, 9 September 1952, *BDEE*, Ser. A, Vol. 3, Part I, p. 24.
18. Letter from Creech Jones to P. Mitchell, 17 October 1946, *BDEE*, Ser. A, Vol. 2, Part III, p. 13; see also 'London conferences: Anglo-American talks on colonial problems', note of a meeting in the Foreign Office of British and US officials, 3 May 1950, *BDEE*, Ser. A, Vol. 2, part II, pp. 467–70.
19. Minute by S. Caine, 23 April 1946, *BDEE*, Ser. A, Vol. 2, Part II, p. 234.
20. 'African development: Beira port and railway', E. Bevin to N. Ronald, 23 October 1948, *BDEE*, Ser. A, Vol. 2, Part II, p. 271.
21. Note by P. Mitchell, 30 May 1947, *BDEE*, Ser. A, Vol. 2, Part II, pp. 140–1.
22. 'Tour in Africa, November–December 1947', memorandum by Lord Montgomery, 19 December 1947, *BDEE*, Ser. A, Vol. 2, Part II, pp. 188–92.
23. Memorandum by Creech Jones, 6 January 1948, *BDEE*, Ser. A, Vol. 2, part II, pp. 196–7.
24. Permanent Under-Secretary's Committee, 'The United Kingdom and the United States', 25 April 1950, *DBPO*, Calendar to Ser. II, Vol. II, p. 139.
25. M. Wright to E. Bevin, 6 May 1950, *DBPO*, Ser. II, Vol. II, p. 245.

26. State Department Bureau of Near Eastern, South Asian and African Affairs, 'Future of Africa', 18 April 1950, *FRUS*, 1950, Vol. V, p. 1527.
27. Memorandum of conversation, 16 April; 1959, *FRUS*, 1958–1960, Vol. XIV, p. 47.
28. Department of Defense, 'The strategic importance of Africa', 25 May 1963, *FRUS*, 1961–1963, Vol. XXI, p. 331.
29. National Security Council, 'Statement of US policy towards Africa south of the Sahara prior to calendar year 1960', August 1957, *FRUS*, 1955–1957, Vol. XVIII, pp. 76–7.
30. Memorandum of discussion in the National Security Council, 14 January 1960, *FRUS*, 1958–60, Vol. XIV, p. 74.
31. National Security Council, 'Statement of US policy towards West Africa', 9 April 1960, *FRUS*, 1958–1960, Vol. XIV, p. 119.
32. Cited in John Madeley, *Trade and the Poor: The Impact of International Trade on Developing Countries*, Intermediate Technology Publications, London, 1992, p. 7.
33. CO International Relations Department paper, 'The colonial empire today: Summary of our major problems and policies', May 1950, *BDEE*, Ser. A, Vol. 2, Part I, p. 361.
34. N. Cheetham to J. Watson, 14 May 1956, *BDEE*, Ser. A, Vol. 3, Part I, p. 237.
35. Final report of the Commonwealth Consultative Committee on South and Southeast Asia, October 1950, *BDEE*, Ser. A, Vol. 2, Part II, p. 168. For the importance to the US of raw materials in South Asia see *FRUS* 11, pp. 16–17, 20–2.
36. Foreign Office, 'Southeast Asia: Agreed minute', undated [May 1950], *DBPO*, Calendar to Ser. II, Vol. II, p. 387.
37. Paper prepared by the tripartite drafting group of the preliminary conversations of the United States, United Kingdom and France, 1 September 1950, *FRUS*, 1950, Vol. III, p. 1174.
38. US Ambassador in the UK to Secretary of State, 11 June 1947, *FRUS*, 1947, Vol. I, pp. 756–7.
39. 'Planning for expansion', Cabinet memorandum by H. Morrison, 2 June 1947, *BDEE*, Ser. A, Vol. 2, Part II, p. 44.
40. 'Development of colonial resources', Cabinet memorandum by Creech Jones, 6 June 1947, *BDEE*, Ser. A, Vol. 2, Part II, p. 45.
41. CO International Relations Department paper, 'The colonial empire today: Summary of our main problems and policies', May 1950, *BDEE*, Ser. A, Vol. 2, Part I, p. 335.
42. 'Colonial development', memorandum by the UK delegation to Commonwealth Economic Conference, 22 September 1952, *BDEE*, Ser. A, Vol. 3, Part III, pp. 172–3.
43. State Department policy statement, 'Great Britain', 11 June 1948, *FRUS*, 1948, Vol. III, p. 1106.
44. R. Loree, National Foreign Trade Council to Secretary of State, 8 February 1949, *FRUS*, 1949, Vol. I, p. 632.

45. CO Information Department paper, 'Notes on capital development in the colonies', October 1955, *BDEE*, Ser. A, Vol. 3, Part III, p. 229.
46. Various minutes, 14 January–18 November 1947, *BDEE*, Ser. A, Vol. 2, Part II, pp. 27–40.
47. Cabinet memorandum by O. Lyttleton, 'Balance of payments of the colonial territories', 19 November 1951, *BDEE*, Ser. A, Vol. 3, Part III, p. 15.
48. O. Lyttleton to R. Butler, 26 November 1951, *BDEE*, Ser. A, Vol. 3, Part III, p. 303.
49. Colonial Office memorandum, 'Colonial development', 19 August 1948, *BDEE*, Ser. A, Vol. 2, Part II, p. 86.
50. Cabinet memorandum by O. Lyttleton, 'Balance of payments of the colonial territories', 19 November 1951, *BDEE*, Ser. A, Vol. 3, Part III, p. 14.
51. Report by the Working Party on Colonial Sterling Assets, 11 September 1953, *BDEE*, Ser. A, Vol. 3, Part III, pp. 63–6.
52. Note by H. Bourdillon, 'Reflections on Colonial Office organisation', 10 May 1948, *BDEE*, Ser. A, Vol. 2, Part I, p. 324.
53. T. Lloyd to H. Brittain, 3 February 1956, *BDEE*, Ser. A, Vol. 3, Part III, p. 98.
54. T. Lloyd to Treasury, 26 July 1948, *BDEE*, Ser. A, Vol. 2, Part II, p. 72.
55. E. Bevin to C. Attlee, 4 October 1947, *BDEE*, Ser. A, Vol. 2, Part II, pp. 53.
56. Minute by N. Brook, 14 January 1948, *BDEE*, Ser. A, Vol. 2', Part II, p. 257.
57. Nassau Adams, *Worlds Apart: The North–South Divide and the international system*, Zed Books, London, 1993, pp. 36–40; see also Reinaldo Goncalves and Luis Carlos Goncalves, 'Alternatives to the world trading system', in John Cavanagh, Daphne Wysham and Marcos Arruda (eds), *Beyond Bretton Woods: Alternatives to the Global Economic Order*, Pluto Press, London, 1994, pp. 212–13.
58. Assistant Secretary of State for International Organisation Affairs to Counselor of the Department of State, 'The case for and against SUNFED', 30 March 1956, *FRUS*, 1955–1957, Vol. IX, pp. 373–5.
59. Secretary of the Treasury to Secretary of State, 26 January 1956, *FRUS*, 1955–1957, Vol. IX, p. 364.
60. Under-Secretary of State for Economic Affairs to Assistant Secretary of State for International Organisation Affairs, 12 August 1961, *FRUS*, 1961–1963, Vol. IX, p. 410.
61. Adams, *Worlds Apart*, p. 59.
62. See Adams, *Worlds Apart*, pp. 75–92; Nassau Adams, 'The UN's neglected brief: "The advancement of all peoples"', in Erskine Childers (ed.), *Challenges to the United Nations: Building a Safer World*, CIIR/St Martin's Press, London, 1994, pp. 41–3.

63. Myriam Vander Stichele, 'World trade: Free for whom, fair for whom?', in Childers, *Challenges to the United Nations*, p. 69.
64. See Adams, *Worlds Apart*, pp. 119–40; and 'The UN's neglected brief', pp. 34–6.
65. See Belinda Coote, *The Trade Trap: Poverty and the Global Commodity Markets*, Oxfam, Oxford, 1992, pp. 49–51; Madeley, *Trade and the Poor*, pp. 45–51.
66. Catherine Gwin, *US Relations with the World Bank, 1945–1992*, Brookings Institution, Washington D.C., 1994, pp. 1, 3.
67. See Kolko, *The Politics of War*, pp. 257–8 for the above quotes.
68. Cited in Gwin, *US Relations with the World Bank*, pp. 4, 7.
69. Memorandum by the Director of the Office of Near Eastern and African Affairs, 4 June 1946, *FRUS*, 1946, Vol. VII, pp. 9–10.
70. Kolko, *Confronting the Third World*, pp. 120–1.
71. Memorandum by the President's Deputy Special Assistant for National Security Affairs to President Kennedy, 18 September 1961, *FRUS*, 1961–1963, Vol. IX, pp. 258–9.
72. Memorandum of conversation, 8 October 1959, *FRUS*, 1958–1960, Vol. IV, p. 351.
73. Minutes of meeting of the Interdepartmental Committee of Under Secretaries on Foreign Economic Policy, 11 April 1963, *FRUS*, 1961–1963, Vol. IX, pp. 361–2.
74. Cited in Susan George and Fabrizio Sabelli, *Faith and Credit: The World Bank's Secular Empire*, Penguin, Harmondsworth, 1994, p. 215.
75. Cited in Kolko, *Confronting the Third World*, pp. 233–5.
76. Cited in Gwin, *US Relations with the World Bank*, pp. 84–5.
77. Current Economic Developments, Issues No. 573, 9 June 1959, *FRUS*, 1958–1960, Vol. IV, pp. 335–6.
78. Secretary of the Treasury to President Eisenhower, 3 December 1959, *FRUS*, 1958–1960, Vol. IV, pp. 360–1. Emphasis added.
79. Jurek Martin, 'Rubin calls for closer IMF surveillance', *Financial Times*, 7 June 1995.
80. *World Bank News*, 22 September 1994.
81. See Gwin, *US Relations with the World Bank*, pp. 54–62, 45.
82. E. Bevin to N. Ronald, 'African development: Beira port and railway', 23 October 1948, *BDEE*, Ser. A, Vol. 2, Part II, p. 271.
83. ODA, 'Fundamental Expenditure Review', July 1995, p. 173.
84. Paul Mosley, 'Britain, the World Bank and structural adjustment', in Anuradha Bose and Peter Burnell (eds), *Britain's Overseas Aid Since 1979: Between Idealism and Self-interest*, Manchester University Press, Manchester, 1991, p. 81.
85. Chalker, Speech to the all-party group on overseas development, 8 November 1989.
86. See Susan George, *The Debt Boomerang: How Third World Debt Harms Us All*, Pluto Press, London, 1992, pp. 85–7, 91–2.
87. House of Commons, *Hansard*, 23 May 1995, Col. 505.

88. OECD, *Development Cooperation*, 1994 report, OECD, Paris, 1995.
89. Oxfam International position paper, 'Multilateral debt: An end to the crisis?', October 1995, pp. 19–20.
90. CO International Relations Department paper, 'The colonial empire today: Summary of our main problems and policies', May 1950, *BDEE*, Ser. A, Vol. 2, Part I, p. 362.
91. Cabinet memorandum by Creech Jones, 'Development of colonial resources', 6 June 1947, *BDEE*, Ser. A, Vol. 2, Part II, pp. 45–7.
92. Colonial Office note on price fixing, March 1947, *BDEE*, Ser. A, Vol. 2, Part II, p. 40.
93. Colonial Office memorandum, 'Colonial Development Corporation', October 1951, *BDEE*, Ser. A, Vol. 3, Part III, p. 277.
94. Minute by O. Lyttleton, November 1951, *BDEE*, Ser. A, Vol. 3, Part III, p. 281.
95. Foreign Office Permanent Under-Secretary's Committee paper, 21 June 1952, *BDEE*, Ser. A, Vol. 3, Part I, p. 17.
96. G. Jebb to A. Eden, 12 January 1953, *BDEE*, Ser. A, Vol. 3, Part I, p. 272.
97. T. Lloyd to W. Strang, 9 September 1952, *BDEE*, Ser. A, Vol. 3, Part I, p. 23.
98. Memorandum by D. Dunnett, 'The Fourth Committee', March 1952, *BDEE*, Ser. A, Vol. 3, Part I, p. 388.
99. Special Ad-Hoc Committee of the State–War–Navy Coordinating Committee, 'Policies and principles for extension of US aid to foreign nations', April 1947, *FRUS*, 1947, Vol. III, pp. 208–9.
100. Memorandum of discussion, State Department, 25 October 1956, *FRUS*, 1955–57, Vol. X, p. 118.
101. National Advisory Council on International Monetary and Financial Problems, 'Investments in less developed areas', 12 December 1955, *FRUS*, 1955–1957, Vol. IX, p. 356.
102. Memorandum from the Chairman of the Policy Planning Council to the Administrator of the Agency for International Development, 17 October 1961, *FRUS*, 1961–1963, Vol. IX, p. 267.
103. Minutes of meeting of the Interdepartmental Committee of Under Secretaries on Foreign Economic Policy, 24 January 1962, *FRUS*, 1961–1963, Vol. IX, p. 426.
104. Memorandum from the President's Deputy Special Assistant for National Security Affairs to President Kennedy, 4 October 1961, *FRUS*, 1961–1963, Vol. IX, p. 262.
105. Report by the Under-Secretary of State for Political Affairs, 15 March 1963, *FRUS*, 1961–1963, Vol. IX, pp. 346–9.
106. Memorandum from the President's Deputy Special Assistant for National Security Affairs to the President's Special Assistant, 5 March 1963, *FRUS*, 1961–1963, Vol. IX, p. 345.
107. Memorandum of conversation, 30 June 1960, *FRUS*, 1958–1960, Vol. XII, p. 677.

108. J. K. Galbraith to President Kennedy, 28 August 1963, *FRUS*, 1961–1963, Vol. IX, p. 86.
109. President's Deputy Special Assistant for National Security Affairs to President Kennedy, 28 February 1961, *FRUS*, 1961–1963, Vol. IX, p. 209.
110. Cited in S. K. Asante, 'International assistance and international capitalism: Supportive or counterproductive?', in Gwendolen Carter and Patrick O'Meara (eds), *African Independence: The First Twenty-five Years*, Indiana University Press, Bloomington, 1985, p. 261.
111. Chalker, speech to the Malaysia, Singapore and Brunei Association, 13 December 1990.
112. Oliver Morrissey, 'The commercialisation of aid: Business interests and the UK aid budget, 1978–88', *Development Policy Review*, Vol. 8, No. 3, September 1990, pp. 314–15.
113. House of Commons, *Hansard*, 13 June 1995, Col. 502.
114. Chalker, speech to Conservative Central Office, 17 September 1993.
115. Lori Udall, 'Grounds for divorce: Why IDA should delink from the World bank', in Cavanagh et al. (eds), *Beyond Bretton Woods*, p. 156.
116. Peter Sullivan, 'Multilateral development banks work and ought to be supported', *International Herald Tribune*, 4 May 1995.
117. Cited in Nick Hildyard, 'Public risk, private profit: The World Bank and the private sector', *The Ecologist*, Vol. 26, No. 4, July 1996, p. 176.
118. Cited in Patrick Bond, 'A five to one return', *African Agenda*, Vol. 1, No. 2, 1995.
119. James Meek, 'Russian talks on IMF loans stall', *Guardian*, 8 February 1995.
120. Herman Cohen, 'Democratic change in Africa', *Dispatch*, 19 November 1990, p. 272.
121. Chalker, speech to the RCDS, 17 January 1991.
122. Chalker, speech to RIIA, 'Britain's aid strategy in the changing world', 18 October 1993.
123. Chalker, 'Promoting the private sector', speech to the CBI, 23 January 1995.
124. Chalker, speech to the Malaysia, Singapore and Brunei Association, 13 December 1990.
125. Chalker, speech to Conservative Central Office, 17 September 1993.
126. ODA, 'Fundamental Expenditure Review', July 1995, p. 18.

## Chapter Four

1. *The Challenge to the South: The Report of the South Commission*, Oxford University Press, Oxford, 1990, pp. 1–8, 35.

2. UNDP, *Human Development Report 1994*, Oxford University Press, Oxford, 1994, p. 63.
3. World Development Movement, 'World poverty: why the world's poor are getting poorer', London, 1995.
4. John Madeley, *Trade and the Poor: The Impact of International Trade on Developing Countries*, Intermediate Technology Publications, London, 1992, p. 6.
5. Cited in Erskine Childers, 'A UN for all our children: A giant undertaking', in Childers (ed.), *Challenges to the United Nations: Building a Safer World*, CIIR/St Martin's Press, London, 1994, p. 202.
6. Cited in *Rural Progress*, Vol. X, No. 1, 1991, p. 1.
7. Dharam Ghai and Cynthia Hewitt de Alcantara, 'Globalisation and social integration: Patterns and processes', *Occasional Paper No. 2*, UN Research Institute for Social Development, Geneva, July 1994, pp. 4–29.
8. Jan Morris, *Farewell the Trumpets: An Imperial Retreat*, Penguin, Harmondsworth, 1978, p. 58.
9. Joan Spero, 'The United States and the global economy', *US Department of State Dispatch*, 26 September 1994, Vol. 5, No. 39, p. 637.
10. Smitu Kothari, 'Global economic institutions and democracy: A view from India', in John Cavanagh et al. (eds), *Beyond Bretton Woods: Alternatives to the Global Economic Order*, Pluto Press, London, 1994, p. 44.
11. Charles Oman, *Globalisation and Regionalisation: The Challenges for Developing Countries*, OECD, Paris, 1994, p. 11.
12. 'Japan and the EC: Trade, Investment and Technology', Speech to the UK Presidency Conference: Europe and the World After 1992, London, 7 September 1992.
13. *IMF Survey*, 12 December 1994, p. 389.
14. David Korten, *When Corporations Rule the World*, Earthscan, London, 1995, pp. 220–1.
15. *Third World Resurgence*, No. 60, August 1995, p. 30.
16. Korten, *When Corporations Rule the World*, pp. 225–6.
17. Ibid., p. 221.
18. Ibid., p. 54.
19. Noam Chomsky, *World Orders, Old and New*, Pluto Press, London, 1994, p. 185.
20. Cited in 'The power of global finance', *Third World Resurgence*, No. 55, p. 18.
21. Wendy Dobson, in James Boughton and K. Lateef (eds), *Fifty Years after Bretton Woods: The Future of the IMF and the World Bank*, IMF/World Bank, Washington D.C., 1995, p. 221.
22. *Third World Resurgence*, No. 60, August 1995, pp. 29–30.
23. House of Commons, *Hansard*, 17 November 1994, Col. 101.
24. *World Bank News*, 2 February 1995, p. 3.

25. Khozem Merchant, 'Indian imports talks collapse', *Financial Times*, 2 July 1997.
26. Kothari, 'Global economic institutions and democracy', p. 41.
27. Oman, 'Globalisation and regionalisation', p. 72.
28. *IMF Survey*, 23 October 1995, p. 317. See also *IMF Survey*, 17 July 1995, pp. 217–20.
29. Michel Camdessus, *Facing the Globalised World Economy: The IMF Experience*, IMF, Washington D.C., October 1996, p. 37.
30. Speech to the RCDS, 17 January 1991.
31. Speech to the Africa Private Enterprise Group, 12 December 1990.
32. Speech by Jacques Attali, UK Presidency conference, London, 7 September 1992.
33. *Japan Times*, 15 September 1991.
34. Cited in Duncan Green, *Silent Revolution: The Rise of Market Economics in Latin America*, Cassell, London, 1995, p. 52.
35. Michel Camdessus and Lewis Preston, in J. Boughton and K. Lateef (eds), *Fifty Years after Bretton Woods*, p. iii.
36. Richard Ellis, 'Business blossoms on a blighted continent', *Sunday Times*, 15 May 1994.
37. Claude Ake, *The New World Order: A View From the South*, Malthouse Press, Lagos, 1992, p. 11.
38. Samir Amin, 'The challenge of globalisation: Delinking', in South Centre, *Facing the Challenge*, pp. 133–4.
39. *International Affairs*, Vol. 67, No. 4, October 1991, p. 730.
40. Paul Rogers, 'A jungle full of snakes?: Power, poverty and international security', in Geoff Tansey et al. (eds), *A World Divided: Militarism and Development After the Cold War*, Earthscan, London, 1994, p. 5.
41. Cited in Amrit Wilson, 'The West's war on population', *Africa World Review*, November 1994, p. 42.
42. UNCTAD, *Trade and Development Report 1994*, UN, New York, 1994, p. xii. Emphasis added.
43. See, for example, John Toye, *Dilemmas of Development: Reflections on the Counter-Revolution in Development Economics*, Blackwell, Oxford, 1993, pp. 12–13, 109–12; UNCTAD, *Trade and Development Report 1994*, UN, New York, 1994, pp. vi–ix.
44. Tony Killick, in J. Boughton and K. Lateef (eds), *Fifty Years after Bretton Woods*, p. 151.
45. Cited in Michael Barratt-Brown and Pauline Tiffen, *Short Changed: Africa in World Trade*, Pluto Press, London, 1992, p. 14.
46. See Ajit Singh, 'How did East Asia grow so fast?: Slow progress towards analytical consensus', *UNCTAD Bulletin*, May 1995, pp. 4–14.
47. See *IMF Survey*, 6 February 1995, p. 48 drawing on a recent IMF analysis.

48. *Uncommon Opportunities – An Agenda for Peace and Equitable Development: Report of the International Commission on Peace and Food*, Zed Books, London, 1994, p. 141.
49. See Mark Curtis, *The Ambiguities of Power*, p. 234; South Commission, *The Challenge to the South*, pp. 69–70; Nassau Adams, *Worlds Apart: The North–South Divide and the International System*, Zed Books, London, 1993, p. 166.
50. See Belinda Coote, *The Trade Trap: Poverty and the Global Commodity Markets*, Oxfam, Oxford, 1992, p. 35.
51. Susan George, *A Fate Worse than Debt*, Penguin, Harmondsworth, 1988, pp. 202, 233–4.
52. See Treasury statement, 'International debt: The way forward', 6 December 1988.
53. Tim Lang and Colin Hines, *The New Protectionism: Protecting the Future Against Free Trade*, Earthscan, London, 1993, p. 13.
54. Oxfam, 'Multilateral debt: The human costs', February 1994, p. 6.
55. House of Commons, *Hansard*, 8 June 1995, Col. 261.
56. See John Toye, *Dilemmas of Development*, pp. 215–21.
57. Korten, *When Corporations Rule the World*, pp. 64, 164.
58. Ibid., pp. 171–2.
59. Walden Bello, *Dark Victory: The United States, Structural Adjustment and Global Poverty*, Pluto Press, London, 1994, p. 85.
60. Chalker, 'Britain and Africa: support for peaceful change', speech to RIIA, 2 March 1995.
61. David Hirst, 'Poised between control and chaos', *Guardian*, 11 February 1995.
62. Cited in Bello, *Dark Victory*, p. 52.
63. See, for example, Oxfam, 'Embracing the future ... Avoiding the challenge of world poverty', July 1994, pp. 4–5; Christian Aid, *Who Runs the World?*, Christian Aid, London, 1994, pp. 4–5; Bello, *Dark Victory*, pp. 32–3.
64. *Africa Recovery*, Vol. 8, No. 1/2, April 1994, p. 8.
65. Ibid., p. 9.
66. See Lori Udall, 'Grounds for Divorce: Why IDA should delink from the World Bank', in Cavanagh et al. (eds), *Beyond Bretton Woods: Alternatives to the Global Economic Order*, Pluto Press, London, 1994, p. 155.
67. Cited in Susan George, *How the Other Half Dies: The Real Reasons for World Hunger*, Penguin, Harmondsworth, 1986, p. 263.
68. Ben Wisner, *Power and Need in Africa*, Earthscan, London, 1988, p. 31.
69. Ben Jackson, *Poverty and the Planet: A Question of Survival*, Penguin, Harmondsworth, 1990, p. 89.
70. Cited in Barry Gough, 'Pax Britannica: Peace, Force and World Power', *Round Table*, No. 314, April 1990, p. 177.
71. *IMF Survey*, 8 November 1993.
72. Cited in *Africa Recovery*, April 1994, p. 9.

73. Julie Wolf, 'Britain has EU's most miserly subsidies', *Guardian*, 23 January 1997.
74. UNDP, *Human Development Report 1994*, Oxford University Press, Oxford, 1994, p. 67.
75. Cited in Noam Chomsky, *Powers and Prospects: Reflections on Human Nature and the Social Order*, Pluto Press, London, 1996, p. 129.
76. NGO Working Group on the World Bank, 'The challenge of poverty eradication', December 1994, p. 9.
77. World Bank, *Global Economic Prospects and the Developing Countries*, World Bank, Washington D.C., 1995, p. 1.
78. *Third World Resurgence*, Issue No. 59, p. 4.
79. Ibid., Issue No. 45, p. 36.
80. Lawrence James, *The Rise and Fall of the British Empire*, Abacus, London, 1994, pp. 171–7.
81. Cited in Amrit Wilson, 'The West's war on population', *Africa World Review*, November 1994, pp. 39–40.
82. Peter Byrd, 'Foreign policy and overseas aid', in A. Bose and P. Burnell (eds), *Britain's Overseas Aid Since 1979*, Manchester University Press, Manchester, 1991, p. 50.
83. 'Africa's debts', *Daily Telegraph*, 21 March 1994.
84. 'Nigeria needs a clear message from Britain', *Independent*, 12 July 1993.
85. 'A moral imperative to help the poor', *Independent*, 18 September 1995.
86. Richard Dowden, 'Postscript: BritAid', *Parliamentary Brief*, Vol. 3, No. 1, Oct 1994, pp. 95–6; see also Frances Raffery, 'Overseas aid and the diva who helps', *Times Educational Supplement*, 6 January 1995, for another eulogy on Lynda Chalker.
87. Ross Clark, 'Rights are wrong', *Sunday Telegraph*, 12 March 1995.

## Chapter Five

1. Edward Krapels, 'The commanding heights: International oil in a changed world', *International Affairs*, Vol. 69, No. 1, January 1993, p. 74.
2. Hassan Hamdan al-Alkim, *The GCC States in an Unstable World*, Saqi Books, London, 1994, p. 141.
3. David Lascelles, 'Gulf's banks bear the brunt', *Financial Times*, 17 August 1990.
4. House of Commons, Foreign Affairs Committee, Third Report, Session 1990–91, *The Middle East after the Gulf War: Volume I*, HMSO, London, 9 July 1991, p. xxv.

5. Memorandum from the Board of National Estimates to Director of Central Intelligence Dulles, 16 March 1959, *FRUS*, 1958–1960, Vol. XII, p. 785. Emphasis added.
6. Circular Airgram from the Department of State to the Embassy in Kuwait and the Embassy in the United Kingdom, 26 January 1962, *FRUS*, 1961–1963, Vol. XVII, p. 439.
7. Message from British Foreign Secretary Lloyd to Secretary of State Dulles, 23 January 1956, *FRUS*, 1955–1957, Vol. XIII, p. 323.
8. Memorandum by Loftus to Pool, 1 June 1945, *FRUS*, 1945, Vol. VIII, p. 54.
9. State Department, 'Middle East oil', September 1950, *FRUS*, 1950, Vol. V, p. 80.
10. David Devereux, *The Formulation of British Defence Policy Towards the Middle East, 1948–56*, Macmillan, London, 1990, p. 12.
11. Department of State, 'The British and American Positions', undated [1947], *FRUS*, 1947, Vol. V, p. 514.
12. State Department, Office of Greek, Turkish and Iranian Affairs, 'Regional Policy Statement: Greece, Turkey and Iran', 28 December 1950, *FRUS*, 1950, Vol. V, p. 264; emphasis in original.
13. Wm. Roger Louis, *The British Empire in the Middle East, 1945–1951: Arab Nationalism, the United States and Postwar Imperialism*, Clarendon, Oxford, 1984, p. 112.
14. Cited in Gabriel Kolko, *The Politics of War: The World and United States Foreign Policy 1943–1945*, Random House, New York, 1968, p. 297.
15. Ibid., p. 309.
16. Cited in Daniel Yergin, *The Prize: The Epic Quest for Oil, Money and Power*, Simon & Schuster, London, p. 393.
17. 'Introductory Paper on the Middle East submitted informally by the United Kingdom representatives', undated [1947], *FRUS*, 1947, Vol. V, p. 569.
18. Cited in Yergin, *The Prize*, p. 427.
19. Ibid., p. 498.
20. Memorandum from November 1943, cited in Louis, *The British Empire in the Middle East*, pp. 47–8.
21. Cited in Kolko, *Politics of War*, p. 308.
22. State Department memorandum, undated [1947], *FRUS*, 1947, Vol. V, p. 547.
23. 'Introductory Paper on the Middle East submitted informally by the United Kingdom representatives', undated [1947], *FRUS*, 1947, Vol. V, p. 570.
24. Cited in Louis, *The British Empire in the Middle East*, p. 60.
25. Cited in Frank Furedi, *The New Ideology of Imperialism: Renewing the Moral Imperative*, Pluto Press, London, 1994, p. 53.
26. E. A. Chapman-Andrews to Mr Younger, FO 371/124968, No. 24/5, 17 September 1951, in *BDEE*, Ser. A, Vol. 2, Part II, p. 380.
27. Louis, *The British Empire in the Middle East*, pp. 60, 141, 159, 621.

28. See, for example, Mohamed Heikal, *Illusions of Triumph: An Arab View of the Gulf War*, Fontana, London, 1993, pp. 265–7, 309–12, 317–18; Said Aburish, *The Rise, Corruption and Coming Fall of the House of Saud*, Bloomsbury, London, 1994, p. 177.
29. Mustafa Alani, *Operation Vantage: British Military Intervention in Kuwait, 1961*, LAAM, Surbiton, 1990, pp. 122–34.
30. Peter Odell, 'International Oil: A Return to American Hegemony', *World Today*, Vol. 50, No. 11, November 1994.
31. David Hirst, 'Jordanians told to uphold peace pact', *Guardian*, 17 November 1994.
32. Dan Smith, 'The New Landscape of European Security', in Chester Hartman and Pedro Vilanova, *Paradigms Lost: The Post Cold War Era*, Pluto Press, London, 1992, p. 29.
33. Muhammad Faour, *The Arab World after Desert Storm*, United States Institute of Peace Press, Washington, D.C., 1993, p. 100.
34. United Nations Development Programme, *Human Development Report 1995*, Oxford University Press, New York, 1995, p. 214.
35. Noam Chomsky, *World Orders , Old and New*, Pluto Press, London, 1994, p. 198.
36. Jan Morris, *Farewell the Trumpets: An Imperial Retreat*, Penguin, Harmondsworth, 1978, p. 265.
37. Ibid.
38. Cited in Brian Lapping, *End of Empire*, Paladin, London, 1985, p. 352.
39. Cited in Anthony Verrier, *Through the Looking Glass: British Foreign Policy in an Age of Illusions*, Jonathan Cape, London, 1983, p. 122.
40. Cited in Louis, *The British Empire in the Middle East*, p. 132.
41. Cited in Chomsky, *World Orders*, p. 202.
42. 'Middle East oil', Cabinet note by Mr Macmillan, CAB 128/78, CP(55)152, 14 October 1955, in *BDEE*, Ser. A, Vol. 3, Part I, p. 136.
43. 'The future of the United Kingdom in world affairs', Memorandum by officials of the Treasury, Foreign Office and Ministry of Defence, CAB 134/1315, PR(56)3, 1 June 1956, *BDEE*, Ser. A, Vol. 3, Part I, pp. 70–1.
44. 'United Kingdom requirements in the Middle East', Report by the Chiefs of Staff for Cabinet Defence Committee, CAB 131/17, DC(56)17, 3 July 1956, *BDEE*, Ser. A, Vol. 3, Part I, p. 151.
45. Cited in Stephen Dorril, *The Silent Conspiracy: Inside the Intelligence Services in the 1990s*, Mandarin, London, 1993, p. 56.
46. Cited in Chomsky, *World Orders*, p. 199.
47. Cited in Louis, *The British Empire in the Middle East*, p. 121.
48. Ibid., pp. 318–19.
49. Ibid., p. 324.
50. State Department, Office of Near Eastern Affairs, 'Regional Policy Statement: Near East', 28 December 1950, *FRUS*, 1950, Vol. V, p. 274.

51. National Intelligence Estimate, 'Nasser and the Future of Arab Nationalism', 27 June 1961, *FRUS*, 1961–1963, Vol. XVII, p. 164
52. Cited in Elisabeth Barker, *The British Between the Superpowers, 1945–50*, Macmillan, London, 1983, p. 51.
53. Devereux, *The Formulation of British Defence Policy*, p. 182.
54. Cited in Noam Chomsky, *The Culture of Terrorism*, Pluto Press, London, 1989, p. 170.
55. Noam Chomsky, *Deterring Democracy*, Vintage, London, 1992, p. 55.
56. Cited in David Holden and Richard Johns, *The House of Saud*, Pan, London, 1982, pp. 192, 197.
57. Cited in Dorril, *The Silent Conspiracy*, p. 353.
58. See Aburish, *The Rise, Corruption and Coming Fall*, pp. 138, 172.
59. National Security Council, 'Statement of US Policy toward Iran', 15 November 1958, *FRUS*, 1958–1960, Vol. XII, p. 605.
60. Gabriel Kolko, *Confronting the Third World: United States Foreign Policy 1945–80*, Pantheon, New York, 1988, p. 225.
61. See Mark Curtis, *The Ambiguities of Power: British Foreign Policy Since 1945*, Zed Books, London, 1995.
62. Fred Halliday, *Arabia Without Sultans*, Penguin, Harmondsworth, 1975, pp. 359–60.
63. Kolko, *Confronting the Third World*, p. 265.
64. Cited in Noam Chomsky and Edward Herman, *The Political Economy of Human Rights – Volume I: The Washington Connection and Third World Fascism*, South End Press, Boston, 1979, p. 14.
65. Ibid., pp. 292–3.
66. Ibid., p. 369.
67. Verrier, *Through the Looking Glass*, p. 108.
68. Dorril, *The Silent Conspiracy*, p. 390.
69. Jonathan Bloch and Patrick Fitzgerald, *British Intelligence and Covert Action: Africa, Middle East and Europe Since 1945*, Junction, London, 1983, p. 113.
70. See Salaam Al-Sahrqi, 'Iran: Unholy Alliances, Holy Terror', *Covert Action Information Bulletin*, No. 37, Summer 1991, p. 53.
71. Memorandum from the Board of National Estimates to Director of Central Intelligence Dulles, 10 November 1958, *FRUS*, 1958–1960, Vol. XII, p. 598.
72. National Intelligence Estimate, 'Stability of the Present Regime in Iran', 26 August 1958, *FRUS*, 1958–1960, Vol. XII, p. 586.
73. National Intelligence Estimate, 'The Outlook for Iran', 3 March 1959, *FRUS*, 1958–1960, Vol. XII, p. 643.
74. National Security Council, 'Statement of US Policy toward Iran', 15 November 1958, *FRUS*, 1958–1960, Vol. XII, pp. 605–7.
75. National Intelligence Estimate, 'The Outlook for Iran', 3 March 1959, *FRUS*, 1958–1960, Vol. XII, pp. 643–4; see also paper prepared by Defense Intelligence Agency, 'An assessment of the military threat to Iran', undated, enclosure to Memorandum from the

Joint Chiefs of Staff to Secretary of Defense McNamara, 29 March 1962, *FRUS*, 1961–1963, Vol. XVII, p. 557.
76. 'The current internal political situation in Iran', enclosure to Memorandum from Morgan to Bundy, 27 March 1961, *FRUS*, 1961–1963, Vol. XVII, p. 57.
77. 'The current internal political situation in Iran', enclosure to Memorandum from Morgan to Bundy, 27 March 1961, *FRUS*, 1961–1963, Vol. XVII, p. 60.
78. Memorandum from the Administrator of the Agency for International Development to the National Security Council, undated [1962], *FRUS*, 1961–1963, Vol. XVII, pp. 514–5.
79. Memorandum from Robert Komer of the National Security Council Staff to the President's Special Assistant for National Security Affairs, 5 October 1961, *FRUS*, 1961–1963, Vol. XVII, p. 286.
80. 'The current internal political situation in Iran', enclosure to Memorandum from Morgan to Bundy, 27 March 1961, *FRUS*, 1961–1963, Vol. XVII, p. 61.
81. Cited in Israel Shahak, 'Israel, Iran, the US and the Bomb', *Covert Action Quarterly*, No. 46, Fall 1993, p. 11.
82. Cited in Charles Kupchan, *The Persian Gulf and the West: The Dilemmas of Security*, Allen & Unwin, London, 1987, p. 152.
83. Mark Curtis, 'Obstacles to Security in the Middle East', in Seizaburo Sato and Trevor Taylor (eds), *Prospects for Global Order, Volume II*, RIIA, London, 1993, p. 77.
84. Cited in Israel Shahak, 'Israel and Syria: Peace through Strategic Parity?', *Middle East International*, No. 490, 16 December 1994, p. 18.
85. Verrier, *Through the Looking Glass*, p. 97.
86. Cited in F. S. Northedge, 'Britain and the Middle East', in Ritchie Ovendale (ed.), *The Foreign Policy of the British Labour Governments, 1945–1951*, Leicester University Press, Leicester, 1984, p. 167.
87. Memorandum by the Ambassador at Large to the Secretary of State, 25 July 1950, *FRUS*, 1950, Vol. V, p. 99.
88. Cited in Chomsky, *Deterring Democracy*, p. 55.
89. Barry Blechman and Stephen Kaplan, *Force Without War: US Armed Forces as a Political Instrument*, Brookings Institution, Washington, D.C., 1978, p. 232.
90. Morris, *Farewell the Trumpets*, p. 266.
91. Ibid., p. 34.
92. Ibid., p. 136.
93. Isabelle Grunberg, 'The Persian Gulf War and the Myth of Lost Hegemony', in Roger Morgan et al. (eds), *New Diplomacy in the Post-Cold War World: Essays for Susan Strange*, St Martin's, London, 1993, p. 253.
94. Cited in V. G. Kiernan, *European Empires from Conquest to Collapse, 1815–1960*, Fontana, 1982, pp. 32, 153–4.
95. J. E. Peterson, *Defending Arabia*, Croom Helm, London, 1986, p. 29.

96. Ibid., p. 81.
97. Cited in Kiernan, p. 200.
98. Cited in Chomsky, *World Orders*, p. 6.
99. Peterson, *Defending Arabia*, p. 18.
100. Jacob Abadi, *Britain's Withdrawal from the Middle East, 1947–1971: The Economic and Strategic Imperatives*, Kingston, Princeton, 1982, pp. 134–5.
101. Jan Morris, *Heaven's Command: An Imperial Progress*, Penguin, Harmondsworth, 1979, p. 99.
102. Jan Morris, *Pax Britannica: The Climax of an Empire*, Penguin, Harmondsworth, 1979, p. 418.
103. Peterson, *Defending Arabia*, p. 29.
104. Kiernan, *European Empires*, p. 196.
105. David Omissi, 'Baghdad and British bombers', *Guardian*, 19 January 1991; Declassified documents on the British use of gas in Iraq, originally released in 1969, were reportedly removed by Whitehall from the Public Records Office, the *Guardian* reported in April 1992 ('Whitehall sits on 1919 Iraq papers', 7 April 1992).
106. Martin Woollacott, 'Getting the dosage right', *Guardian*, 19 January 1993.
107. Cited in Fan Yew Teng, 'Humanitarian and Human Rights', *Third World Resurgence*, No. 51, undated, p. 37.
108. Peterson, *Defending Arabia*, p. 19.
109. Cited in Ibid., p. 106.
110. Chomsky, *World Orders*, pp. 199–200; William Blum, *The CIA: A Forgotten History*, Zed Books, London, 1986, pp. 93–5.
111. Blum, *The CIA: A Forgotten History*, Zed Books, London, 1986, p. 92.
112. Devereux, *The Formulation of British Defence Policy*, p. 125.
113. Kolko, *Confronting the Third World*, pp. 71–2.
114. See Bloch and Fitzgerald, *British Intelligence and Covert Action*, p. 125; Verrier, *Through the Looking Glass*, p. 158.
115. Michael Stewart, *Life and Labour: An Autobiography*, Sidgwick & Jackson, London, 1980, pp. 232–3.
116. Robin Allen, 'Qatar palace coup presages more aggressive exploitation of gas field', *Financial Times*, 28 June 1995.
117. Richard Johns, 'Sharjah coup undermines deferral uncertainty', *Financial Times*, 19 June 1987.
118. William Blum, 'Hit List', *Covert Action Quarterly*, No. 46, Fall 1993, p. 9.
119. Noam Chomsky, 'International Terrorism: Image and Reality', in Alexander George (ed.), *Western State Terrorism*, Polity Press, Cambridge, 1991, p. 26.
120. Dorril, *The Silent Conspiracy*, pp. 391–2.
121. Cited in Michio Kaku and Daniel Axelrod, *To Win a Nuclear War: The Pentagon's Secret War Plans*, Zed Books, London, 1987, p. 32.
122. Cited in ibid., p. 168.

123. Blechman and Kaplan, *Force Without War*, p. 238.
124. Kaku and Axelrod, *To Win a Nuclear War*, pp. 168–71.
125. Ibid., pp. 225–6.
126. Cited in Heikal, *Illusions of Triumph*, p. 370.
127. Paul Rogers, 'A note on the British Deployment of Nuclear Weapons in Crises', pp. 2, 7–8; see also Milan Rai, *Tactical Trident: The Rifkind Doctrine and the Third World*, Drava papers, London, 1994, pp. 8, 15.
128. For postwar US nuclear war-fighting plans see Kaku and Axelrod, *To Win a Nuclear War*.
129. Martin Navias, cited in Rai, *Tactical Trident*, p. 7.
130. *Statement on the Defence Estimates 1966*, cited in Rai, *Tactical Trident*, p. 7.
131. Enclosure to Memorandum from the Joint Chiefs of Staff to Secretary of Defense McNamara, 29 March 1962, *FRUS*, 1961–1963, Vol. XVII, pp. 559–60.
132. Christopher Bellamy, 'Anglo-French deal likely for missiles', *Independent*, 27 December 1990.
133. See Rai, *Tactical Trident*.

## Chapter Six

1. 'Gulf states urged to do more for collective security', European Wireless File, *News Alert*, 24 September 1992.
2. Michael Wilkes, '"What Friends are for" – British Defence Policy in the Gulf', *RUSI Journal*, Vol. 139, No. 3, June 1994, pp. 43–6.
3. 'British advisers fuel Gulf anger', *Guardian*, 30 January 1995.
4. Harold Macmillan, *At the End of the Day, 1961–1963*, Macmillan, London, 1973, p. 272.
5. *Guardian*, 17 November 1994.
6. Cited in J. E. Peterson, *Defending Arabia*, Croom Helm, London, 1986, pp. 41–2.
7. Telegram from the Consulate General in Dhahran to the Department of State, 30 October 1955, *FRUS*, 1955–1957, Vol. XIII, p. 284.
8. Telegram from the Department of State to the Embassy in the United Kingdom, 23 November 1955, *FRUS*, 1955–1957, Vol. XIII, p. 292.
9. Peterson, *Defending Arabia*, p. 104.
10. Gregory Gause, *Oil Monarchies: Domestic and Security Challenges in the Arab Gulf States*, Council on Foreign Relations Press, New York, 1994, pp. 69, 71.
11. Ibid., p. 73.
12. 'Traditions built on shifting sands', *Financial Times*, 21 April 1995.

13. Kathy Evans, 'Oil keeping alive gunship tradition in the sheikhdoms', *Guardian*, 10 August 1990.
14. Adel Darwish, 'Female politicians come to the fore in Oman's world', *Independent*, 22 November 1994.
15. State Department memorandum, January 1956, *FRUS*, 1955–1957, Vol. XIII, p. 320. Emphasis added.
16. Memorandum of a conversation, White House, 30 January 1956, *FRUS*, 1955–1957, Vol. XIII, p. 329.
17. Anthony Verrier, *Through the Looking Glass: British Foreign Policy in an Age of Illusions*, Jonathan Cape, London, 1983, p. 184.
18. Thomas McNaugher, *Arms and Oil: US Military Strategy and the Persian Gulf*, Brookings Institution, Washington D.C., 1985, pp. 87–8.
19. See, for example, Peterson, *Defending Arabia*, p. 176.
20. Cited in Said Aburish, *The Rise, Corruption and Coming Fall of the House of Saud*, Bloomsbury, London, 1994, p. 168.
21. See Charles Kupchan, *The Persian Gulf and the West: The Dilemmas of Security*, Allen & Unwin, London, 1987, pp. 85–7, for further evidence.
22. House of Commons, Foreign Affairs Committee, Session 1990–91, Third Report, *The Middle East after the Gulf War, Vol. II*, HMSO, London, 9 July 1991, p. 240.
23. House of Commons, Foreign Affairs Committee, Session 1990–91, Third Report, *The Middle East after the Gulf War, Vol. I*, HMSO, London, 9 July 1991, p. xiii.
24. State Department memorandum, 31 March 1958, *FRUS*, 1958–1960, Vol. XII, pp. 774–5. Emphasis added.
25. Don Oberdorfer, 'US and Saudis find a way', *International Herald Tribune*, 1 June 1992.
26. 'US will store weapons in Qatar', *International Herald Tribune*, 21 March 1995.
27. 'US strengthens presence in the Gulf', *Guardian*, 29 October 1994.
28. Gause, *Oil Monarchies*, p. 141.
29. 'More armour in the Middle East', *Financial Times*, 28 October 1994.
30. Cited in Wm. Roger Louis, *The British Empire in the Middle East, 1945–1951: Arab Nationalism, the United States and Postwar Imperialism*, Clarendon, Oxford, 1984, p. 327.
31. Cited in ibid., p. 363.
32. Statement by Edward Djerejian, 30 June 1992, in USA, House of Representatives Committee on Foreign Affairs, Subcommittee on Europe and the Middle East, One hundred second Congress, Second session, *Developments in the Middle East*, USGPO, Washington D C., 24 and 30 June 1992, p. 86.
33. Cited in Muhammad Faour, *The Arab World after Desert Storm*, United States Institute of Peace Press, Washington D.C., 1993, p. 89.
34. Ibid.

35. Statement by Edward Djerejian, 30 June 1992, in USA, House of Representatives Committee on Foreign Affairs, Subcommittee on Europe and the Middle East, One hundred second Congress, Second session, *Developments in the Middle East*, USGPO, Washington D.C., 24 and 30 June 1992, p. 86.
36. 'Weapon-toting West bleeds Saudis dry', *Guardian*, 17 December 1994.
37. 'La France at les Emirats arabes unis signent un accord de sécurité', *Le Monde*, 19 January 1995.
38. *Human Rights Watch World Report 1995: Events of 1994*, HRW, New York, 1994, p. 294.
39. Statement of John Kelly in USA, House of Representatives Committee on Foreign Affairs, Subcommittee on Europe and the Middle East, One hundred second Congress, First session, *United States Policy toward the Middle East and Persian Gulf*, USGPO, Washington D.C., 17 and 26 June 1991, p. 15.
40. Ibid., pp. 31–2.
41. 'Clinton forms new Gulf fleet to police Iran', *Guardian*, 4 July 1995.
42. *The Middle East Military Balance, 1992–1993*, Jaffee Centre for Strategic Studies, Tel Aviv University, 1993, pp. 449–52.
43. SIPRI, *SIPRI Yearbook 1993*, Oxford University Press, Oxford, 1993, pp, 498–517; *Yearbook 1994*, Oxford University Press, Oxford, 1994, pp. 514–547.
44. Kupchan, *The Persian Gulf and the West*, p. 39.
45. Ibid., pp. 147–8.
46. Cited in Isabelle Grunberg, 'The Persian Gulf War and the Myth of Lost Hegemony', in R. Morgan et al. (eds), *New Diplomacy in the Post-Cold War World: Essays for Susan Strange*, St Martin's, London, 1993, p. 253.
47. State Department memorandum, 29 June 1961, *FRUS*, 1961–1963, Vol. XVII, p. 170.
48. Kupchan, *The Persian Gulf and the West*, pp. 57–9.
49. Cited in Gabriel Kolko, *The Politics of War: The World and United States Foreign Policy 1943–1945*, Random House, New York, 1968, p. 306.
50. Peterson, *Defending Arabia*, p. 148.
51. McNaugher, *Arms and Oil*, pp. 165, 171.
52. Cited in Kupchan, *The Persian Gulf and the West*, p. 146.
53. Cited in Fred Halliday, *Arabia Without Sultans*, Penguin, Harmondsworth, 1975, p. 475.
54. National Security Council, 'Statement of US Policy Toward Iran', 15 November 1958, *FRUS*, 1958–1960, Vol. XII, pp. 611, 613.
55. Statement by the United States and United Kingdom Groups, undated [1947], *FRUS*, 1947, Vol. V, p. 613.
56. Gause, *Oil Monarchies*, p. 68.

57. Amnesty International, *Repression Trade (UK) Ltd: How the UK makes Torture and Death its Business*, AI, London, January 1992, pp. 14, 16.
58. Sarah Cunningham, 'Path cleared for huge Saudi deals', *The Times*, 5 January 1996; 'Qatar weapons deal for UK', *Financial Times*, 18 November 1996.
59. Robert Pelletreau, 'A Review of Developments in the Middle East', *Dispatch*, Vol. 5, No. 41, 10 October 1994, p. 684.
60. Cited in Jochen Hippler, *Pax Americana?: Hegemony or Decline*, Pluto Press, London, pp. 102–3.
61. Mark Nicholson, 'Kuwait cashes in on its $10bn defence prize', *Financial Times*, 2 February 1993.
62. 'Arms fair opens in Gulf', *Financial Times*, 20 March 1995; Bernard Gray, 'Much show and few orders at Gulf arms fair', *Financial Times*, 23 March 1995.
63. David White, 'France beats Britain and US to win $3. 5bn UAE tank deal', *Financial Times*, 15 February 1993.
64. Aburish, *The Rise, Corruption and Coming Fall*, pp. 9–41.
65. Cited in Louis, *The British Empire in the Middle East*, p. 177.
66. McNaugher, *Arms and Oil*, p. 137.
67. Hassan Hamdan al-Alkim, *The GCC States in an Unstable World*, Saqi Books, london, 1994, p. 37.
68. Cited in Louis, *The British Empire in the Middle East*, pp. 174, 177, 192.
69. Aburish, *The Rise, Corruption and Coming Fall*, p. 148.
70. *Human Rights Watch World Report 1994: Events of 1993*, HRW, New York, 1993, p. 330.
71. State Department memorandum, 19 March 1950, *FRUS*, 1950, Vol. V, p. 1132.
72. President Eisenhower to King Ibn Saud, 15 June 1953, *FRUS*, 1952–1954, Vol. IX, pp. 2541–2.
73. Cited in Daniel Yergin, *The Prize: The Epic Quest for Oil, Money and Power*, Simon & Schuster, London, 1993, p. 497.
74. State Department memorandum, 7 February 1957, *FRUS*, 1955–1957, Vol. XIII, p. 477.
75. Cited in Kupchan, *The Persian Gulf and the West*, pp. 127–8.
76. Cited in Mark Curtis, 'Obstacles to Security in the Middle East', in Seizaburo Sato and Trevor Taylor (eds), *Prospects for Global Order, Volume II*, RIAA, London, 1993, p. 77.
77. Cited in Elaine Sciolino, 'Saudi Arabia, its purse thinner, learns how to say "no" to US', *New York Times*, 4 November 1994.
78. David Gore-Booth, Assistant Under-Secretary of State at the Foreign Office, cited in David White and Victor Mallett, 'UK seeks £1bn from Saudis on arms deal', *Financial Times*, 8 June 1991; Foreign Office, Foreign Policy Document No. 162, *General Information on Saudi Arabia*, London, October 1986, p. 20.

79. Jeremy Hanley, *Hansard*, House of Commons, 24 January 1996, Cols 457–9.
80. Ian Pallister, 'Defence accord doubled Saudi combat air force', *Guardian*, 10 October 1994.
81. Michael Binyon, 'Trade tied up with diplomatic niceties [sic]', *The Times*, 23 September 1993.
82. Cited in Sciolino, 'Saudi Arabia'.
83. Cited in Aburish, *The Rise, Corruption and Coming Fall*, p. 161; State Department memorandum, 7 February 1957, *FRUS*, 1955–1957, Vol. XIII, p. 476.
84. Speech by Prince Khaled bin Sultan to the Royal Institute of International Affairs, London, 16 May 1995.
85. National Intelligence Estimate, 'The Outlook for Saudi Arabia', 19 April 1960, *FRUS*, 1958–1960, Vol. XII, p. 759.
86. Memorandum from the Under-Secretary of State to the Secretary of State, 20 December 1955, *FRUS*, 1955–1957, Vol. XIII, p. 304.
87. Faour, *The Arab World after Desert Storm*, p. 45.
88. Testimony of Andrew Whitley of Middle East Watch, in USA, House of Representatives Committee on Foreign Affairs, Subcommittee on Europe and the Middle East, One hundred second Congress, Second session, *Human Rights in the Middle East*, USGPO, Washington D.C., 15 September 1992, p. 75.
89. Ibid., p. 79.
90. 'US rights group attacks Saudi political reforms', *Independent*, 18 May 1992.
91. David Hirst and Kathy Evans, 'Saudi shura gets cautious welcome', *Guardian*, 23 August 1993.
92. Mark Nicholson, 'Saudis widen political horizons', *Financial Times*, 24 August 1993.
93. Kathy Evans, 'Saudis welcome shake-up in king's cabinet', *Guardian*, 3 August 1995.
94. *Human Rights Watch World Report 1995: Events of 1994*, HRW, New York, 1994, pp. 299–300.
95. Ibid., pp. 300–2.
96. Aburish, *The Rise, Corruption and Coming Fall*, p. 76.
97. Ibid., p. 295.
98. Ibid., p. 56.
99. UNDP, *Human Development Report 1994*, Oxford University Press, Oxford, 1994, pp. 129, 134.
100. UNICEF *State of the World's Children 1995*, Oxford University Press, Oxford, 1995, p. 67.
101. *Human Rights Watch World Report 1995*, p. 304.
102. Cited in Halliday, *Arabia Without Sultans*, p. 54.
103. Enclosure to Report by the Subcommittee on Rearmament to the State–War–Navy Coordinating Committee, 21 March 1946, *FRUS*, 1946, Vol. I, p. 1159; see also State Department memorandum, 19 March 1950, *FRUS*, 1950, Vol. V, pp. 1139–40.

104. Memorandum from the Secretary of State to the President, 7 February 1957, *FRUS*, 1955–1957, Vol. XIII, p. 478.
105. Cited in Yergin, *The Prize*, p. 428.
106. State Department memorandum, 7 February 1957, *FRUS*, 1955–1957, Vol. XIII, p. 471.
107. Halliday, *Arabia Without Sultans*, pp. 58–9.
108. McNaugher, *Arms and Oil*, p. 130.
109. Martin Walker and David Pallister, 'Saudi bomb targets US military role', *Guardian*, 14 November 1995.
110. McNaugher, *Arms and Oil*, pp. 162–3.
111. Peter de la Billiere, *Storm Command: A Personal Account of the Gulf War*, HarperCollins, London, 1993, p. 104.
112. Peterson, *Defending Arabia*, pp. 195–6.
113. Al-Alkim, *The GCC States*, p. 139.
114. Aburish, *The Rise, Corruption and Coming Fall*, pp. 77, 157.
115. Michael Sheridan, 'Slump in oil prices rocks the Kingdom', *Independent*, 15 October 1994.
116. Ibid., p. 116.
117. Michael Binyon, 'Hurd dismisses exiles' claims of Saudi instability', *The Times*, 7 October 1994.
118. 'London exile plots Saudi revolution', *Independent*, 23 May 1995; see also Leslie Plommer and Kathy Evans, 'Saudi dissident fights expulsion', *Guardian*, 28 November 1994.
119. *Hansard*, House of Lords, 11 January 1996, Col. 262.
120. 'Arms' bosses secret plot' and 'Web that links weapons and Whitehall', *Guardian*, 6 January 1996.
121. Paul Lewis, 'Saudi envoy takes on Riyadh', *International Herald Tribune*, 15 June 1994.
122. Michael Binyon, 'Saudi defector makes asylum plea to Britain', *The Times*, 30 June 1994.
123. Ibid., p. 201.
124. Bernard Gray, 'BAe in £500m sale to Saudi Arabia', *Financial Times*, 9 September 1994.
125. Aburish, *The Rise, Corruption and Coming Fall*, p. 202.
126. Alan Travis, 'Saudis to buy Tornados in £5bn arms deal with Britain', *Guardian*, 29 January 1993.
127. Bernard Gray, 'BAe in £500 sale to Saudi Arabia'.
128. Robin Ballantyne, 'Trading in torture', *Spur*, March/April 1995, p. 4.
129. See Aburish, *The Rise, Corruption and Coming Fall*, pp. 203–4.
130. Ibid., p. 103.
131. Patrick Tyler, 'Gulf security pact stalled by dispute over Saudi army', *International Herald Tribune*, 14 October 1991.
132. Don Oberdorfer, 'US and Saudis find a way'.
133. Patrick Bishop, 'The Queen welcomes the Emir of Kuwait', *Daily Telegraph*, 24 May 1995.
134. David Fairhall, 'Defence deal struck in Gulf', *Guardian*, 28 November 1996.

135. Mohamed Heikal, *Illusions of Triumph: An Arab View of the Gulf War*, Fontana, London, 1993, p. 220.
136. Sami Yousif, 'The Iraqi–US War: A Conspiracy Theory', in Haim Bresheeth and Nira Yuval-Davis (eds), *The Gulf War and the New World Order*, Zed Books, London, 1991, p. 58.
137. Verrier, *Through the Looking Glass*, pp. 184–6.
138. See Mark Curtis, *The Ambiguities of Power: British Foreign Policy Since 1945*, Zed Books, pp. 105–8.
139. Verrier, *Through the Looking Glass*, p. 171.
140. Noam Chomsky, *World Orders, Old and New*, Pluto Press, London, 1994, p. 195.
141. Message from Foreign Secretary Home to Secretary of State Rusk, 28 June 1961, *FRUS*, 1961–1963, Vol. XVII, p. 168.
142. Memorandum from Talbot to McGhee, 29 December 1961, *FRUS*, 1961–1963, Vol. XVII, pp. 377–8.
143. Cited in Curtis, 'Obstacles to Security in the Middle East', p. 75.
144. Robert Fisk, 'US evidence links emirate's ruling family with death squads murdering Palestinians', *Independent*, 27 April 1991.
145. Cited in Hugh Davies, 'Britain's military advisers may stay', *Daily Telegraph*, 4 May 1991.
146. Charles Hoots, '"Collaborators" on jail fast in Kuwait', *Guardian*, 25 May 1995.
147. Michael Kramer, 'Kuwait: Back to the past', *The Times*, 5 August 1991.
148. Faour, *The Arab World after Desert Storm*, pp. 42–3.
149. Jeremy Hanley, *Hansard*, House of Commons, 23 October 1995, Col. 803.
150. *Human Rights Watch World Report 1994: Events of 1993*, HRW, New York, 1993, pp. 313–16.
151. *Human Rights Watch World Report 1995*, p. 293.
152. See Curtis, *Ambiguities of Power*, pp. 98–100.
153. Prime Minister Macmillan to President Eisenhower, 19 July 1957, *FRUS*, 1955–1957, Vol. XIII, p. 227.
154. Brian James, 'At the desert coast of Sultan Qaboos', *The Times*, 7 April 1990.
155. Tony Geraghty, *Who Dares Wins: The Story of the SAS, 1950–1980*, Fontana, 1981, pp. 157–8.
156. Cited in Bridget Bloom, 'Discreet relationship', *Financial Times*, 11 November 1985.
157. Great Britain, FCO, Foreign Policy Document No. 164, *General Information on Oman*, London, October 1986, p. 20.
158. Khozem Merchant, 'Defence on a tight budget', *Financial Times*, 20 November 1991.
159. Stephen Dorril, *The Silent Conspiracy: Inside the Intelligence Services in the 1990s*, Mandarin, London, 1993, pp. 269–70.
160. Jeff Gerth, 'A web of CIA links emerges in Oman', *International Herald Tribune*, 28 March 1985.

161. Halliday, *Arabia Without Sultans*, pp. 447, 461.
162. Robert Fisk, 'Secret terror stifles wind of change', *Independent*, 20 February 1996; 'British advisers fuel Gulf anger', *Guardian*, 30 January 1995.
163. Michael Sheridan, 'Violent Shia protests embarrass Bahrain', *Independent*, 20 December 1994.
164. 'Des centaines d'opposants seraient incarceres sans jugement', *Le Monde*, 10 May 1991.
165. Michael Binyon, 'Amnesty protests at Bahrain killing', *The Times*, 1 April 1995; Amnesty International press release, 5 May 1995.
166. BHRO, 'Arbitrary arrest, torture, unlawful killing', press release, 3 April 1995.
167. Ian Black, 'Hurd hits out at fundamentalists', *Guardian*, 7 April 1995.
168. Michael Binyon, 'Four die at political rally in Bahrain', *The Times*, 7 January 1995.
169. Michael Sheridan, 'Cleric's deportation stirs unrest in Bahrain', *Independent*, 21 January 1995.
170. *Hansard*, House of Lords, 5 June 1995, Cols 1251, 1254–5.

## Chapter Seven

1. 'Changes at the UN's top table', *Independent*, 11 June 1993.
2. 'A diplomat for all seasons', *Independent*, 23 November 1991.
3. See Mark Curtis, *The Ambiguities of Power: British Foreign Policy Since 1945*, Zed Books, London, 1995.
4. Ibid., pp. 157–65.
5. Rajaram Panda, 'Japan, Germany and the Security Council', *India Quarterly*, Vol. XLVIII, No. 4, October–December 1992, pp. 52–3.
6. 'The system's choice', *Guardian*, 23 November 1991.
7. 'The possible and the defensible', *Independent*, 16 July 1993.
8. 'Paying for Peace', *The Times*, 7 May 1992.
9. IISS, *Strategic Survey 1991–1992*, Brassey's for the IISS, London, 1992, p. 11.
10. Paul Wilkinson, 'Flaws in the no-fly zone', *Guardian*, 8 January 1993.
11. C. P. Hope, 'Anglo-American talks on colonial questions', 3 July 1952, FO 371/101383, No. 7, *BDEE*, Series A, Vol. 3, Part I, p. 260.
12. Minute by Viscount Hood, 3 September 1945, *DBFPO*, Series I, Vol. II, p. 47.
13. Memorandum by the Director of the Office of Near Eastern and African Affairs, 'The present situation in the Near East – A danger to world peace', undated [1946], *FRUS*, 1946, Vol. VII, pp. 2–3.
14. Permanent Under-Secretary's Committee, 'The United Kingdom and the United Nations', 25 April 1950, *DBFPO*, Calendar to Series II, Vol. II, p. 146.

15. Foreign Office to O. Franks, 23 January 1951, *DBFPO*, Series II, Vol. IV, p. 324.
16. G. Jebb to A. Eden, 12 January 1953, FO 371/107032, No. 1, *BDEE*, Series A, Vol. 3, Part I, p. 274
17. O. Franks to A. Eden, 'Anglo-American conversations on the United Nations, 22–26 September 1952', 6 October 1952, FO 371/101386, No. 85, *BDEE*, Series A, Vol. 3, Part I, p. 260.
18. G. Jebb to A. Eden, 12 January 1953, FO 371/107032, No. 1, *BDEE*, Series A, Vol. 3, Part I, p. 271.
19. Anthony Eden, 'Persia: Memorandum by the Secretary of State for Foreign Affairs', 5 August 1952, PRO, CAB 129/54, CP(52) 276.
20. Foreign Office memorandum for Permanent Under-Secretary's Committee, 'The United Kingdom and the UN', 7 June 1950, CO 537/5701, No. 25, *BDEE*, Series A, Vol. 2, Part I, p. 482.
21. Frank Furedi, *The New Ideology of Imperialism: Renewing the Moral Imperative*, Pluto Press, London, p. 79.
22. Minute by Lord Salisbury, 16 February 1953, DO 35/5056, No. 6, *BDEE*, Series A, Vol. 3, Part II, p. 5.
23. Cabinet memorandum by Lord Swinton, 'Commonwealth membership', 11 October 1954, CAB 129/71, C(54)307, *BDEE*, Series A, Vol. 3, Part II, pp. 30, 34, 36.
24. Colonial Office, 'The colonial empire today: Summary of our main problems and policies', May 1950, CO 537/5698, *BDEE*, Series A, Vol. 2, Part I, pp. 354–5.
25. Colonial Office, 'The colonial empire today: Summary of our main problems and policies', May 1950, CO 537/5698, *BDEE*, Series A, Vol. 2, Part I, pp. 357–8.
26. C. P. Hope, 'Anglo-American talks on colonial questions', 3 July 1952, FO 371/101383, No. 7, *BDEE*, Series A, Vol. 3, Part I, p. 259.
27. George Drower, *Britain's Independent Territories: A Fistful of Islands*, Dartmouth, Aldershot, 1992, p. 42.
28. Ibid., p. 44.
29. D. I. Dunnett, 'The Fourth Committee', [March 1952], FO 371/101363, No. 48, *BDEE*, Series A, Vol. 3, Part I, p. 388.
30. Joint Strategic Survey Committee, 'United States assistance to other countries from the standpoint of national security', 29 April 1947, *FRUS*, 1947, Vol. I, p. 748.
31. Policy Planning Staff, 'Review of current trends: US foreign policy', 24 February 1948, *FRUS*, 1948, Vol. I, pp. 526, 528
32. Anthony Parsons, 'The United Nations after the Gulf War', *Round Table*, No. 319, July 1991, p. 267.
33. See Curtis, *Ambiguities of Power*, pp. 122–5; see also William Minter, *King Solomon's Mines Revisited: Western Interests and the Burdened History of Southern Africa*, Basic Books, New York, 1986, pp. 131–4.
34. Cabinet, 'Relations with South Africa', 28 September 1950, CAB 128/18, CM 62(50)4, *BDEE*, Series A, Vol. 2, Part IV, p. 295; see also Lord Salisbury, 'Relations with the Union of South Africa in

the context of the United Nations', 24 September 1952, CAB 129/55, C (52)306, *BDEE*, Series A, Vol. 3, Part I, p. 352.
35. Cabinet memorandum by Gordon Walker, 16 April 1951, CAB 129/45, CP(51)109, *BDEE*, Series A, Vol. 2, Part IV, p. 315.
36. See Curtis, *Ambiguities of Power*, pp. 121–2.
37. See ibid., pp. 121–5.
38. Agrippah Mugomba, *The Foreign Policy of Despair: Africa and the Sale of Arms to South Africa*, East African Literature Bureau, Kampala, 1977, p. 55.
39. Commonwealth Secretariat, *South Africa: The Sanctions Report*, 1990, pp. 61–3; Commonwealth Secretariat, *South Africa: The Sanctions Report*, Penguin, Harmondsworth, 1989, p. 47.
40. Ed Vulliamy, 'How the CIA intercepted SAS signals', *Guardian*, 29 January 1996.
41. Foreign and Commonwealth Office, *Table of Vetoed Draft Resolutions in the United Nations Security Council, 1946–1987*, Foreign Policy Document No. 183, January 1988.
42. Jonathan Steele, 'Israeli attack on Qana was deliberate, says Amnesty', *Guardian*, 24 July 1996.
43. Noam Chomsky, *Letters from Lexington: Reflections on Propaganda*, Common Lowage Press, Maine, 1993, p. 5.
44. Noam Chomsky, *World Orders, Old and New*, Pluto Press, London, 1994, p. 208.
45. Chomsky, *Letters from Lexington*, p. 5.
46. Panda, 'Japan, Germany and the Security Council', pp. 52–3.
47. *Human Rights Watch World Report 1995*, p. 289.
48. Carmel Budiardjo, 'Indonesia: Mass extermination and the consolidation of authoritarian power', in Alexander George (ed.), *Western State Terrorism*, Polity Press, Cambridge, 1991, p. 203.
49. Noam Chomsky and Edward Herman, *The Political Economy of Human Rights – Volume I: The Washington Connection and Third World Fascism*, South End Press, Boston, 1979, p. 158.
50. For sources, see Curtis, *Ambiguities of Power*, pp. 220–1.
51. Cited in Noam Chomsky, *Deterring Democracy*, Vintage, London, 1992, p. 200.
52. Cited in Chomsky and Herman, *The Washington Connection*, p. 157.
53. Cited in Carmel Budiardjo and Liem Soei Liong, *The War against East Timor*, Zed Books, London, 1984, p. 10.
54. *TAPOL Bulletin*, No. 116, April 1993, p. 2.
55. *TAPOL Bulletin*, No. 122, April 1994, p. 20.
56. For sources see Curtis, *Ambiguities of Power*, p. 153.
57. *Hansard*, House of Commons, Vol. 712, 1964–65, 11 May 1965, Col. 266.
58. Barry Blechman and Stephen Kaplan, *Force Without War: US Armed Forces as a Political Instrument*, Brookings Institution, Washington D.C., 1978, p. 332.

59. Cited in William Blum, *The CIA: A Forgotten History*, Zed Books, London, 1986, p. 314.
60. Foreign and Commonwealth Office, *Table of Vetoed Draft Resolutions in the United Nations Security Council, 1946–1993*, Foreign Policy Document No. 249, January 1994, p. 44.
61. Ibid., p. 42.
62. Thomas Weiss and Kurt Campbell, 'Military humanitarianism', *Survival*, Vol. XXXIII, No. 5, September–October 1991, p. 451.
63. FCO, *Table of Vetoed Draft Resolutions*, p. 36.
64. Anthony Nutting, *No End of a Lesson: The Story of Suez*, Constable, London, 1967, p. 58.
65. Cited in Geoff Simons, *The United Nations: A Chronology of Conflict*, Macmillan, London, 1994, pp. 122–3.
66. State Department to Embassy in the UK, 23 November 1955, in *FRUS*, 1955–57, Vol. XIII, p. 292.
67. Cited in Simons, *The United Nations*, p. 119.
68. See Curtis, *Ambiguities of Power*, pp. 102–5.
69. Anthony Eden, *Full Circle*, Cassell, London, 1960, p. 13.
70. Cited in Erskine Childers, 'Introduction', in Childers (ed.), *Challenges to the United Nations: Building a Safer World*, CIIR/St Martin's Press, London, 1994, pp. 12–13.
71. Chomsky, *Deterring Democracy*, pp. 96–7.
72. Michio Kaku and Daniel Axelrod, *To Win a Nuclear War: The Pentagon's Secret War Plans*, Zed Books, London, 1987, pp. 300–1.
73. Cited in Noam Chomsky, 'International terrorism: Image and reality', in Alexander George (ed.), *Western State Terrorism*, Polity Press, Cambridge, 1991, p. 29.
74. Cited in Simons, *The United Nations*, p. 146
75. John Dickie, *'Special' No More – Anglo-American Relations: Rhetoric and Reality*, Weidenfeld and Nicolson, London, 1993, pp. 201–2.
76. Maggie O'Kane, 'Report condemns sanctions on Iraq', *Guardian*, 18 May 1996.

## Chapter Eight

1. United Nations, Department of Public Information, 'Resolutions and Decisions Adopted by the General Assembly During the First Part of its Forty-Sixth Session', 17 September to 20 December 1991, press release GA/8307, January 1992, p. 27.
2. United Nations, Department of Public Information, *Yearbook of the United Nations 1992, Volume 46*, UNDPI, New York, 1993, pp. 733–4.
3. Ibid., pp. 42–3.
4. Ibid., pp. 51–2.
5. Ibid., pp. 72–3.

6. United States Department of State, *Voting Practices in the United Nations, 1993*, Washington D.C., 31 March 1994.
7. Ibid., p. 42.
8. Ibid., pp. 42, 45–6.
9. United States Department of State, *Voting Practices in the United Nations, 1996*, Washington D.C., 1997, pp. 1, 12–14, 35–41.
10. Martin Khor, 'Security Council a tool of major powers, say South countries' and 'South countries call for Security Council reforms', *Third World Resurgence*, Issue No. 51, November 1994.
11. Erskine Childers, 'United Nations Mechanisms for Intervention and Prospects for Reform', Paper presented to the Life and Peace Institute, Sigtuna, Sweden, May 1992, pp. 7–8.
12. Annika Savill, 'UK finds a way to hold on to the mother of all seats', *Independent*, 7 January 1992.
13. George Jones and Ian Brodie, 'Britain seeks UN meeting with Russia', *Daily Telegraph*, 2 January 1992.
14. Ibid., p. 164.
15. Geoff Simons, *The United Nations: A Chronology of Conflict*, Macmillan, London, 1994, p. 302.
16. Alejandro Bendana, 'Means and Ends and the United Nations', in Elizabeth Ferris (ed.), *The Challenge to Intervene: A New Role for the United Nations*, Life and Peace Institute, Uppsala, Sweden, 1992, pp. 135–6.
17. See also Mark Curtis, *The Ambiguities of Power: British Foreign Policy Since 1945*, Zed Books, London, 1995, especially chapters 1 and 2.
18. International Commission on Peace and Food, *Uncommon Opportunities: An Agenda for Peace and Equitable Development*, Zed Books, London, p. 20.
19. For instructive discussion of Security Council reform see especially articles by Martin Khor and Chin Oy Sim in *Third World Resurgence*, No. 51, November 1994.
20. 'An anachronism that works', *Independent*, 28 January 1993.
21. 'An international interest', *Independent*, 31 January 1992.
22. Erskine Childers, 'The United Nations System', in Childers (ed.), *Challenges to the United Nations: Building a Safer World*, CIIR/St Martin's Press, London, 1994, p. 20.
23. Leonard Doyle, 'Washington opposes spy role for UN', *Independent*, 20 April 1992.
24. Clinton, cited in Elaine Sciolino, 'The peacekeeping front: Clinton is pulling back', *International Herald Tribune*, 7 May 1994.
25. Lake, 'Yes to an American role in peacekeeping, but with conditions', *International Herald Tribune*, 7 February 1994.
26. Joint Chiefs of Staff to the United States representatives on the Military Staff Committee, 'Guidance as to command and control of the armed forces to be placed at the disposal of the Security Council of the United Nations', *FRUS*, 1946, Vol. I, pp. 796–8.

27. *The Expanding Role of the United Nations and its Implications for United Kingdom Policy: Observations by the Secretary of State for Foreign and Commonwealth Affairs*, HMSO, London, October 1993, p. 6.
28. See Edward Johnson, 'British proposals for a United Nations force, 1946–48', in Ann Deighton (ed.), *Britain and the First Cold War*, Macmillan, London, 1990.
29. David Howell, 'Strong nations, strong UN', *The House Magazine*, 26 June 1995, p. 17.
30. Lake, 'Yes to an American role in peacekeeping'.
31. Madeleine Albright, 'Building a Consensus on International Peacekeeping', *US Department of State Dispatch* (hereafter *Dispatch*), Vol. 4, No. 46, 15 November 1993, p. 790.
32. Madeleine Albright, 'The Clinton Administration's Policy on Reforming Multilateral Peace Operations', *Dispatch*, Vol. 5, No. 20, 16 May 1994, p. 316.
33. Madeleine Albright, 'Myths of Peacekeeping', *Dispatch*, Vol. 4, No. 26, 28 June 1993, p. 464.
34. Albright, 'Building a Consensus on International Peacekeeping', p. 791.
35. 'Two UN's at war with each other', *Independent*, 13 Aug 93.
36. Albright, 'The Clinton Administration's Policy on Reforming Multilateral Peace Operations', p. 316.
37. European Wireless File, News Alert, 'Clinton Administration policy on reforming peace operations', 5 May 1994.
38. Warren Christopher, 'American Leadership and Effective UN Peacekeeping', *Dispatch*, Vol. 6, No. 5, 30 January 1995, p. 59.
39. Albright, 'The Clinton Administration's Policy on Reforming Multilateral Peace Operations', p. 315.
40. University of London, Centre for Defence Studies, *The Framework of United Kingdom Defence Policy*, CDS, London, 1995, p. 122.
41. Simon Duke, 'The State and Human Rights: Sovereignty versus Humanitarian Intervention', *International Relations*, Vol. XII, No. 2, August 1994, p. 27
42. Ibid., p. 27.
43. See Curtis, *Ambiguities of Power*, pp. 216–17.
44. European Wireless File, News Alert, 'Somalia effort offers a chance to "make a difference"', 6 December 1992.
45. *Statement on the Defence Estimates 1995*, Cmnd. 2800, HMSO, London, May 1995, p. 23.
46. Trevor Taylor, 'West European security and defence cooperation: Maastricht and beyond', *International Affairs*, Vol. 70, No. 1, January 1994, p. 7.
47. Elizabeth Ferris, 'Intervention, Sovereignty and the United Nations', in Ferris (ed.), *The Challenge to Intervene*, p. 16.
48. Cited in A. G. Noorani, 'Bush and his designs', *Third World Resurgence*, No. 26, p. 44.

49. British Army Staff College Research Paper, 'Can the UN, the military and non-governmental organisations work together?', draft, undated, p. 15.
50. David Rieff, 'The Illusions of Peacekeeping', in *World Policy Journal*, Vol. XI, No. 3, Fall 1994, p. 17.
51. Barbara Amiel, 'There is a Rwandan in all of us', *Sunday Times*, 3 July 1994.
52. Anthony Bevins, 'Hurd urges UN to take 'imperial' role', *Independent*, 19 September 1992.
53. Frank Furedi, *The New Ideology of Imperialism: Renewing the Moral Imperative*, Pluto Press, London, 1994, pp. 108–13.
54. Philip Sabin, 'British defence choices beyond 'Options for Change'', *International Affairs*, Vol. 69, No. 2, April 1993, pp. 269, 271.
55. Adam Roberts, 'Humanitarian war: Military intervention and human rights', *International Affairs*, Vol. 69, No. 3, July 1993, pp. 442, 448.
56. John Chipman, 'The future of strategic studies', *Survival*, Spring 92, p. 116.
57. Robert Art, 'A US military strategy for the 1990s: Reassurance without dominance', *Survival*, Vol. 34, No. 4, Winter 1992–93, p. 6.
58. Francoise Bouchet-Saulnier, 'Justice dumb in the face of genocide', *Guardian*, 6 April 1995.
59. This section builds on Mark Curtis, 'Britain's bit part in Rwanda's tragedy', *Africa Analysis*, 27 January 1995, p. 15.
60. Guy Vassall-Adams, *Rwanda: An Agenda for International Action*, Oxfam, Oxford, 1994, p. 36.
61. Larry Elliott, 'Fury greets US block on peace force', *Guardian*, 18 May 1995.
62. Vassall-Adams, *Rwanda*, pp. 43, 58; see also Richard Dowden, 'Don't blame the UN for an American mess', *Independent*, 18 May 1995.
63. Alain Destexhe, 'The third genocide', *Foreign Policy*, No. 97, Winter 1994–95, p. 10; Stanley Meisler, 'Dateline UN: A new Hammarskjold?', *Foreign Policy*, No. 98, Spring 1995, p. 194.
64. Cited in Larry Elliott, 'US and Russia sink plans to send 5,500 troops', *Guardian*, 13 May 1994.
65. Destexhe, 'The Third Genocide', p. 11.
66. Paul Rogers, 'It can't be too late for the West to get its act together', *Observer*, 31 July 1994.
67. Vassall-Adams, *Rwanda*, p. 44.
68. Holly Burkhalter, 'The question of genocide: The Clinton administration and Rwanda', *World Policy Journal*, Vol. XI, No. 4, Winter 1994/5, p. 51.
69. Human Rights Watch Africa, *Genocide in Rwanda: April–May 1994*, Vol. 6, No. 4, May 1994, p. 10.
70. Richard Dowden, 'More children are massacred as US backs Rwanda mission', *Independent*, 18 May 1995.

71. James Bone and Catherine Bond, 'Rwanda minister snubbed at UN over massacre', *The Times*, 13 May 1994.
72. *Human Rights Monitor*, No. 25–26, p. 5.
73. Madeleine Albright, 'The tragedy in Rwanda: International cooperation to find a solution', *Dispatch*, Vol. 5, No. 26, 27 June 1994, p. 438.
74. See, for example, Human Rights Watch, *Rearming with Impunity: International Support for the Perpetrators of the Rwandan Genocide*, HRW, New York, May 1995, Mark Huband, 'Militiaman claims France trained Rwanda's killers', *Guardian*, 22 June 1994; Chris McGreal, 'Paris stands by as arms pour through eastern Zaire', *Guardian*, 23 June 1994.
75. Report of the Secretary-General on security in the Rwandese refugee camps, S/1994/1308, 18 November 1994.
76. Douglas Hurd, *Hansard*, House of Commons, 2 November 1994, Col. 1554.
77. Hurd, *Hansard*, House of Commons, 17 November 1994, Col. 140.
78. Douglas Hogg, *Hansard*, House of Commons, 7 December 1994, Cols 267–8.
79. Statement by the President of the Security Council, S/PRST/1994/75, 30 November 1994.
80. Chalker, *Hansard*, House of Lords, 23 January 1995, Col. 63.
81. Alain Destexhe, 'So Doctors Without Borders is leaving the Rwanda refugee camps', *International Herald Tribune*, 10 February 1995.
82. Inigo Gilmore, 'First British troops in Rwanda assess humanitarian goals', *The Times*, 3 August 1994.
83. Nicholas Soames, *Hansard*, House of Commons, 9 December 1994, Col. 416.
84. *Hansard*, House of Commons, 31 October 1994, Col. 1210.
85. Destexhe, 'So Doctors Without Borders is leaving', 10 February 1995.
86. Cited in Victoria Brittain, 'French aid agency urges Rwandan genocide trials', *Guardian*, 25 January 1995.
87. Douglas Hurd, Speech to the Overseas Development Institute, London, 6 February 1995, p. 7.
88. Julian Bedford, 'Hutu soldiers repulsed after invading Rwanda', *Independent*, 12 January 1995.
89. ODA press release, April 1994.
90. Douglas Hurd, Speech, 15 June 1994, in *Arms Control and Disarmament Quarterly Review*, No. 34, July 1994, p. 45.
91. For example, *The Times* commented editorially on the slaughters in Rwanda, writing that the killings were due to 'ethnic hatred'. There was a 'history of slaughter between the minority Tutsi and the majority Hutu tribes' and what was occurring was 'Rwanda's madness'. Further, 'it is not clear who fans the flames. Which parties would be asked to cease fire against whom?' 'Carnage in Africa', *The Times*, 11 April 1994.

92. See Destexhe, 'The Third Genocide'; African Rights, *Rwanda – Who is Killing, Who is Dying, What is to be Done?*, African Rights, London, May 1994.
93. Lindsey Hilsum, 'UN suppressed warning of Rwanda genocide plan', *Observer*, 26 November 1995.
94. African Rights, *Rwanda*, pp. 10–11.
95. Destexhe, 'The Third Genocide', pp. 13–14.
96. Douglas Hurd, Speech to the 49th General Assembly of the United Nations, New York, 26 September 1994.
97. Douglas Hogg, *Hansard*, House of Commons, 2 November 1994, Col. 1558.

# Index